THE CONCISE OXFORD H
INDIAN BUSINESS

THE CONCISE OXFORD HISTORY OF
INDIAN BUSINESS

DWIJENDRA TRIPATHI
JYOTI JUMANI

OXFORD
UNIVERSITY PRESS

OXFORD
UNIVERSITY PRESS

Oxford University Press is a department of the University of Oxford.
It furthers the University's objective of excellence in research, scholarship,
and education by publishing worldwide. Oxford is a registered trademark of
Oxford University Press in the UK and in certain other countries

Published in India
by Oxford University Press
YMCA Library Building, 1 Jai Singh Road, New Delhi 110001, India

© Oxford University Press 2006

ISBN-13: 978-0-19-568429-2
ISBN-10: 0-19-568429-X

Printed in India by Replika Press Pvt Ltd.

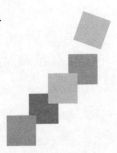

CONTENTS

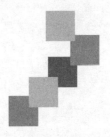

PREFACE TO THE CONCISE EDITION

THE OXFORD HISTORY OF INDIAN BUSINESS, HAS BEEN HAILED BY REVIEWERS as the first comprehensive and authoritative work on the subject. It also had very good reception in the market. Encouraged by this, the publishers suggested a concise version for the benefit of the non-specialist reader. I liked the idea, but found myself incapable of the task. For, no author can easily determine what can be deleted from his work without damage to its essential character. Fortunately, Jyoti Jumani agreed to my and the publishers' suggestion to undertake the responsibility. This volume is the result.

The concise volume faithfully follows the original in every respect—coverage, content, and even linguistic flavour. However, the relatively recent periods, particularly the post-Independence phase, have received somewhat greater attention than in the original, and a new chapter, 'In the Aftermath of Liberalization', has been written specially for this volume. Momentous changes have taken place in the wake of the opening of the economy since the original was written; hence a fresh look.

The idea of bringing out a concise volume of *The Oxford History of Indian Business* would have never occurred to me but for the suggestion from Nitasha Devasar of Oxford University Press, and but for her gentle push, the idea would never have gone beyond the suggestion stage. Further, but for Jyoti Jumani's painstaking effort, the idea would never have become reality. To them thus belongs the real credit for this volume.

I must acknowledge the debt of some other persons in shaping this book. Inputs from V.L. Mote greatly helped in structuring the chapter on liberalization.

He also took the trouble of going through the draft of this chapter and made very useful suggestions. Usha Jumani, as usual, was generous with material and ideas pertaining to recent times. Harish Damodaran furnished some factual details. R. Ramamurthy helped in myriad ways, and Neeraj Lal procured some illustrations.

I am grateful to all of them for their help. The responsibility for any shortcoming in the treatment of the subject, however, must necessarily remain mine.

Ahmedabad   Dwijendra Tripathi
August 2006

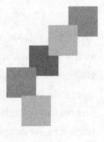

PROLOGUE

THE TERM 'BUSINESS' IN A BROAD SENSE ENCOMPASSES ALL ACTIVITIES and transactions of goods and services with an eye on profit. However, the emphasis in this account is on such activities and exploits that defined the contours of Indian business from time to time—activities and exploits that set the tone, influenced the trends, and impacted the processes of transition. History, all history, after all is concerned with the process of change manifested in the shifting contours.

The focus of the volume is on the modern period or that phase of Indian history which witnessed the shaping of the features and characteristics that distinguish Indian business today—during which period the country made the transition to an industrial economy. Interaction between Indian and European business was a critical factor in this development. While India did not blindly imitate the West, the manner in which Indians organized and managed their undertakings underwent a great deal of modification as a result of their interactions with the European companies—or independent businessmen who followed in their footsteps—which began to spread their tentacles into the Indian Ocean lands around the turn of the seventeenth century. As there was a considerable time lag before the Indian business world began to experience their impact this volume concentrates on post-1700 India. Incidentally, the starting point of this volume also conforms to the conventional scheme of periodization for Indian history in general.

PLATES

Note· Plates 1–19 have been reproduced from
The Oxford History of Indian Business (OUP, 2004).

ABBREVIATIONS

A&M	Acquisitions and Mergers
ACC	Associated Cement Companies
AEL	Adani Exports Limited
AMCO	Assam Match Company
ASSOCHAM	Associated Chamber of Commerce
ATM	Automated Teller Machine
BI	British India Steam Navigation Company
BISCO	Bengal Iron and Steel Company
BPO	Business Process Outsourcing
BSE	Bombay Stock Exchange
C-DOT	Centre for Development of Telematics
CEO	Chief Executive Officer
CIMMCO	Central Indian Machinery Manufacturing Corporation
DCM	Delhi Cloth Mills
DSA	Deccan Sugar and Abkari Company
FACT	Fertilizers and Chemicals Travancore Ltd
FDI	Foreign Direct Investment
FERA	Foreign Exchange Regulation Act
FICCI	Federation of Indian Chambers of Commerce and Industry
FII	Foreign Institutional Investor
GAPL	Gujarat Adani Port Ltd
HCL	Hindustan Computers Ltd
HINDALCO	Hindustan Aluminium Company

HLL	Hindustan Lever Limited
ICI	Imperial Chemical Industries
ICICI	Industrial Credit and Investment Corporation of India
IDBI	Industrial Development Bank of India
IDPL	Indian Drugs and Pharmaceutical Corporation Ltd
IFCI	Industrial Finance Corporation of India
IIM-A	Indian Institute of Management Ahmedabad
IISCO	Indian Iron and Steel Company
IPCL	Indian Petrochemicals Corporation Ltd
IRCI	Industrial Refinance Corporation of India
ITC	Indian Tobacco Company
ITI	Indian Telephone Industries
KDCMPUL	Kaira District Corporation Milk Producers' Union Ltd
L&T	Larsen & Toubro
MIT	Massachusetts Institute of Technology
MMC	Machinery Manufacturer Organization
MRIL	Mcleod Russel India Ltd
MRTP	Monopolies and Restrictive Trade Practices
NOCIL	National Organic Chemical Industries Ltd
NPC	National Planning Committee
NSE	National Stock Exchange
NSIC	National Small Industries Corporation
O&K	Orenstein and Koppel
OECD	Organization of Economic Cooperation and Development
ONGC	Oil and Natural Gas Corporation
OVL	ONGC Videsh Ltd
P&O	Pacific and Orient
PIL	Polyolefin Industries Ltd
PSE	Public Sector Enterprises
SEBI	Securities and Exchange Board of India
TCS	Tata Consultancy Service
TELCO	Tata Engineering and Locomotive Company
TEXMACO	Textile Machinery Corporation
TISCO	Tata Iron and Steel Company
TUSCAL	The United Steel Corporation of Asia Limited
USFDA	United States Food and Drug Administration
VSNL	Videsh Sanchar Nigam Ltd
WIMCO	Western India Match Company

CHAPTER 1

THE BACKDROP: INDIAN BUSINESS c.1700

AT THE TURN OF THE EIGHTEENTH CENTURY, THE MUGHAL EMPIRE UNDER Emperor Aurangzeb encompassed practically the whole of the Indian subcontinent. India was a predominantly agrarian society at this time. Though it was counted among the most industrialized countries of Asia, it was the agricultural sector that generated the bulk of output and employment. The manufacturing sector, confined largely to textile goods and handicrafts, occupied very limited space in the total economy. This determined to a large extent the character of Indian business in the eighteenth century.

THE STATE OF THE MARKET

The state of the market was another major factor that affected business operations, both in range and complexity. With its vast size and population, India could have provided a huge market for goods and services. But the subcontinent was a congeries of scattered markets, instead of a single integrated theatre of transactions. To make matters worse, facilities for moving goods and services were woefully restricted, as successive governments including the Mughals had virtually ignored the need to develop roads and highways for commercial purposes.

All that India could boast of in the name of physical infrastructure, indispensable for the smooth operation of long-distance trade, were a few trade routes and riverways which were serviceable only in some parts of the year. The Indus and the Ganges, the principal waterways in north India, were navigable only during the monsoons, while many stretches of the principal rivers in south India remained unfit for commercial traffic all through the year owing to rocky terrain. Though there were some trade routes, served by branch roads going into deep interiors, they were woefully inadequate for a country of continental proportions. And even these were *kachcha* (unpaved) lines in most cases, which made them unusable for wheeled traffic, especially during the monsoons. In this scenario, pack animals were the most convenient means of transport.

The means of communication, inadequate and inefficient, were beset by two major difficulties. The first was safety on the roads. The danger of theft and violence was usually too great for smooth passage of small or unprotected convoys. Merchants, therefore, usually preferred moving in caravans, which sometimes took months to form. However on numerous occasions the carvans were subjected to blackmail, extortion, and even physical assault en route to their destinations, even while the Mughal star still shone bright. By AD 1700, when the Empire had already passed its prime, conditions had definitely worsened.

Another constraint to movement was the existence of an intricate web of custom barriers, or *chowkies* as they were called in popular parlance. Having existed for centuries, these chowkies had multiplied severalfold with the passage of time, largely on account of repeated political fragmentation. Goods passing through territories under different rulers were understandably subject to customs clearances at the borders. But consignments were liable to duty payment at multiple points even if they transited within the jurisdiction of a single ruler or chieftain. So deeply entrenched had the system already become that even the rise of the Mughals made no dent in it, and the collection points increased rather than decreased with the weakening of the Empire. Provincial rulers, local chieftains, and even powerful zamindars could extract imposts for goods passing through their territories. Thevenot, who visited India in the first quarter of the eighteenth century, counted sixteen customs points within a distance of less than sixty miles. To compound the hardships created by customs barriers were the rates, or lack of them, of duties and harassment by corrupt customs officials. As hardly any item was exempt from duty, officials had a wide berth to demonstrate their loyalty to the Empire and also enrich themselves in the process. The extensive and intricate web of customs barriers, coupled with the way officers in charge behaved, unduly prolonged the duration of transit and increased the cost of transport, resulting in a rise in the price of the commodity at the destination.

A plethora of currencies circulating in different parts of the country was yet another factor the merchants had to contend with. The Indian economy had become fairly well monetized by the end of Akbar's reign (1556–1605) and the process continued to gain momentum under his successors. The currencies issued by the previous regimes, however, did not disappear and continued to circulate along with the Mughal coins. In fact, in some regions, the currencies associated with the older regimes were more common than the Mughal rupee, for example *mahmudis* in the west, particularly Gujarat, and *pagodas* in the south. In addition, some foreign currencies were also in circulation, particularly in the port towns through which foreign commerce was conducted with the adjoining regions.

No fixed rate governed the exchange between the various currencies in circulation. Their relative value was determined by their metal content and the prevailing price of the metal in a given market. To further complicate matters, the purchasing power of a currency varied in the same market depending on the age of the coin; the older the coin the less its value to allow for depreciation due to wear and tear. The situation as regards weights and measures was still more chaotic. Standards varied not only between region and region, province and province, or district and district, but sometimes even between two neighbouring villages. In some places, the standards used for buying were different from those used for selling the same article. Measures too presented a similar situation. For instance, *gaz*, a basic measuring unit, signified different lengths, depending on the fabric being measured.

Because of these socio-economic realties, India at the turn of the eighteenth century was, as it had always been, a vast conglomerate of regional or local markets. They differed in size, depending on the nature of the merchandise. Consumer goods such as foodgrains, which perished faster and entailed relatively higher transport cost because of the volume involved, usually had a narrower range of movement while specialized products such as indigo, saltpetre, spices, precious metals, and textiles commanded markets of somewhat larger size. Although a total absence of interlinkages would be hard to conceive, markets for the two categories of goods were fairly independent of one another. Only in areas connected by sea or riverways were the markets somewhat more integrated.

The merchants had to adjust to these realities of the market. Those whose operations were largely limited to dealing in foodgrains and articles of general use operated within a more limited area. They had limited resources and their business power was limited. Not surprisingly, the names of only a few in this category have survived. In fact, practically all those about whose business exploits we learn something from contemporary sources concentrated on trading in goods and services, the markets for which extended far beyond their immediate vicinity or neighbourhood. They wielded great power within their respective regions and had business linkages with their counterparts elsewhere in the land. Some of them were active even in seaborne trade.

MERCHANTS AND THEIR OPERATIONS

One of the most influential merchants of this period was Seth Hira Nand Sahu, the founder of what would come to be known as the house of Jagat Seth. Although the family was nowhere near as powerful as it was to become soon after Aurangzeb's death, Hira Nand was a force to reckon with in and around Patna, then a prominent centre of trade, from where he operated. As Patna, situated on the Ganges, was well connected with other trade centres in eastern India, Sahu found it easy to spread his network. Originally from the desert of Rajasthan, he had moved to the east with little resources of his own in the last decade of the seventeenth century, but had already acquired a great deal of fortune and influence before the decline of the Mughal Empire set in. The mainstay of his operations was banking or moneylending, but he also had extensive trading business.

The Gujarat region, at the other end of the country, had a much larger number of merchants with great business power. This is so because the region had long been the centre of the most thriving commercial life in India, and its long coastline had a number of major ports. At the turn of the eighteenth century, Surat was still the most important port in the entire land and boasted of a vigorous business community, with, among others, some of the most prominent shipowners in the country. One of them, Abdul Ghafur, is reputed to have owned more than twenty sailing ships, and trade carried on by him was reputed to be equal to that of the English East India Company. He was active in foreign commerce as well as inland trade, and had attained a position similar to that of the legendary Virji Vora, the colossus of business in western India until his death around 1680. Other prominent business families of the city included the Chellabys, Parekhs, Rustomjis, and Travadis. The Chellabys were primarily shippers, engaged in procuring freight for the Red Sea and Persian Gulf ports. The Parekhs and Rustomjis were brokers while the Travadis were bankers.

Though not a port town, Ahmedabad too had a vigorous business community. The biggest of the Ahmedabad merchants was Khushalchand, grandson of Shantidas Zaveri, a contemporary of Virji Vora, whose position in Ahmedabd in the seventeenth century was similar to the latter's in Surat. Primarily jewellers, the Zaveris also carried on banking business, occasionally obliging the English East India Company with loans. Khushalchand and his family enjoyed immense power and influence in Gujarat. Among other great merchants of Ahmedabad were Vanmalidas Tapidas, Kapurchand Bhansali, and Padam Gopal. Ahmedabad also had a class of brokers who offered various kinds of support to the merchants in their business dealings.

While Surat owed its position as a busy business centre largely to its being a port, Ahmedabad's importance was due to its location on major trade routes that connected it with port towns on the one hand, and principal commercial centres in the interior like Multan in the north and Agra in the east, on the other. As a consequence, the city had become a major emporium of goods from various parts of India and the world. Ahmedabad was also known for its textile manufactures—cotton, silk, and wool. Silver and gold brocades produced here were in great demand in India as well as abroad, and the gold and silver jewellery made by its craftsmen was famed for its intricacy. Other flourishing industries included dyeing and bleaching, embroidery and needlework, inlaying of precious stones, and paper making. One of the principal commodities of Ahmedabad market was indigo, produced in large quantity in Sarkhej, now a suburb of the city. Saltpetre, a commodity available in plenty in and around Ahmedabad, and an indispensable input for producing gunpowder, was in great demand in India and abroad.

Broach and Cambay, once major centres of commerce in western India, were already past their prime, and Bombay was still far from the glory it would achieve within a few decades. Few merchants belonging to these places were at the hub of Indian business at the beginning of the eighteenth century. Neither have the names of any merchants operating in the north and north-west endured even though these regions did have a number of business centres such as Lahore, Burhanpur, Agra, and Multan. In contrast, the names of many big merchants operating from the Coromandel coast are mentioned in the records of the European trading companies. Prominent among them were Malay Chetti, Kasi Viranna, and Sunca Rama Chetti.

It seems that the most prominent merchants were concentrated in major ports or their hinterland which, linking the country with the commercial world outside, provided some definite locational advantage. These merchants operated on a large scale while those in the interior were more limited in their reach and the volume of their business. Also a host of traders existed whose business dealings were confined to local markets or village fairs. The business class of India at the turn of the eighteenth century, thus, comprised a hierarchy of traders and merchants operating at different levels and scales.

The bigger traders—the merchant princes, as they are sometimes called—dealt mostly in commodities of interest to the European companies or those in demand in external markets. They concentrated on export items like indigo, spices, and textile goods; they also participated extensively in inter-regional trade. Much of the competitive strength of these merchant princes was due to the fact that they acquired their merchandise from places, both far and near, where the prices were relatively low.

For help in procuring and selling their goods, the merchant princes employed the services of brokers, known as *dalal* or *wakil*. The broker was not an employee but a businessman in his own right, working for a merchant under certain arrangements. Besides the brokers, there were *shroffs* or *sarafs* who specialized in exchanging currencies. They thrived because a variety of coins were in circulation, and determining the value of one vis-à-vis another required a great deal of expertise. To procure their merchandise, particularly textile goods, the merchants very often advanced funds to the primary producer to carry on his operation. The primary producer, availing of the advance, would be under an obligation to deliver goods of specified quality and quantity at a mutually agreed price and time, usually fixed when the money was advanced.

Extensive involvement of merchant princes in inter-regional trade and external commerce made it necessary for them to remit large sums to far-off places. This was difficult, given the means of communication in the subcontinent. The *hundi* system, a well-entrenched credit institution in vogue all over the country, stood them in good stead in this respect. Hundi was a sort of bill of exchange drawn by a party on his agent or correspondent elsewhere asking the latter to pay to the drawee a specified sum of money the equivalent of which the drawer had already received. This precluded cash movement, although the remittance charges understandably were quite high. This line of business was dominated by shroffs, but general merchants were not absent from the scene. Most of the merchants operating at regional or local levels also combined moneylending with trading, and they too, like their more powerful brethren, made use of the hundi system whenever necessary.

One class of businessmen which does not easily fit into our hierarchy of merchants consisted of itinerant traders. Comprising a group of tribes known collectively as *banjaras*, they dealt mainly in grains and moved from place to place, carrying their merchandise and personal effects on oxen, and living in camps. They moved in caravans, and their customers consisted of rural folk. At the turn of the eighteenth century, however, the banjara business was on the decline.

Thus the basic character of Indian business around this time was commercial rather than industrial. Trading or moneylending or both dominated business at every level. Manufacturing was largely in the hands of artisans who were often dependent on merchants to provide finances for their operations and buy their products, although the artisans also sold directly to the final consumer. Noted for their skill—Dacca muslins, Ahmedabad brocades, and Patan saris can be cited as examples—the artisans and craftsmen could produce limited goods as the production technology was labour intensive. Steeped in trading and moneylending, the merchants, even those with vast financial resources, showed no interest in promoting industrial undertakings or attempting technological innovation. Liquidity preference and low-risk ventures were the hallmarks of business behaviour in India around this time.

This should not be interpreted to mean that the mercantile community lacked business acumen or material ambition. Given the fragmented state of the market and prospects of large profits in trade, the lack of industrial initiative makes perfect sense. The available technology too was not amenable to large-scale production or economies of scale. By all accounts, Indian merchants at every level were as shrewd and calculating as merchants anywhere else, including their European counterparts. In fact, it is the profit motive more than anything else that determined their business strategies. It is very often suggested that the Hindu ethos with its focus on otherworldliness cannot generate a sufficiently strong will to achieve material progress. This does not apply even remotely to the Indian businessmen of our period, even though most merchants belonged to the castes and groups normally identified with business under the Hindu social division—Jains and Vaishnava banias in the west, Khatris in the north-west, Jains and Agrawal banias in the north and east, and Chettiers and Komatis in the south. Most of the Muslim traders were centred in the Sindh-Gujarat region. Belonging to three major groups— Bohras, Khojas, and Memons—they were converts from Hindu trading castes and still retained some of their pre-conversion customs and practices, including usury. The Parsees, who would later emerge prominently on the Indian business scene, were at this time a primarily agricultural community clustered in Surat–Navsari area. Likewise, Rajasthani traders, who would soon spread their tentacles into various parts of India and be collectively called Marwaris, were still confined by and large to their homeland and its neighbourhood.

Whatever their social origins, the merchant class could expect little by way of protection from the state. Even though some businessmen at individual level had very close ties with imperial bureaucracy and thus could depend on various kinds of support from the government, the community as a whole could not anticipate, under the prevailing system of governance, how the authorities would deal with issues affecting business. No legal framework governing the course of business existed, there was no contract law, and nothing prevented the government from curbing the freedom of enterprise at will. It was not uncommon for highly placed functionaries of the government to indulge in business activities of their own, and on many occasions in the latter half of the seventeenth century some provincial governors, taking advantage of their official position, brought the whole trade in certain commodities under their personal monopoly.

The merchant classes under these conditions had to utilize traditional channels to regulate their ranks and enforce a measure of discipline. In most places, age-old caste fora such as panchayat (caste assembly) served this purpose. In certain regions, however, there were trade associations as well. We know of the existence of such agencies in the major commercial centres of Gujarat. Known as *mahajan*, they were essentially occupational pressure groups representing all those who were engaged in the trade of a particular commodity. Mahajans were mainly concerned with professional matters; unlike caste panchayats, they had little to do with the socio-cultural problems of their members.

Foreign Elements

Indian merchants did not have the Indian market entirely to themselves. They had to compete as well as collaborate with the European East India Companies on one hand and traders of other lands operating on Indian soil on the other. Among the East India Companies, the English and the Dutch were most active. A latecomer on the scene, the French East India Company was still consolidating its position in the Indian markets while Portugal, once the most formidable force in Indo-European trade, had ceased to be of much consequence. All the three major European companies operated from their 'factories' or fortified settlements at or near some major Indian ports: the English at Surat, Bombay, Madras, and Calcutta; the Dutch at Surat, Cochin,

Pulicut, Masulipatnam, and Hooghly; and the French at Surat, Pondicherry, and Hooghly. In addition they also had subordinate stations in the interior.

Even though these companies enjoyed monopoly rights over trade between their respective countries and India by virtue of charters granted to them by their respective governments, all trade between Europe and India was not carried on through these companies alone. Their employees, too, traded on their personal accounts like individual merchants. This was patently illegal, but for various reasons, the company managements could not enforce strict discipline in this regard. Besides, there were a small number of interlopers who, taking the risk and defying the monopoly rights of the companies, carried on clandestine trade.

The European companies, their servants, and the interlopers were not the only foreign elements in Indian business. There were others who had preceded them. The Arab and Egyptian merchants, who controlled India's export trade with the Red Sea countries at the time of Portuguese penetration of India, were still active on the west coast in and around Calicut, although their influence had considerably waned with the decline of the port city. For most of them, India had ceased to be a foreign land because their families had long been living in the country. Another group of foreign merchants active in most of the major Indian ports and their hinterland were the Armenians. Their national origin is still unknown, and we do not know why they are called Armenians. Regarded as the most ancient merchants of the world, they were highly skilled arbitrage dealers, noted for very flexible and geographically mobile forms of commerce.

Most merchants, both Indian and foreign, were involved in inland trade as well as in India's trade with other countries—particularly with those in the Red Sea and Persian Gulf areas, Central and South East Asia, and China.

The Indian merchants by and large operated as sole proprietors or sometimes in partnership. In contrast, the European companies trading with India were all joint stock organizations. They also differed from the Indian traders both in the scope and scale of their operations. As Indians had limited use for European goods while the demand in Europe for Indian goods, particularly textiles, was enormous, the European companies could not generate sufficient finances to procure merchandise in India through imports from home. They, therefore, developed a trading network encompassing several Asian countries, based on, to use a present-day terminology, the concept of comparative advantage. They would, for instance, generate resources to buy cloth in Gujarat or the Coromandel coast by selling spices procured in South East Asia through the sale of goods from China and silver from Japan. The profits from inter-Asian trade along with the bullion imported from Europe were used to procure Indian textiles, indigo, saltpetre, and other goods to be exported to Europe. Thus, while the Indian merchants either operated within India or participated in bilateral trade between India and some other countries, the trading activities of the European companies were multilateral in character. The scale of the European companies' operations, consequently, was much larger and their geographical spread much wider.

Within India, however, the position of Indian merchants was supreme. Their operations, both in scale and scope, suggest that while commercial capitalism had sufficiently matured in India by the beginning of the eighteenth century, the conditions for the transition to the next stage of capitalist development had not yet emerged.

CHAPTER 2

MERCHANTS DURING
THE IMPERIAL CRISIS

THE COLLAPSE OF THE MUGHAL EMPIRE WITHIN JUST A FEW YEARS AFTER the death of Aurangzeb in 1707 brought about practically no change in the business situation. This was so because the business fortunes were not linked with the fortunes of the Empire. With a well-organized treasury and revenue administration, the Empire was not overly dependent on wealthy merchants for funds, and the merchants expected little by way of any special protection from the government. Though the Mughal emperors occasionally sought to protect the interests of some loyal merchants, the Empire, by and large, had a neutral stance towards business, and the territorial unity that the Mughal might had wrought was of no special advantage for mercantile pursuits.

In one respect, however, there was a radical change. Merchants and bankers became almost indispensable for the functioning of the new regimes that arose on the ruins of the Empire in various parts of the subcontinent—the Nawabs of Bengal and Oudh in the east and north, the Sikhs in the north-west, the Marathas in the west, and the Nizam in the south to mention only the most prominent ones. Most of the successor states lacked the financial solvency of the Great Mughals and lacked an efficient revenue-collection machinery to which the financial might of the Empire was largely due. Rich merchants and bankers offered an answer to both these problems. They could advance money to the state in exchange for the right to collect land revenue from specified areas. Most of the successor states resorted to this system, known as *potedari*, to tackle their financial problem.

The new political scenario, thus, invested the Indian merchant with a new sense of power and influence. While the geographical range of his operations as well as the traditional sources of his profit remained more or less undisturbed, the addition of the state to the list of his clients brought about a very significant change in his material position. Not only did his moneylending operations receive a great fillip as a result of the state's dependence on him for funds; he also now emerged, because of his proximity to the governing system, as a central figure in the unending power games that riddled the subcontinent with the fading of the Mughal glory.

Native princes and chieftains were not the only players in these power games; the European trading companies, notably the English and the French, were becoming inseparable parts of these. This is because by now they had transcended the narrow limits of trade and were conjuring up territorial designs. During the heyday of the Mughal Empire, they had remained content with efforts to expand commercial spaces, as they could hardly have nurtured any political ambition in a realistic sense then. In the wake of the break-up of the Empire and the confusion prevailing after the death of Aurangzeb, not to entertain the thought of carving out political power for themselves would indeed have been unnatural. The merchants' interaction with the European Companies had been essentially of commercial nature until the onset of the eighteenth century. While fashioning their moves, they now had to take note of the growing political postures of what had hitherto been merely trading organizations. These moves were usually determined by considerations of short-term gain rather than a long-term perspective. Neither any sense of nationalism nor the thought that the European Companies, if allowed to gain political power, would eventually pose a serious threat to its own business interests ever entered into the calculations of the Indian mercantile class. Also, the European Companies, appearing to be honest brokers or the champions of fair trade, did not arouse much suspicion in native business circles. A few examples drawn from different parts of the country may substantiate these general observations.

WESTERN INDIA

With reference to business developments in the first half of the eighteenth century, western India can be divided into two distinct parts. While the northern part, comprising the Gujarat region, was a theatre of the most vigorous business activity, the southern part, most of which was under the control of the Maratha chiefs, had only small and petty traders. Land revenue was the principal source of income for the Maratha state, and the *kamvisdars* or revenue collectors advanced funds to the government before the actual collection—sometimes for several years in advance. Large amounts, required to finance military expeditions, were also raised through loans from moneylenders and traders. All this gave great fillip to the moneylending business. In many cases the profits from moneylending were reinvested in trade, creating a multiplier effect on the business situation in general.

Moneylending, and therefore trading and allied businesses, received further impetus when the Peshwa, with his capital at Poona, emerged as the de facto head of the Maratha state after 1725. In their bid to build an all-India empire, the Peshwas had to fight a number of wars, entailing endless need of funds. The moneylender, under these conditions, virtually became an integral part of the administrative apparatus, very often accompaniying the army to attend to the financial need of the campaigns. The government naturally granted various kinds of concessions to traders and moneylenders. All this led to considerable expansion of the business horizon in the Maratha country and drew many new entrants into business, including high-caste Brahmans. Expansion of business opportunities also attracted big merchants from Gujarat and other neighbouring areas to the Peshwa territories—particularly Poona, the capital. As new seats of Maratha power emerged as a result of the Maratha sardars establishing their own principalities, virtually independent of the Peshwa Durbar but still professing allegiance to it, these outsiders became even more important. For, the Gaikwads, the Scindias, and the Holkars, with their headquarters at Baroda, Gwalior, and Indore, found it expedient to pay their annual tributes to the Poona court through these bankers who had offices at Poona as well as in the capitals of these feudatory states. As a result Poona gradually emerged as a principal centre of hundi transaction.

Among the Gujarati bankers who opened their offices at the Peshwa headquarters were the Haribhaktis whose career illustrates in many ways the importance of big merchants in the Maratha kingdom. Founded by two brothers, Hari and Bhakti, this house had become fairly important in the financial life of the Gaikwad state by the middle of the eighteenth century. Some time after the Third Battle of Panipat (1761), the Haribhaktis established a branch at Poona to exploit the profitable opportunities which proximity to the seat of the suzerain power seemed to offer. They also continued to function as potedars for the Gaikwads and help them tide over the state's financial difficulties. As the Peshwa glory faded by the turn of the century, the Poona branch was closed down leaving the Haribhaktis to concentrate wholly on their business affairs at Baroda where royal patronage helped their business considerably.

By this time the East India Company had already carved out a significant position for itself in the political life of western India, and the Haribhaktis and other potedars of the state considered it expedient to ingratiate themselves with the ascendant alien power. The administration of the state, never in a particularly good shape, was now in total disarray. Most of the districts had already been mortgaged, or their revenue farmed out. The security against which the potedars used to honour claims vis-à-vis the state was thus practically non-existent. Under these conditions, the potedars, including the Haribhaktis, refused to advance further loans to the government in 1802 and relented only after the English East India Company gave a guarantee for the repayment of the loans. In return the Gaikwad ruler agreed to many humiliating conditions that, in effect, resulted in the virtual subjugation of the kingdom to the alien power.

Only a few years after the Baroda bankers had placed their trust in the English East India Company to protect their business interests, merchants at Ahmedabad did likewise. Ahmedabad was then under the joint control of the Peshwas and the Gaikwads. The merchant bankers of the city had advanced large sums to the Maratha rulers against the security of the land revenue, which the government was unable to pay. They now looked to the rising British sun as their possible saviour. It is not surprising, therefore, that they rejoiced over the British annexation of the city in 1817, following the Peshwa rout in the last and decisive Anglo-Maratha war. Significantly, one of the principal reasons cited by the alien power for annexing the city was the financial embarrassment of the Gaikwads and their inability to honour the shroffs' claims against them.

The Surat merchants aligned with the British even more openly. As Mughal control weakened and the Maratha demand for tribute became more frequent, the local government resorted to all sorts of means to extort money from the business class. Having failed to persuade the authorities to change their ways, a large majority of the merchants formally pledged their allegiance to the English Company, and it is on their appeal that the British forces captured the castle, the administrative headquarters, and placed a puppet at the head of government. In this fashion, the Company emerged as the real power in 1759. A grateful Company appointed the banking house of Travadi Arunji Nathji, a major supporter of the rebellion, as its official bankers in recognition of the services rendered. With the Company gaining a firm foothold in western India with the assistance of the merchants began an era of collaboration between business and the British power that had momentous consequences for the country.

EASTERN INDIA

Less than two years before the English success in Surat, the Company had already established itself as a critical force in the polity and economy of Bengal, nay of the whole country. This too became possible because of the assistance the British received from a small but influential group of merchants. The beginnings of the events that culminated in this development can be traced back to 1717 when the English Company secured the right of free trade, that is exemption of its goods from custom duties, within Bengal through an imperial *farman*. This caused little difficulty as long as the Bengal *subedar*s (viceroys) remained loyal to the imperial court. However, as the power of the Empire declined, the subedars, styling themselves as nawabs, became virtually independent of the Delhi Durbar, though theoretically still owing allegiance to it. The revenue of the province now began to be collected through a system in which the house of Jagat Seth, perhaps the most powerful business house in India at that time, played a pivotal role.

As mentioned earlier, the founder of this house was Hira Nand Sahu. One of Hira Nand's seven sons, Manekchand, had left Patna, Hiranand's headquarters, at the turn of the eighteenth century and settled down at Dacca, the capital of Bengal province, where he established a flourishing business. More importantly, he developed such close links with the then governor of the province, Murshid Quli Khan, that when the governor transferred his administrative headquarters to Murshidabad in 1703, Manekchand considered it prudent to move along with him—now as government banker and treasurer. He was also given control over the government mint and thus the right to strike coins on behalf of the administration. He now had an additional source of profit—the power to control the money supply as well as the exchange rate. According to one estimate, Manekchand's annual earning from minting coins was Rs 3.5 lakh. Even more important than the control over the mint was the fact that Manekchand was the most critical link in the revenue-collection machinery of the province. The nawabs assigned revenue collection to the rajas and zamindars who had to deposit the collection at government headquarters by a given date. As they could seldom collect the entire amount on time, they were dependent on Manekchand to stand security for the shortfall, on payment of 10 per cent commission. Profits from this source alone were around rupees ten lakh annually. The Mughal emperor honoured Manekchand with the title of Seth in recognition of his services to the state.

Under the leadership of Fateh Chand, the adopted son and successor of Manekchand, the house reached its pinnacle. He held the keys to the treasury and received the revenues and payments on behalf of the government. Emperor Farukhsiyar honoured him with the title of Jagat Seth in perpetuity by which his descendants as well as his house would be remembered by posterity. Edmund Burke, the renowned British statesman, described him as the 'Rothschilds of India'.

By the time Nawab Murshid Quli Khan, whose links with the house had fortified his own as well as the banker's position, died in 1725, Fateh Chand had become indispensable to the ruling clique. He along with the nawab's two top officials, virtually governed Bengal, and made or unmade nawabs at will. It was largely due to his machinations that Alivardi Khan secured the nawabship of Bengal in 1739, dethroning another contender. Within two years after Alivardi had assumed the nawabship, the Marathas started raiding Bengal. Fateh Chand's *kothi* was plundered twice, and lakhs taken away. These raids, however, made little dent on his wealth. In the words of a contemporary European observer: 'So amazing a loss which would distress any monarch in Europe affected him so little that he continued to give government bills of exchange at sight [*darshani hundi*] of full one crore at a time'.

The English and French East India Companies had by this time already started fishing in the troubled political waters of India. Suspicious of their motives, the nawab maintained cordial relations with the prominent merchants—Hindus, Muslims, Armenians—who in turn backed him and, despite mutual rivalry, acted as mediators between the nawab and the European Companies. Leaving behind the complex business-politics nexus, Alivardi died in 1756. Sirajuddaula, his successor, had neither the temperament nor the ability to play a balancing role between mutually conflicting interests. He had contempt for the English, hated the house of Jagat Seth, and alienated a large number of persons whose support had sustained Alivardi's government. Only two prominent merchants, Khoja Wajid and Amirchand, retained Siraj's favour.

Eventually, all disgruntled elements joined hands to eliminate the common enemy, and hatched a conspiracy to replace Sirajuddaula. Robert Clive and W. Watts of the English East India Company and the Jagat Seth were among the main actors in the drama. Even Khoja Wajid joined the conspirators and Amirchand was won over by a false promise of a large financial reward. All preparations culminated in the Battle of Plassey in 1757 in which Clive, commanding a small force of the English Company, defeated Siraj's army, let down by treachery and duplicity of his own men who were secretly in league with the conspirators. The young nawab was killed on the battlefield, and the conspirators placed their own man, Mir Jafar, on the throne.

The victory at Plassey brought enormous power and prestige to the English Company and marked the beginning of a process that culminated in the British conquest of almost the entire subcontinent within the next sixty years. Just a few decades earlier, no one could have imagined that a mere merchant, whatever his wealth and financial clout, would have the power to change the course of history—of India and Britain both.

OTHER PARTS OF THE COUNTRY

The story of the business-politics nexus in many other parts of India is more or less similar, although merchants and bankers elsewhere did not play as critical a role in shaping the political developments in the mid-eighteenth century as their counterparts in Surat and Bengal did. Through the north Indian bankers the British gradually gained access to the countrywide hundi network to transmit funds from the Calcutta region to Bombay, perennially in deficit, to finance the wars of conquest in western India. We also know of several bankers, such as Manohardas Dwarkadas and Travadi Arjunji Nathji of Surat and Mannu Lal and Beni Prasad of Benares, who financed the British military operations against the Indian rulers. The state of Hyderabad in the south presents yet another example of the shifting loyalties of Indian merchant princes. The banking community had remained among the most trusted allies of the successive nizams ever since the founding of the kingdom in 1724. Whenever the state needed money, it turned to the *sahukar*s who happily obliged with loans. This pattern remained more or less undisturbed almost up to the end of the eighteenth century. But after the Company established its supremacy in that part of the country, the sahukars refused to advance any money to the nizam except through the English agency house of Palmer and Co., which enjoyed the patronage of the Company government. The nizam's government had to pledge the land revenue of several villages in repayment of these debts.

Close liaison also existed between rich merchants and the Rajput rulers in various independent states that emerged in Rajasthan in the wake of the Mughal decline. This, however, was not an entirely new development. Even during the heyday of the Mughal Empire, merchants and moneylenders served as revenue officers both at pargana and state levels, known variously as potedar, *amir*, and *amin*. Some of them worked as *modi* or the suppliers of provision to the army. As the imperial power declined and the Maratha incursion into the Rajputana states became more frequent, the rulers increasingly found it more expedient to fall back on the system of *ijara* (revenue farming) to ensure that their government had easy access to ready cash. This sometimes resulted in the rulers being in heavy debt to their sahukars-cum-*ijaradars*. The East India Company, after it gained political ascendancy in the region, stood by the merchants in their claims against their native patrons. But because of a long tradition of interdependence between the political and financial elite in the region, the Rajputana sahukars seldom became as alienated from the native rulers and drew as close to the Company authorities as elsewhere in India.

IMPACT OF THE BRITISH ASCENDANCY

The Rajputana sahukars in consequence suffered much less as the relevance of the Indian merchant class for the designs of the alien conquerors diminished. In Bengal, all those merchant collaborators, without whose complicity the British victory at Plassey would have been impossible, lost their commercial privileges, and therefore business powers, within barely a few years of the British success. The Company servants now entered in a big way the trade in salt, saltpetre, and opium on which traders like Khoja Wajid and Amirchand previously had a near monopoly. The Jagat Seths lost all their sources of profit, power, and prestige, and were eventually reduced to penury.

The treatment meted out to the bankers and merchants in other parts was no different. The Nawab of Oudh had borrowed a large sum from the bankers of his state to meet, among other things, the expenses of the British forces stationed in his capital. However, the Company authorities, while acknowledging the validity of the bankers' claims, did little to help them to recover the money. The Hyderabad bankers suffered the same fate, and the guarantee given to the Baroda sahukars for the loans advanced to the Gaikwad rulers was never honoured. With the attainment of political paramountcy in the subcontinent by 1820, the Company had little need for merchant bankers.

The real decisive blow to the position of the merchant princes in the financial life of the country, however, came in the form of currency reforms introduced by the new government. With the establishment of district treasuries, where the Company's bills could be encashed without hassle, and the introduction of the modern postal system, dependence on the hundi for remitting funds was substantially reduced. The Company's silver rupee was declared to be the legal tender throughout India in 1835. This eventually crippled the moneychanging business—another major source of the sahukars' profit. Within a space of less than thirty years after the emergence of British supremacy, thus, the Indian merchant princes, who rose to prominence as the Mughal Empire disintegrated, were once again cut down to size, as another empire began to take shape. At the lower levels of the spectrum, however, the traders and moneylenders continued with their traditional activities in their traditional ways, unconcerned about the rise and fall of empires.

CHAPTER 3

TOWARDS TRANSITION

THE EMERGENCE OF THE ENGLISH EAST INDIA COMPANY AS AN UNRIVALLED political force in the subcontinent coincided with a momentous development in England—the 'Industrial Revolution'. The term refers to far-reaching changes in the methods of production and consequent social and economic structures, as new scientific inventions and technological innovations radically altered the manufacturing processes. The use of steam for power, replacing the conventional sources such as wind and water, marked the beginning of this revolution. Although a greatly improved steam engine developed by James Watt in 1765 was the most visible symbol of the change, some equally important inventions such as Richard Arkwright's spinning frame (1769), James Hargreave's spinning jenny (1770), Samuel Crompton's mule (1779), and Edmund Cartwright's powerloom (1783) transformed Yorkshire and Lancashire into thriving centres of textile production. Around the same time the use of coke in iron production brought into prominence the Black Country, comprising districts with large coal and iron ore deposits in West Midlands and Staffordshire.

A cumulative result of all this was the rise of the factory system of large-scale machine production and greater economic specialization. By 1850, industry had become a dominant factor in Great Britain, a country that had been largely agricultural until the middle of the eighteenth century. The growing British hegemony in India after 1750 provided an easy market for the products of the burgeoning British factory system.

REVERSAL OF ROLES

Cotton manufacturing was among the greatest beneficiaries of the new technology. Prior to 1760, the machines used by the British cotton producers were nearly as simple as those in India. But the 'calicoes', as the Indian textile goods were known in Europe, enjoyed considerable price advantage in the British market. The coming of the new machines, producing goods in much greater quantity and at much greater speed than manual labour could do, brought about a complete reversal of the situation. To further add to its competitive advantage, Britain continued with its policy of tariff protection to domestic industry against imports from India.

The exports of Indian textiles, the single largest item in India's list, to Britain fell drastically. What, however, hurt India most was that the products of British mills made deep inroads into its domestic market as well. Meanwhile, the Industrial Revolution spread to other industries in Britain such as iron and steel and chemicals, enabling British factories to continually expand the markets for an increasingly large variety of their products in India. The result was that within less than half a century after the beginning of the Industrial Revolution, India's superiority in international commerce became a thing of the past.

This caused a complete transformation in the character of Indian business. The large urban merchants through whom the European Companies previously used to procure Indian goods for export to their own countries and other markets now became the distributors of imported products brought in by the European, chiefly British, traders. The business operations of the Indian merchants, however, must have received a fillip on the whole, as the volume of imports registered an upward trend in the wake of the consolidation of industrial transition in England. As the proceeds from the sale of British products in India and the accumulating revenue from the territories that gradually came under the British control after 1757 were more than sufficient to procure whatever India still had to offer to other countries—saltpetre, silk goods, raw silk, curios, etc.—the import of precious metals to finance procurements in India, as was earlier the case, virtually stopped. For the same reasons, borrowings from Indian bankers could now easily be dispensed with. Consequently, their relevance for the Company's commercial operations, as the suppliers of goods and credit, suffered considerable erosion. Prominent Indian merchants could no longer dictate terms to the European

Companies as Virji Vora, Shantidas Zaveri, the Jagat Seths, and the Mallyas did in the good old days.

THE RISE OF AGENCY HOUSES

The Industrial Revolution in England, coupled with territorial acquisitions in India, thus greatly strengthened the position of the English East India Company. Its monopoly rights on trade with India, however, came under a vigorous offensive as the rise of the factory system brought to the fore a new class of entrepreneurs in England, eager to benefit from the populous markets of the subcontinent, who swelled manifold the ranks of the Company's critics. The criticism against the Company's monopoly became still shriller after Britain lost its colonies in North America in 1776. To mollify its critics, the Company became much more liberal in granting licences to British citizens to operate as free merchants in the subcontinent.

Consequently, the number of British subjects engaged in private trade with India became much larger. Many servants of the Company resigned their jobs to swell the ranks of free merchants. Campaigns against the Company's privileges, however, continued unabated, leading finally to the abolition in 1813 of its two-hundred-year-old monopoly on Indian trade. Free merchants coming out to India for business grew in number. They explored new and less competitive areas for gain, tried out new methods of doing business, and demonstrated a great deal of drive and aggressiveness. Their interaction with native merchants was often close and vigorous.

The most popular form of organization that the free merchants adopted for their business was the agency house. It was so called because an agency house acted as a business agent of others from whom it charged a fee for its services; also every agency house was an 'agent' of a firm in London. Usually of ordinary means, the free merchants did not bring their own start-up capital; their main source of finance was the deposits from the Company servants. Agency relationship with the firms back home helped the free merchants to act, in the absence of any other exchange facility between Britain and India, as a safe medium of remittance of funds by the Company servants to their families back home. It was something akin to the hundi system operating at the international level. Interest-free advance from their constituents back home was another source of business finance for the agency houses.

The agency houses were understandably headquartered in the three Presidency cities of Calcutta, Bombay, and Madras where a large number of Europeans lived. With the powerful presence of the East India Company in Bengal after the Battle of Plassey, Calcutta had a much larger number, followed by Bombay. The first agency house in India, however, was Forbes & Co. founded in Bombay by John Forbes of Newe in England as early as 1767. But the city being still in the development stage, the second agency house in Bombay did not come into being until 1790 by which time Calcutta had as many as fifteen firms of this genre. Madras, with very limited commercial opportunities at this stage, had probably only one agency house at this time, founded by Thomas Parry who had arrived in the city just about two years earlier. Then the numbers went up very rapidly, particularly in Calcutta where there were as many as twenty-nine such houses by 1803, while Bombay and Madras had around a dozen such firms. Many of them were relatively small establishments which either folded up because they could not withstand competition or merged with more successful concerns. The number of agency houses in all the three Presidency cities as a result continued to fluctuate.

Agency houses were partnership firms. Though primarily trading houses, they also acted as bankers, bill brokers, shipowners, insurance agents, surveyors, and importers and exporters. They normally avoided entering those areas of commerce in which Indians were deeply entrenched and could thus offer stiff competition. Experimentation with relatively unexplored lines of business was the most striking feature of the strategy the agency houses adopted. The beginning of coal mining in India was entirely due to this propensity. The first attempt in this direction was made in 1775 by a firm formed by two Britons, but the beginning of a regular coal mining operation had to wait until 1820 when Alexander & Co. started exploring in the Raniganj area of the present-day state of Jharkhand. The beginnings of steam navigation in 1828 gave a new impetus to coal mining as coal provided fuel to the steamers plying on the Ganges and other rivers in the Bengal area. However, not all their experiments were successful and attempts to launch cotton manufacturing on modern lines by two agency houses in Bengal proved to be sheer adventure. A free merchant in Madras, Edward Heath, even wrestled with the impossible task of steel making.

Being unfamiliar with the land, its customs, and language, the European promoters of agency houses had to depend on Indian agents to assist them in business dealings in myriad ways. Generically knows as *banian*, the Indian agent was not a mere factotum. In many ways, he was the lynchpin of the entire operation. Without him no sales or purchases of goods could be made and no shipments could be organized. He was responsible for the quality and quantity of goods purchased or shipped through him. He was also a link between the Europeans and indigenous bankers. In most cases, the banian carried on his own trading operations as well. The term banian, it need be added, had a purely professional connotation and had nothing to do with the bania caste. Anyone engaged in the activities mentioned, regardless of his caste, was called banian.

Agency houses in general maintained very close relations with the Company government. They advanced funds to the Company in its hour of need, and on many occasions exported goods on its behalf and financed the movement of troops to far-off places. The Company government in turn assisted the agency houses with loans whenever they were in financial straits, which was quite often. In fact, without government support, it would have been difficult for many of them to survive. A remarkable degree of interdependence thus characterized the relations between the government and the agency houses.

Brief case studies of three prominent houses, one from each Presidency city, would provide a clearer understanding of the process of their emergence and the range of their operations.

Some Case Studies

Forbes & Co. of Bombay was the oldest of all the agency houses in the subcontinent. Its founder John Forbes came to Bombay in 1764 as a civil servant. Set up in 1767, it remained the only European mercantile firm in western India until 1790, when Bruce Fawcett & Co., another agency house, made its appearance. Both firms worked very closely with each other and even joined hands occasionally to monopolize the trade in certain commodities. In fact, many in Bombay looked upon these two companies as a single enterprise. The same kind of harmony marked the relations among other firms which came into being later. The flourishing commerce of the city had enough room for all to prosper.

The main areas of the operations of Forbes & Co. were, besides agency business, shipping, moneylending, and general trading. Shipping, however, was its special interest. Owning a number of ships, the company carried raw cotton from India and China to Britain for use in the mills at Lancashire and Manchester, and brought textile goods to be sold in these countries. It also exported tobacco, ivory, and spices from India. The Napoleonic Wars (1806–15) gave a great setback to European shipping, which encouraged Forbes & Co. to enter shipbuilding in right earnest.

The firm had numerous Parsee brokers who helped the firm in its transactions with Indian and foreign merchants. Brokers and agents also looked after the firm's business interests in China, which was a large consumer of opium imported from India. The trade in opium was so profitable that most of the mercantile firms in Bombay participated in it in some way or the other. Charles Forbes was against this trade in principle. However, his firm in Bombay could not always restrain from indulging in it, although opium export never became a major part of the Forbes operations.

Forbes & Co. maintained very close and cordial relations with the government of the East India Company, and supplied, jointly with Bruce Fawcett & Co., huge sums to the government at low rates of interest during the wars with the Maratha chiefs from 1799 to 1806. The Forbes loans are usually regarded as the forerunner of the public loan systems that the government launched in 1813.

At the time of the birth of Forbes & Co. in Bombay, Madras was in an extremely undeveloped state, being more of a British naval base than a commercial centre. It was not surprising under these conditions that the city had no agency house until 1789, when Thomas Parry founded one in partnership with the agent of a London-based company. The firm of Chase and Parry acted as a real estate agent, bought and sold navy bills, and traded in Madeira wines. The partnership also acted as agents for ships, lotteries, booksellers, and insurance firms. Its main business, however, was banking. Deposits were taken in and utilized to finance the firm's transactions. Soon after the birth of the partnership, the Third Anglo-Mysore War between the East India Company and Tipu Sultan broke out. Chase and Parry made handsome profits by supplying provisions to the huge army the British had assembled against the valiant Tipu. It was a promising beginning indeed.

In the next thirty-five years before his death in Madras in 1824, Parry would change several partners as a result of which the name of the firm would keep changing. Experimentation with relatively unexplored lines was the hallmark of his approach. While continuing with his traditional businesses, Parry decided to launch entirely on his own in 1805 what was a sort of industrial venture. This was a tannery, the first of its kind in Madras. He imported hides from Colombo, Penang, and the Cape of Good Hope and supplied leather goods to the Company troops, and also exported such goods to many countries.

Depression caused by the Napoleonic wars continued to plague business prospects but Parry's agency businesses as also his industrial concerns survived. After the end of the Napoleonic wars, when the business environment improved, Parry's fortunes under different partnerships took an upward turn, and by the beginning of the second decade of the nineteenth century, he was counted among the most prosperous and influential persons of the city. Entrusting most of the managerial responsibilities to his partners, Parry then practically retired from business. He died of cholera in 1824 at the age of 56, and lies buried at Cuddalore. The present Parry's Corner in Madras, where the Welsh adventurer had set up his headquarters as early as 1815, is still a mute reminder of his business endeavours.

At the time of Parry's death, there were more than a dozen prominent mercantile firms in Madras. At least two of these, besides Parry & Co., would continue to play a significant role in the business life of the region. Binny & Co. founded by John Binny, a Scotsman, exactly ten years after the birth of Parry & Co. had similar business interests, although its founder was far less adventurous and colourful. George Arbuthnot of a distinguished Scottish lineage founded Arbuthnot & Co. in 1809 with general trading and banking as the mainstay of its business. Apart from these major firms, there were a large number of private traders belonging to a variety of nationalities—Indian, Portuguese, Armenian, Chinese, Persian, Arabian, and natives of many European countries. The business community of the city had become quite variegated, and the city fairly populous since Thomas Parry's arrival thirty-seven years ago.

Unlike Forbes in Bombay and Parrys in Madras, Palmer & Co. was not the first agency house founded in Calcutta, but it developed into the largest and most powerful enterprise of its times. The founder of the firm John Palmer, whose father had served the English East India Company in many responsible positions, came to Calcutta sometime during the 1780s. For a number of years after his arrival, Palmer operated either alone or in partnership. Beginning with 1810, however, the name of the firm appears simply as Palmer & Co., suggesting that the founder was strong enough to dispense with partnership.

Within just a few years Palmer & Co. emerged as the most dominant enterprise in the city. Shipping, insurance, and general trading, besides agency business, were its major interests. But on occasions, it also experimented with some novel ideas, such as the establishment of a European-type bank called Calcutta Bank. This, however, was not the first institution of its kind in India. The pioneering role in this respect had been played by Alexander & Co. with the establishment of the Bank of Hindustan sometime during the 1770s followed by the Commercial Bank of Mackintosh & Co., another agency house. The publication of the *Calcutta Journal* was yet another unconventional venture promoted by Palmer & Co. Cruttenden & Co. was the only agency house which had preceded Palmer in the publishing business.

Whatever the stages of growth or the sequence in which various lines were added to his business portfolio, there is no doubt that Palmer's firm had emerged as fairly creditworthy by 1805, and was among the first to offer freight services to ship Bengal cotton to China, an export market the Company was keen to promote. Opium was another commodity that had great demand in China. Imperial edicts prohibiting its imports into the Celestial Empire had little effect in the face of large-scale popular addiction. The East India Company, however, did not carry the commodity in its own ships, even though it had the monopoly over the production and sale of the drug. Private traders and speculators, who bought it at the Company's periodical auction sales at Calcutta, transported it clandestinely to China in country ships. Palmer & Co. came to control such a large share of this trade that it was popularly referred to as the 'opium king'. On a few occasions, the firm also exported grains and saltpetre to China.

Boosting exports from Indian territories to China was important for the Company's authorities because that would obviate the need to import bullion into that country to procure Chinese goods including tea, for which there was great demand in Great Britain. Palmer & Co. also had a great hold on the export of indigo to Europe because of which it was called the 'indigo king' of Bengal. Coastal trade was another major source of profits for the house. The Indian and Arab traders, who once reigned supreme in the Indian Ocean, held on to their dominant position in the commerce between the various port cities of the country almost up to the middle of the eighteenth century. However, the British free merchants and agency houses had practically displaced the Indians and Arabs by the end of the century. Palmer & Co., a major instrument as well as beneficiary of this change, and many other agency houses in India extended their operations to other territories in the Indian Ocean that fell into British hands around this time, such as Ceylon, Malaya, New South Wales, the Cape of Good Hope, and Mauritius. On many occasions, they also transported foodstuffs to tide over temporary scarcity in the metropolitan country.

ON TO DISASTER

What has been detailed here is only a representative sample of the range of business interests of Palmer & Co., indeed of most of the prominent agency houses. Practically no sphere of business that promised a reasonable profit escaped their attention. The abolition of the East India Company's monopoly on trade with India under the Charter Act of 1813 gave a further push to their operations. In fact, within just a few years after the new Charter, the agency houses and private merchants displaced the East India Company from its position of supremacy in the commercial sphere. The Company now concentrated on the administration of the territories acquired in India rather than commercial pursuits.

Indigo was one of the commodities that had become the backbone of the trade between India and England by the time the new Charter was adopted. This was a consequence of the declining production of the commodity in the West Indies following the slave uprisings in 1791. Europe needed the article in great quantity, and the soil and climate of the northern Indian plains were ideally suited for its cultivation. Many British subjects took to indigo production in Bengal, and practically all the major agency houses in Calcutta became intimately involved with the financing of indigo production.

The period between 1819 and 1825 witnessed an almost uninterrupted boom in indigo trade, bringing huge profits to the agency houses. Expecting the boom to continue, they invested a large amount of resources in indigo production. Conditions, however, turned unfavourable in 1825–6 for a variety of reasons. Trading conditions continued to remain depressed both in India and England for the rest of the decade. Consequently, several agency houses became bankrupt. Palmer & Co., the 'Indigo King of Bengal', held its own for some time. But when the price of indigo experienced a precipitous fall, consequent upon an abundant crop in 1829, the firm found it difficult to weather the storm. Its private bank was the first casualty. A few months later, on 4 January 1830, the house itself, unable to meet the claims against it, closed its doors for good.

The failure of the largest of the agency houses generated a strong wave that engulfed most of the others, and by the beginning of 1834, all principal houses had disappeared from the scene, leaving the commerce of Bengal in the hands of minor firms. Only a few, like Gillanders Arbuthnot (established in 1819), managed to survive and prosper until the end of the colonial rule.

The causes of the failure of the Calcutta houses are obvious. With overdependence on the savings of the Company servants and wealthy Indians, they had a slender and uncertain capital base. This in itself would not have caused a problem, had they kept their speculative propensities under check. Their involvement in indigo production and trade crossed the bounds of all business prudence. The only source they could look to for succour was the Company government with whom they had maintained cordial relations, and whom they had helped in various ways. The government did try to salvage the situation, but there was a limit beyond which the government could not help without jeopardizing its own financial stability. It is significant that the agency houses in Bombay and Madras, whose operations remained by and large consistent with their resources, continued to survive, and some of them even grew into respectable industrial firms in due course of time.

While the British agency houses dominated the business scene in eastern India for well over three decades before they met their doom, Indian merchants were not entirely absent from the scene. But their operations were much more limited both in scope and scale. The names of Sheikh Gullam Hussain and Ram Dulal Dey appear in the Company records. The former sent rice and gruff goods to England in 1813, and the latter a variety of articles to Malta a little later. Both used their own ships. We do not know much about Hussain or his position in the Calcutta business, but Dey by all accounts was a force to reckon with. He had made his millions by working as a banian or factor to an American trader and exercised great influence in the Indian business circles. According to one estimate, as many as 155 vessels received supplies worth more than Rs 410 lakh through Dey's office between 1797 and 1821. An extremely cautious man in business dealings, he was not at all affected by the unsettled business conditions of the 1820s. He died in 1825 bequeathing considerable wealth to his two sons, Ashutosh and Promothanath, who continued to be active in the Calcutta business for another two decades. Other prominent Indians in business were Udit Narain Pal, Comul Lochun Basak, and Gopaldas Manohardas. However, in the range and complexity or territorial reach of their operations the Indian merchants, even the biggest of them, could seldom match, much less surpass, the British houses of agency. The first quarter of the nineteenth century in eastern India, without question, belonged to these houses.

MESSENGERS OF CHANGE

Whatever the failings of the agency houses, they did broaden the horizon of Indian business. The relatively unconventional lines in which they perceived opportunities for gain, the manner in which they assembled their resources, and the aggression with which they pursued their interests opened up new vistas for business, pointing to new avenues of enterprise, and to new ways of exploiting them.

The message of the operations of the agency houses and free merchants could not have been lost on Indian merchants. Private alien operators, unlike officials of the East India Company, had very close interaction with the Indian mercantile community. Their Indian banian was a very critical resource, deeply involved at every functional level of business from procurement to shipment of goods. He thus had the opportunity to watch the operations of his foreign clients from close quarters and imbibe some of their business methods and attitudes. Even the merchants not directly associated with the agency houses must have felt the impact of the demonstration effect of their business endeavours. In the process, the agency houses and free merchants became role models for an influential section of the Indian business community in Calcutta which developed great trust and admiration for them. Dwarkanath Tagore, unquestionably the most influential Bengali of his times, told a public meeting in 1834: 'Twenty years ago the Company treated us as slaves. Who raised us from this state but the merchants of Calcutta?... It was to the merchants, agents, and other independent English settlers that the natives of Calcutta were indebted for the superiority they possess over their countrymen in the Mofussil'. While a section of the European community in Calcutta condemned the agency houses and free merchants for their dishonesty and chicanery, many Indians admired their entrepreneurial capabilities.

The demonstration effect of the business performance of the agency houses and admiration for them was reinforced by a number of salutary developments. The beginnings of secular education was one of these. Although a formal declaration introducing English education had to wait until 1835, the process of secularization had begun much earlier, of which the establishment of the Hindu College in Calcutta in 1817 was probably the most visible symbol. By the end of the first quarter of the century, the impact of Western ideas and new education was already noticeable in Bengal. The growing disregard for time-honoured customs and traditions by English-educated Bengali youth caused much anguish to parents and guardians. But on the positive plane, the new education, to quote R.C. Majumdar, 'instilled into the minds of Indians a spirit of rational enquiry into the basis of the their religion and society'.

For those who were influenced by this spirit, occupational choice was purely a function of economic consideration, and deviation from caste norms in choosing one's career or pursuing a calling constituted no infringement of religion. Admittedly, only a small group of people had felt this influence, but they were sufficient in number to fill the vacuum created by the fall of the agency houses in the business life of eastern India. A host of firms promoted by them emerged soon after the eclipse of major agency houses. These firms, mostly partnership concerns, had business lines similar to those of the old agency houses. They were mainly interested in export business, and were involved directly or indirectly in the production of export commodities such as indigo, sugar, and silk.

The most prominent of these new firms were promoted jointly by Indian and English businessmen, and these were the most influential enterprises in Bengal during the 1930s and 1940s. Of these Carr, Tagore & Co.; Oswald, Seal & Co.; and Rustomji, Turner & Co. emerged as the most powerful. Significantly, the Indian partners in all three firms—Motilal Seal, Rustomji Cowasji, and Dwarkanath Tagore—had close prior business contacts with Englishmen whose enterprising spirit they admired. European liberalism, that was slowly seeping into Bengali life and thought, struck a sympathetic chord in them; and movements like the Brahmo Samaj, aimed at cleansing Hindu society of dogma and superstition, had their implicit or explicit support. Dwarkanath Tagore, the senior partner in Carr, Tagore & Co. was by far the most prominent businessman of his times in eastern India. He was also among the most influential citizens of Calcutta. Born into a Brahman zamindar family, he had been educated in an English school and had developed some measure of legal expertise through personal effort. The well-known agency house, Mackintosh & Co., had a Tagore for its banian for a number of years. Several Tagores also held high offices under the Company government. The reform movement taking shape in Bengal under the leadership of Rammohan Roy found a great champion in Dwarkanath who emerged as a prominent leader of the Brahmo Samaj, next only to the founder himself. A supporter of India's political connection with Britain, he was particularly impressed by the business endeavours of the agency houses and developed close relations with many of them including Mackintosh & Co. and Palmer & Co.

During most of the 1820s, when the agency houses were passing through a turbulent time, Dwarkanath was in the employ of the Company government, occupying a high office. However, he had developed an influential position for himself in the Calcutta business circles by 1829 when Mackintosh & Co. decided to wind up its Commercial Bank and promote the Union Bank entirely independent of the mercantile interest of the firm. Though Dwarkanath was not among the directors of the new bank, he, together with his friends and associates, held substantial shares and made sure that his brother Ramnath was elected treasurer.

As commercial crisis deepened in Calcutta in the late 1820s, resulting in widespread business failures, Tagore began to conjure up his business dreams. His association with John Palmer had brought him in contact with one

William Carr who had come to India as early as 1824 and joined Palmer & Co. as a partner. Impressed by Carr's talents, business experience, and mercantile knowledge, Tagore asked him to join as partner in launching Carr, Tagore & Co. in 1834, the largest firm of its kind in Calcutta and the first biracial enterprise in India. Dwarkanath perhaps believed that having a European partner would provide a certain measure of respectability to the firm. Perhaps because of the same consideration 'Carr' preceded 'Tagore' in the name of the company, even though Dwarkanath was the moving spirit behind this venture, the principal provider of capital, and the most dominant figure in its management. William Carr in fact was a mere sleeping partner in the firm.

Export trade was the mainstay of Tagore's business. As Britain and Europe were the principal destinations for its cargoes, Carr, Tagore & Co. had its own correspondents in London and La Havre to whom the consignments were sent and who handled the business in their respective cities. Like the British houses, Tagore's firm too operated on the basis of backward integration to control the production and processing of the commodities it exported, namely indigo, sugar, silk, silk piece-goods, saltpetre, hides, rice, timber, and rum. The chief source of these goods was his landed estate, which became a valuable tool in his hands to control the supply of goods that Carr, Tagore & Co. exported. Apart from these activities, that were similar to those of the agency houses, Tagore's company helped promote a number of joint stock concerns and managed them in the name of the shareholders, even though the joint stock principle was yet to be enshrined in the law of the land. The process started in 1836 when Tagore purchased what was the largest coal mine in the country, Raniganj Colliery in Burdwan, from Alexander & Co. Bengal Coal Company that he organized in 1843 incorporating Raniganj Colliery, virtually controlled the supply of fuel in the entire Presidency. Soon after his entry into coal mining, Tagore promoted four joint stock enterprises, all of which were dependent on Bengal Coal Company for fuel. These were Calcutta Steam Tug Association, Bengal Salt Company, Steam Ferry Bridge Co., and India General Steam Navigation Company.

Apart from the companies he fully controlled, Tagore had a finger in many other pies. In fact, few joint stock companies in Calcutta were formed without his direct or indirect support, or in which he or his partners were not involved in some way or the other. No one in Calcutta, Indian or European, equalled, much less surpassed, the business power of this Bengali Brahman during his lifetime. Admittedly, the ideas for all his ventures did not originate with Dwarkanath himself; some were the brainchild of his British partners and associates. But it was largely due to his position in the Calcutta business world and his financial clout that they became a concrete, visible reality.

Tagore's companies, however, exploited by and large the fields that had been made familiar by the British agency houses. His attitude to riskier or more unfamiliar lines was one of caution and ambivalence. Tea plantation was one such area. In their attempt to develop tea cultivation in India, the officials of the East India Company had established experimental tea gardens in the Assam hills under government control and ownership during the early 1830s. By 1838, the Company government was ready to hand over its gardens to private enterprise. Dwarkanath initially showed some interest in acquiring these gardens, but stepped aside when a group of London-based merchants formed Assam Company and made a bid to exploit this unique opportunity. He dealt with potential competition from London in another field in a similar fashion. Interested in building a railway line, Dwarkanath founded Great Western of Bengal in 1844, but the route he chose clashed with one proposed by the London promoters of another company. Instead of putting up a fight, Dwarkanath preferred to let the rival concern absorb his firm.

Why did he give his rivals in tea plantation and railway development a virtual walkover? Was it because of his concern to avoid a conflict between the British and Indian wings of imperial citizenry? It is well known that Dwarkanath had very high opinion of the entrepreneurial capabilities of the British. It is not unlikely that the material resources and managerial skills available to him did not give him sufficient confidence to compete with the British organizers of enterprises in the lines of business with which he was entirely unfamiliar. If this was so, events proved that he was not wrong in his assessment of the situation. For, both the ventures from which he withdrew had precarious, uncertain existence for years to come before they attained a measure of stability.

MANAGERIAL FAILURES

Whether the above companies would have fared better in Tagore's hands is extremely doubtful. For, barring Calcutta Steam Tug Association and Bengal Coal Company, both of which operated in a monopolistic situation, none of his other concerns fared particularly well. Steam Ferry Bridge and Bengal Salt Company wound up within just a few years of their formation; India General Steam Navigation maintained a rather precarious existence during Tagore's lifetime; and Carr, Tagore & Co. was normally identified with jobbery, manipulation, and cliquism in the Calcutta business world. Dwarkanath's forte, obviously, was enterprise creation rather than enterprise management. To be fair to him, however, it must be added that the second quarter of the nineteenth century was not an age of efficient management in Calcutta business any more than the first quarter had been. The disaster that overtook the British agency houses at the end of the 1820s apparently did not provide a lasting lesson to the generation that followed.

Nothing illustrates this better than the career of Union Bank, the largest business institution of its time, in which almost the entire business world of Calcutta had high stakes. Dwarkanath was not among its directors at the time of its birth in 1829, but soon became the most powerful voice in its management. Although the government refused to grant the bank a charter of limited liability and was never particularly helpful, the bank maintained steady progress during the first decade despite a few minor crises. A buoyed management, with the powerful support of Dwarkanath, decided in 1839 to increase the share capital from Rs 15 lakh to Rs 1 crore, enter the exchange business, and advance loans to indigo producers against the properties, equipment, and produce of the factories as well as against the personal security of the borrowers.

The new basis of advancing credit exposed the bank to serious hazards. This became patently clear barely three years later when a number of firms, heavily indebted to the bank, failed. But the management ignored the warning signals and the bank's involvement with indigo exporters continued to grow. So deeply involved with the indigo producers did the bank become during the next two years that it lost its original character of a commercial bank. In the meantime, the continually declining prices of indigo were leading the bank into an increasingly deeper quagmire from which there seemed to be no escape. This was the situation in 1847 when Great Britain, because of a junction of diverse circumstances, was hit by a deep commercial crisis. Many mercantile houses closed down. A large number of them had business connections with the Calcutta firms that were heavily indebted to Union Bank. The distress inevitably spread to Calcutta where as many as sixteen houses fell within a week. The bank lost heavily in the process. Enquiries revealed a sorry mess of misappropriation, mismanagement, and misuse of a public institution for private gain. Unable to withstand the combined pressure of all these unfavourable factors, the bank declared itself insolvent in January 1848. Along with the Bank, a host of firms went down the drain, including Carr, Tagore & Co. and all other Indo-British partnerships that had come into being after the crisis of the early 1830s. A host of British firms mainly engaged in importing manufactured goods from Britain also disappeared from the scene. It is somewhat strange that the kind of crisis that had brought ruin to the British agency houses at the beginning of the 1830s repeated itself within less than two decades with much greater fury. And this time, it engulfed the entire business world of Calcutta.

LASTING CONTRIBUTION

Dwarkanath Tagore, who had played such a critical role in building—as also unwittingly destroying—this world did not live to see his dream crashing. He had died about two years before the commercial crisis of 1847 set in. There is no doubt that as Carr, Tagore & Co. developed into the most dominant enterprise in eastern India, far ahead of the contemporary European companies in Calcutta, respect for the Indian businessman in the eyes of his European counterparts went up several notches. Never before or since in colonial India did the Indian businessman have a greater sense of equality with his European counterparts as he had in Bengal of the 1830s and 1840s. This was largely due to the environment Dwarkanath and his ilk had shaped by their conduct and action.

This kind of equality was admittedly bound to be short-lived, as it was in basic conflict with the colonial ethos where equality between the governing and governed classes in any sphere can only be ephemeral. But Dwarkanath's experiment in organizing and managing joint stock enterprises within the rubric of a single managerial structure was a lasting contribution to Indian business and management. The attempt to launch joint stock firms in the face of legal handicaps was a bold innovation in itself, without precedence in Indian business, with the exception of Union Bank in the birth of which Dwarkanath himself had played a leading role. But to conceive of a single firm promoting a string of enterprises with interlocking capital and a common management was a truly revolutionary concept indeed. Although the genesis of the concept lay in some of the agency houses managing the properties and affairs of others for a fee, nobody had ever used this idea to create fairly large corporate systems. In a country where capital, managerial resources, and risk-taking attitude were all in short supply, this was perhaps the best way to advance the cause of business. Dwaraknath's companies had much too brief an existence to validate this concept or invest it with a general acceptability. But without question his experiment was the incubator for a form of management—the managing agency system—that would provide the basic framework for managing India's industrial firms in the not too distant future. The court of history, thus, may adjudge Tagore to be the father of modern Indian business.

No Bengali, however, came forward to build upon the essentials of Dwarkanath's legacy. The disaster that swept Calcutta business at the end of the 1840s would continue to keep Bengalis off modern business for decades to come, leaving the field almost exclusively for foreign operators or immigrants from other parts of India to exploit. Bengal still had moneyed men, including the descendants of Dwarkanath Tagore and Motilal Seal, but what was lacking was the will to re-enter a world that looked both frightening and distant. Bengalis did not withdraw from the business scene altogether—Ashutosh Dey & Co. and Ram Gopal Ghosh & Co. were still among the leading agency houses in Calcutta during the 1850s—but the verve and the optimism of the 1840s had disappeared, perhaps never to return.

In contrast, the crisis of the 1840s had at best a temporary impact on the business plans and operations of the Europeans. Old houses like Gillanders Arbuthnot continued to consolidate their positions, while new firms continued to emerge. In fact some of the European houses that came into being during the 1840s would develop into formidable concerns and important players in Indian business. These included Kilburn & Co. originally formed by a Russian national, C.E. Schoene, in 1842 but taken over by E.D. Kilburn seven years later, and Mackinon Mackenzie formed by William Mackinon and Robert Mackenzie in 1847. The former specialized in the import-export trade in the initial stages, but developed into a prominent managing agency with extensive interest in tea, insurance, and shipping. The latter started as general merchants, but later launched a shipping line which eventually metamorphosed into the powerful British India Steam Navigation Company (BI) registered in London.

As a result of the exertions of firms like these and others that followed, the expatriates re-established their dominance on the business scene of eastern India after a brief interregnum of less than two decades, while the natives retreated into the background. Had the natives emulated the finer points of Dwarkanath's enterprising spirit, perhaps eastern India, and not western, would have been the first to witness the rise of modern industries in the country.

CHAPTER 4

THE WESTERN SCENARIO

THE BUSINESS SCENE IN WESTERN INDIA IN THE FIRST HALF OF THE
nineteenth century was in complete contrast to the east. Here the European
agency houses never carved out a dominant presence, Indo-British business
partnerships were unheard of, and business failures were comparatively few.
The region undeniably had many prominent businessmen, but none came
close to the power and prestige of Dwarkanath Tagore. Business life revolved
around conventional trading and moneylending. Families belonging to
certain castes and clans dominated the scene, and attempts to form joint stock
concerns were few and far between. In short, business life in this region was
much more stable and less exciting than in the eastern part.

BUSINESS STABILITY

The business stability in western India was due to many factors. The region,
particularly its northern part, roughly comprising the present state of Gujarat,
had a long and deeply entrenched commercial tradition. Many families and
clans had remained engaged in trading and moneylending on a big scale for
centuries. Departure from these lines in which they were so firmly established
would have meant an opportunity loss for them. Caution would have prevented
them from experimenting with new lines, the future of which was still
uncertain. With the occupational division of society still remaining largely
undented, new entrants to business came from similar social backgrounds
and, therefore, with similar attitude to risk taking. They preferred to perpetuate
rather than disturb the well-established ways of doing things.

In the southern part of the region, comprising roughly the western districts of the present-day Maharashtra, business development was at a stage where departure from conventions was not easily possible. With limited British possessions in the region well up to the end of the second decade of the nineteenth century, British businessmen had a limited presence. The demonstration effect of their pursuits would have been but limited. The growing city of Bombay, where the British set the tone, was the only area in the region that demonstrated some forward trends, but neither in terms of volume nor in complexity of business did it come anywhere close to the populous metropolis of the east.

The traditional mercantile classes under these conditions still occupied a prominent place in the business life of the region. The special financial requirements of the government of the Bombay Presidency added to their clout. The Presidency, as is well known, remained a chronically deficit area, dependent on remittances from Bengal to meet the cost of administration, almost up to the middle of the century. Only the shroffs and bankers could facilitate these remittances through their hundi network. This must have invested them with some clout. On the whole, however, the business environment had considerably worsened since the disintegration of the Mughal Empire. The region's trade with West Asia—Red Sea and Persian Gulf littorals—and Europe had declined; its long distance overland links with the rest of the country had been ruptured; and the volume of trade between the west coast and Bengal had substantially declined. The Indian merchants in western India, as elsewhere, did have a brief period of glory under the successor states that arose on the ruins of the Mughal Empire. But they had become increasingly inward looking, thanks to the region's weakened commercial links with other parts of the country and the world.

THE RISE OF BOMBAY

Then the almost insatiable need of opium in the Celestial Empire opened up a whole new world of opportunities for merchants in Ahmedabad, Surat, Broach, Cambay, Baroda, Bombay, and even the smaller centres of trade. As mentioned earlier, opium had become a major item of export to China from Bengal by the end of the eighteenth century, as the Chinese were too passionately addicted to the drug to honour official injunction against its use. The British, in the meanwhile, had developed a tremendous fondness for tea, the consumption of which had been steadily rising. Imports of opium from the British possessions in India generated the resources to pay for the exports of Chinese tea to Britain. A large proportion of the opium exported from Bengal was produced in areas that were under the direct jurisdiction of the East India Company. The Company government, therefore, exercised monopolistic control over the production and sale of the drug, and the exporters of Bengal opium usually acquired the commodity from auction sales periodically organized by the Company authorities.

In contrast, the export of opium from western India remained a clandestine affair for a long time as the Bombay government had imposed severe restrictions on private trade in the commodity. But the Bombay government was hardly in a position to bring the production and sale of the drug under its exclusive control as practically all opium-producing areas in western and central India lay in territories governed by independent Indian rulers and chiefs until the end of the second decade of the century. The city of Ujjain, the most important centre of opium trade in the western region, was not under the Company's direct control. From the wholesalers in the producing regions to the stockists at various centres of trade, the merchants in western India formed a long and intricate supply chain for exports. Operating clandestinely, it ended at such ports on the west coast as were still not under the British control: Karachi, Cambay, Bhavnagar, Broach, and Daman. So efficiently did this network for exporting opium to China function that the British authorities had no inkling of it until the onset of the nineteenth century.

The Company authorities tried to check the export of opium from western India in a variety of ways, but to no avail. An exasperated government eventually resorted, in 1831, to what may be called a system of regulated trade. Anyone interested in exporting opium from Bombay and other British possessions had to obtain a pass—something like an export permit—and agree to pay a heavy export duty. This brought the Bombay-based merchants into the business of opium export in a big way. The city had in the meantime grown substantially because of immigration of a large number of people from Gujarat, and to a lesser extent, the Maratha country.

The immigrants belonged to a variety of social groups, but the most conspicuous and prominent of them were the Parsees. Many Gujarat towns such as Surat, Broach, Navsari, and Cambay had a large concentration of Parsees. In these towns, the Europeans, particularly the English, had depended on the services of people belonging to this community as middlemen, agents, and brokers since the beginning of their commercial contacts with India. The Parsees possessed the knowledge of the land and its language, and being a small minority it was relatively easy for them to deal with the foreigners and mediate between different interests and political powers. As Bombay was emerging as the hub of commerce, the Parsees gravitated to it and established themselves as guarantee brokers, contractors and suppliers for troops, importers and exporters, shipbuilders, general traders, and even moneylenders. The less fortunate among them worked as weavers, carpenters, artisans, liquor brewers, and retailers of imported alcoholic drinks. Generally associated with agriculture until then, the Parsees with their growing involvement in Bombay's trade and commerce, gradually metamorphosed into a business community.

Exploiting the emergent business opportunities, many Parsee migrants had already carved out a dominant position in the business life of Bombay much before the removal of restrictions on opium export from this port. The Wadias were perhaps the most prominent. Originally from Surat, the family had an artisan background. Known for their skill in carpentry, they were invited as the master shipbuilder when the East India Company established the Bombay Dockyard in 1736. But it was only after the later generations of the family turned to trade during the 1780s, exporting cotton to China among other things, that the Wadia fortunes took a really upward swing. A large number of other Parsee families had also emerged as successful traders and shippers by the time the policy of regulated trade in opium was introduced. Most of them worked very closely with European firms in a variety of ways.

Next to the Parsees to be lured to Bombay were the Gujarati banias, both Hindus and Jains. As the prevailing caste rules would not permit them to undertake sea voyages, they remained practically aloof from export business, but became active in the coastal trade, bringing to the city the products of Gujarat and Konkan including raw cotton to feed the export trade to China, and cotton piece goods for the Arabian Sea and Persian Gulf markets.

Another class of Hindu merchants came from the Kutchh-Kathiawar region. These were the Bhatias, Lohanas, and Bhansalis. They started moving to Bombay around the beginning of the nineteenth century and remained confined to modest trade in general merchandise. The Muslim immigrants from the Kutchh-Kathiawar region were Bohras, Khojas, and Memons. As a class, the Konkani Muslims seem to have been more successful in Bombay business during this period than the Muslim immigrants from Gujarat. The most prominent of them all were the Roghays whose founder Muhammad Ali bin Muhammad Hussain Roghay was known as Nakhoda (shipmaster) as he owned a large number of ships. With the exception of the Konkani

Muslims, immigrants from the Maratha country were rather poorly represented in the business life of the developing city.

Besides the major groups of businessmen mentioned, Bombay, during the first quarter of the nineteenth century, also had a small Jewish population, the descendants of a small group that had come to India a long time ago to escape persecution. Most of them worked as carpenters, masons, and small traders. David Sassoon, a Jewish immigrant from Baghdad, joined them in 1832. Belonging to a family that had occupied a prominent position in Baghdad for generations, he had to migrate to India because conditions for the Jewish minority in Baghdad had become much less hospitable by the end of the eighteenth century. With an eye on a two-way export and import business between India and Persia, he set up a trading firm, David Sassoon & Sons.

Bombay by this time had already developed into a respectable commercial centre. The lifting of the ban on opium trade and export from Bombay in 1831 boosted business prospects still further. For much of the drug produced in the Malwa area now found its way legitimately to Bombay through the same commercial network that had been feeding the illegal transhipment to other ports on the west coast. The result was a growing and close integration between Bombay and its vast hinterland, as a consequence of which the city soon developed into the premier entrepôt of not only Malwa opium but also of the entire produce of south-west India. Bombay previously had been developing at a normal pace; its progress was now so fast that by the middle of the nineteenth century it became the hub of business and commercial life in western India.

THE MERCHANTS OF BOMBAY

Enormous profits were being made as a result of the successively rising exports of opium to China after 1831. Those who had already joined the export trade in the commodity stepped up their operations while a large number of new entrants came forward to reap the harvest. The Parsees, who had remained dominant in the field, retained their position. The China trade became almost synonymous with Parsee families such as the Readymoneys, the Kamas, the Banajis, the Jejeebhoys, and the Petits. The Bombay-based exporters to China operated on their own accounts as well as on behalf of others, particularly up-country merchants. The British agency houses too preferred to ship opium through the Indian merchants to avoid the risk involved in the contraband trade—let us not forget that the import of the drug in China was unlawful—of a commodity subject to great price fluctuation. Most Bombay exporters organized the sale of their cargoes in China through the British agency houses in that country which charged commission for their labours. Opium exports to China yielded substantial profits—certainly higher than moneylending, internal trade, and real estate transactions. Part of the money earned through these businesses was used to acquire landed property, as there were few other areas of investment. In the process the Parsees, the most dominant group in the city's commercial life, also emerged as the largest landholders in the city.

Strangely enough, despite all their commercial success and close interaction with Europeans, who had a strong presence in Bombay, the Parsees formed no joint ventures with them which was a characteristic feature of the Calcutta business during the 1830s and 1840s. A few banking firms set up as joint stocks were the only examples of common participation by Indian and British businessmen. The move to establish banking firms was partly a result of the setback in the fortunes of a number of Bombay-based agency houses, consequent upon the abolition of the East India Company's monopoly on trade with the East in 1833. The prosperity of these houses was closely linked with the Company's trading privileges; once these were taken away, they found it difficult to stand on their own feet. The banks were expected to replace the agency houses as a repository of the savings of the European business community in the city and a source of business finance. Whether and to what extent the banking institutions served this purpose is debatable, but their emergence had little impact on the business of the traditional shroffs and Indian merchants whose operations in most cases represented an amalgam of trading, banking, brokerage, and agency business.

However, those like the Parsee merchants and Konkani Muslims, who had built their fortunes on China trade, received a setback during the 1840s because of two developments taking place beyond the borders of India. One was the Treaties of Nanking (1842) and Tientsin (1858) that opened China to the rest of the world and permitted free imports of opium. The China traders of Bombay now faced a challenge from many quarters, including European firms. The second was the growing use of steamships in international commerce, rendering the age-old sailing vessels obsolete in the process. The competitive advantage of the China traders of Bombay, who had for decades depended on sailing vessels, was further eroded.

The impact of these changes on the structure of Bombay commerce was so swift that by 1850 the Indian merchants had lost their hold on the China trade—the principal source of their prosperity—which now passed into the hands of European traders. Bombay, however, did not witness the kind of widespread business failures that Calcutta experienced during the 1840s. Unlike the Calcutta firms, the Bombay merchants largely traded with their own capital, and the returns from their banking, brokerage, and real estate businesses were sufficient to sustain them even as their export operations shrank. Their commercial difficulties of the 1840s, therefore, caused only a temporary setback. Instead of withdrawing from the scene as their counterparts in Calcutta did, they were now looking for new avenues of investment and profit.

THE CAREER OF JAMSETJI JEJEEBHOY

The career of Jamsetji Jejeebhoy illustrates in many ways the trials and triumphs of Indian merchants in Bombay during the first half of the nineteenth century. It also reflects some broad features of the organization and mechanics of the Bombay business. Born in 1783 as the son of a poor Parsee weaver at Navsari, Jamsetji moved to Bombay at the age of 12 to live with his maternal uncle who traded in used bottles. Soon he caught the attention of one of his cousins, a China trader, who despatched him to China as his agent in 1802. He made three more trips to China as the agent of other Parsees during that decade. Through these assignments as also through exporting cotton to England during the Napoleonic wars, he had acquired a small fortune by the end of the second decade of the nineteenth century and earned a prominent place for himself among the city's trading community. By 1822 we find him exporting a large cargo of opium to China for a British firm.

By the time Jamsetji started shipping opium on behalf of his European client, the Bombay government had already introduced the auction sale of the drug as one of the measures to check the illegal trade. By 1826 he himself was participating in such auction sales to acquire the commodity for export. He had also become the owner of a large fleet of ships by this time. Large-scale trade, shipping, and opium export to China remained the cornerstone of his business for the most part of his life.

The strategic framework of his operations was what is known as consignment trade, consisting of three basic elements: the consignor who financed the cargo, the shippers responsible for the management of the voyage, and the resident agents who organized the sale at the other end. While the resident agents were compensated through commission on sales, the shippers claimed a share in the profits as reward for their labours. Jamsetji's consignors included not only the Bombay-based mercantile houses, but also some of the most prominent merchants of Ahmedabad such as Vakhatchand Khushalchand, Hatheesing Kesarising, and Karamchand Premchand. A great-grandson of the illustrious Shantidas Zaveri and a forerunner of the present Lalbhai family, Vakhatchand was a *nagarsheth* of Ahmedabad; Hatheesing presided over a large banking firm; and Karamchand Premchand, also a banker, was an ancestor of the famous Sarabhai family of the later times.

What it means is that Jamsetji had a large network of traders and merchants at the commercial and producing centres that fed his shipping operations. At the other end of the spectrum was the famous mercantile house of Jardine Matheson & Co. at Canton that organized the sale of the goods brought by his ships. Jamsetji and William Jardine had been friends since both were young and without any great achievement to their credit. The personal bond later resulted in a lifelong business arrangement as Jardine's partnership firm, established jointly with James Matheson, grew into one of the most powerful agency houses at the Chinese port. The firm handled almost one-third of the entire opium arriving at Canton from Bombay, and the largest quantity of tea exported to Britain. So close were Jamsetji's relations with the British agency house that Jardine Matheson & Co. often waived its commission on Jamsetji's own consignments and sometimes also on those belonging to his close friends.

Although Bombay understandably was the nerve centre of Jamsetji's operations, he also exported a substantial quantity of opium and cotton to China from Calcutta, and cotton from Madras. His affairs at Calcutta were handled by Jardine Skinner & Co. in which William Jardine's brother, David, was a partner. He also had close connections with another Calcutta house, Lyall Matheson & Co., in which James Matheson's brother was a partner. Charles Skinner (whose brother John was a partner in Jardine Skinner & Co.), looked after the Calcutta firm's interests in Bombay. The Canton-based firm of Jardine Matheson & Co., thus, had close associates at Calcutta as well as Bombay. Jamsetji had no direct stakes in these firms, but he was as much an integral part of this network as any of the owners. He often volunteered advice on the internal affairs of their firms and they valued his advice. Jamsetji's position vis-à-vis the Jardine-Matheson-Skinner combine was thus more like that of a partner than a mere business associate. His links with the Bombay government were equally strong. And yet Jamsetji had to contend with what he termed as 'widespread prejudice' and discriminatory laws against the country ships in England.

Jamsetji, like other Indian exporters to China, had little difficulty in remitting his sale proceeds back home as long as the English East India Company had a monopoly on the China trade. For, he could easily obtain from the Company treasury at Canton the bills of exchange for equivalent value drawn either at the Court of Directors in London or the Company government in Calcutta. With the abolition of its monopoly on the China trade, the Company could absorb relatively lesser funds, and therefore, issued much fewer bills. To get around the problem, Jamsetji resorted to several expedients. On one hand, he urged his agents at Canton to send *sycee*, ignots of Chinese silver, in payment. On the other hand, he began exporting Chinese tea and silk to London. He also tried to reroute his funds from China to India via Britain by importing Chinese goods into Britain and British goods into India. None of these arrangements, however, proved entirely satisfactory. Shippers like Jamsetji, who operated on short-term credit extended by their consignors, had no easy answer to the challenge posed by an interlocking international credit network and a new breed of European and American competitors who had entered the China trade in the wake of the opening of China.

Jamsetji continued to run his operations profitably despite this challenge, but he could do little to counter the technological superiority of steamships which had become increasingly popular by the beginning of the 1840s. Reading the writings on the wall, Jamsetji started selling his ships. A few of them were burnt in mysterious fires in Bombay and Calcutta harbours. The process of elimination by sale or fire culminated in Jamsetji's large fleet of vessels being reduced to two by the end of the decade. This meant a total collapse of the very foundation of Jamsetji's business. True, he had other sources of profit, but most of these were directly or indirectly linked with his shipping operations. The end of his shipping career or the slackening of his other businesses as a consequence, however, made little dent on his power and prestige in the business world of Bombay. He had been knighted in 1842 at the heyday of his career; he became the first Indian to earn a still more coveted honour, a baronetcy, in 1857, several years after the end of his shipping business. Even after his death two years later, his family remained, largely because of his legacy, a powerful force in the social life of the city.

While the opening of China marked the decline of Jamsetji's operations, it proved to be a turning point in the fortunes of David Sassoon. Between his arrival in Bombay in 1832 and the Treaty of Nanking in 1842, he had mainly concentrated on developing a multilateral trade between India, Persia, Mesopotamia (now a part of Iraq), and Britain. These operations were sufficient to build a small fortune, but were not sufficient to earn for Sassoon a place among the front-ranking businessmen of the city. Though China always attracted him, it was not until 1844, two years after the Treaty of Nanking, that he started exploring the business possibilities in that country.

David's second son, Elia, took charge of the China operations and established branches at Canton, Hong Kong, and Shanghai. With Shanghai as their base, the Sassoons now entered the opium trade in a big way and established themselves firmly in this line within barely five years after their entry into the field. Instead of owning their own ships, they used the facilities owned by other merchants and thus avoided the fate that overtook Jejeebhoy's operations. In this fashion the Sasoons attained a near monopoly position in opium export. Simultaneously, they continued to explore the Chinese markets for the products of India, and expand their operations to other regions in South East Asia where they developed a vigorous interest in spice trade. Significantly, the Sassoons were the first among the Bombay mercantile houses to open a branch in Japan—at Yokohama—within barely four years after that country ended its centuries-long isolation from the rest of the world in 1853.

Despite all that Bombay gave them, the Sassoons always identified themselves with the Western world, never with India. Not surprisingly, David Sassoon decided to acquire a British citizenship in 1853, barely a few years after he had attained an unrivalled position in the Bombay trading circles. Bombay, however, remained the nerve centre of the Sassoons' operations, although they would open a branch in London in 1858, and their Chinese branches would continue to flourish. Exploiting the opportunities that arose in the wake of the consolidation of the British rule, they would continue to grow from strength to strength. In this process, their racial linkages with the Western world stood them in good stead—the kind of linkages few Indian merchants were in a position to build.

Other Centres

Jamsetji, Sassoon, and a vast majority of people in business in western India and elsewhere were the representatives of an age when commercial capitalism ruled the roost in the country; when success in trade and moneylending was the maximum an ambitious businessman could dream of. In other parts of India, where conditions were less favourable for large-scale trade, there were merchants operating at regional or local levels. One area that presented a somewhat different picture was Sind. Shikarpur in this province was home to powerful bankers and traders like Ramdas Hinduja, Daya Ram Lohana, and Narayan Das Bhatia; and a large number of Shikarpuri merchants were active in Central Asian trade. Karachi too was developing as a major centre of trade and attracting immigrants from the neighbouring regions, including Gujarat, after the province came under British occupation in 1843. British territorial expansion seems to have provided some impetus to inland migration in pursuit of business opportunities.

The spurt in the number of Rajasthanis moving to other parts of the country suggests the same thing. Inter-state movement of merchants had been a common feature of business life in the Rajputana kingdoms before the rise of the British supremacy. Sometimes famine conditions or such other natural calamities influenced their decisions, while on many occasions the merchants were lured by the concessions and facilities for business offered by a ruler. The Rajputana merchants moved to the neighbouring regions also, but only a few of them were moving to far-off regions in search of better business opportunities before the British established their hegemony over the entire land. After that, there was a steady rise in the number of such migrants, and their destinations were not confined to the nearby places alone.

Also, while the early emigrants belonged almost exclusively to the thinly populated, arid region of Marwar, greener pastures elsewhere now began to invite residents of other parts of Rajputana as well. They went in all directions, to all places that promised better business prospects, and which already had a nucleus of settlers from their homeland to help them settle down. Calcutta, however, became their preferred destination, perhaps because it was the headquarters of the Company government and a centre of vigorous commerce. Also a small but active group of immigrants from the Rajputana area, most of them from Marwar region, had been operating in business there for several decades, including the illustrious Jagat Seth family. Since these early adventurers had never severed their links with their native place, they served as some sort of a resource group for the new comers.

The immigrants did not form a homogenous group. The native Bengalis, however, referred to the entire Rajasthani diaspora by the generic name of Marwari after the name of the region from where the earlier settlers had come. This was understandable in view of the fact that all immigrant traders from Rajasthan shared a common lifestyle, spoke the same language, wore similar kind of clothing, and specialized primarily in trading and moneylending. They remained a discrete community by themselves since most of the immigrants maintained their links with their original homeland, and their distinctive social and linguistic characteristics prevented their integration with the local Bengali population. In due course, the term 'Marwari' would come to signify a discrete business community comprising all businessmen of Rajasthani origin operating from outside Rajasthan.

It is appropriate to add here that the Rajputana traders who decided to move to other places in search of better opportunities were as a rule small operators, persons of modest means, who did not see much future for themselves in their native places with limited business opportunities. Prominent traders and bankers, enjoying the patronage of the Rajput chiefs and occupying respectable positions in society, continued with their operations in their homeland but started setting up branches of their firms in other parts of India. In the process an increasingly larger number of Marwari businesses, primarily trading and moneylending, emerged in practically all parts of India, including such far-off places as Assam, Madras, and even Burma.

Almost unnoticed by these commercial barons, big and small, a new age was dawning in Indian business around the middle of the nineteenth century. Much more than mere financial power and commercial acumen would be required to perceive and exploit the opportunities in the new environment.

CHAPTER 5

BIRTH PANGS OF MODERN INDUSTRIES

DESPITE ALL THE HUSTLE AND BUSTLE, OF WHICH THE PRECEDING CHAPTERS provide a fair glimpse, continuity rather than change was the hallmark of Indian business well up to the middle of the nineteenth century. This is because the existing infrastructural facilities were not capable of inducing new direction in the business scene. They were also too inadequate for effective governance of the vast land. More importantly, without improvement in these facilities, the resources of the country could not have been efficiently harnessed for service of the metropolitan country, which is the very raison d'etre of colonialism. India's new masters, therefore, lost little time after establishing their undisputed sway over the entire country to launch a programme aimed at achieving two interlinked purposes: to securely tighten the imperialist noose around their new possession and to augment the capacity of their new principality to serve the economic interests of Great Britain to the maximum possible extent. A more business-friendly climate was an unintended byproduct of the measures to achieve these twin ends.

VEHICLES OF CHANGE

To provide for safe and speedy movement was the first prerequisite to make sure that troops rushed quickly to thwart any possible threat to the British hold on the country, and that the export of raw material from India for the use of British industry and imports into India of industrial products from Britain experienced the least possible impediments. This required a two-pronged approach: removal of constraints that reduced the usefulness of the existing facilities for communication on one hand, and organization of new facilities on the other. The abolition of transit and town duties between 1836 and 1844 and the assault on the thugs and pindaris fall in the first category of measures. As the first important step towards the unification of currency, the Company rupee was declared as the legal tender throughout British India. Attempts to reform weights and measures were also made, though they never fully succeeded. These reforms, however, were hardly enough to link the various parts of India. Very few new road lines had been planned and still fewer completed as late as 1842—and that too for mainly military needs.

This was the setting when Lord Dalhousie, perhaps the most imperialistic of all Governor Generals, took over charge of the colony. He gave a new impetus to road construction and development of railways in India. Underlining the importance of improving the transport system in India for the economic interest of Great Britain, he once wrote to the top management of the East India Company in one of his numerous communications:

Great tracts are teeming with produce they can not dispose of; others are scantily bearing what they would carry in abundance if only it could be conveyed whither it is needed. England is calling aloud for the cotton which India does already produce in some degrees and would produce sufficient in quality and plentiful in quantity if only there were provided the filling means of conveyance for it from distant places to the several ports adapted for its shipment.

The opening of the first railway line in 1854 was largely due to Dalhousie's energetic initiative. That was the beginning of one of the largest railway networks that the world would ever have. The father of the present-day post and telegraph system in India, he also added his might to the cause of promoting Western learning through the medium of the English language— a programme initiated by Lord William Bentinck, one of his predecessors. The first three universities in India—one in each Presidency city—were in fact established under Dalhousie's regime.

As a result of the growing opportunities for modern secular education coupled with the growing interaction between Englishmen and Indians at various levels, European liberal values made further inroads into Indian life and thought. The critical and questioning attitude towards religion and society, that had manifested itself in the rise of the Brahmo Samaj in Bengal in the late 1820s, now spread to other parts of the country, striking gentle but effective blows at Indian rituals and customs. Beginning with the 1830s, practically every community and region in the country, with the possible exception of the south, experienced in some measure the impact of reformist tendencies. Institutions like the Gujarat Vernacular Society, established in 1848 by the joint effort of forward-looking Indians and English officials, were also a vehicle of education about modern science and technology. The process of change had gained sufficient momentum by the middle of the nineteenth century.

The introduction of a new judicial system had much wider appeal. Not only the educated middle classes but also the property owners in general, including the business interests, welcomed the setting up of law courts on British lines to dispense justice based largely on the principles of European jurisprudence. This meant that a body of laws defining the rights and privileges of individuals, rather than traditions and usages, would guide the administrators of justice in deciding criminal and civil cases, including property matters. Codification of laws and a total overhaul of the administrative machinery for justice went hand in hand, underscoring the new rulers' determination to reduce, if not altogether eliminate, the possible arbitrariness of the state. One particular legal measure must have been of special interest to the business community. This was the first company law ever adopted in India. Modelled broadly on the prevailing English law, Act XLIII of 1850 merely sought to legitimize most of the existing business practices rather than place any meaningful restrictions on the working of the firms. But it marked the beginning of a process that would have important bearing on the future directions of Indian business. Seven years later, the limited liability principle was introduced through an amendment to this Act.

Whatever their intended purpose, these developments were cumulatively leading India into a new age, the impact of which no sphere of life could entirely escape. In the realm of business, various administrative measures, providing for efficient governance of the colony and effective exploitation of its resources in the interests of the metropolitan country, served to enlarge the size of the market on one hand, and make for greater security investment on the other. At the same time, growing contact with European liberalism and technology, thanks to the spread of modern education and personal interaction, was expanding the horizon of perceivable business opportunities at least for a section of Indians. In other words, the climate for enterprise, in terms of both material as well as ideational aspects, was slowly but steadily undergoing a metamorphosis around the mid-nineteenth century, generating in the process new ideas for business. Although the full impact of the British ruling presence on business life in India would be felt only later in the century, some signs were visible even during the 1840s and 1850s.

EARLY STIRRINGS

The subcontinent as a whole, understandably, did not uniformly experience the impact of these changes. As trade and commerce in the northern and southern parts of the country had made very limited progress until then, the capital base was still too weak for the message of the slowly transforming environment to register with the business interests operating in these areas. The objective conditions in eastern India, particularly Bengal, were more favourable for experimenting with new business ideas, but having burnt their fingers during the 1830s and 1840s, the Bengalis were cautious about taking further initiatives, and found the opportunities in the civil services much more alluring. This perhaps is the reason that the Indians in eastern India gave the Scottish promoters a walkover, as it were, when a clear opportunity presented itself to mount jute manufacturing on modern lines during the early 1850s. The Indians had all the advantages in this respect: the raw material was produced at their doorstep; labour was cheap; and despite the turmoil of 1840s, there were still moneyed people in Bengal, capable of making large investments. But no native entrepreneur came forward to promote jute manufacturing in Bengal when the flex and hemp cloth manufacturing industry in Britain suffered a mortal blow with the Crimean War (1854–6) cutting off the supply of raw material from Russia. The Scottish promoters lost no time in capturing the entire field and established an ironclad monopoly on jute manufacturing in Bengal that would not be breached until the 1920s. The native business interests in Calcutta remained scrupulously aloof from all modern ventures.

Western India, in contrast, reacted much more positively to the new opportunities. A long history of trade and commerce had already led to substantial capital accumulation in the Bombay-Gujarat region. Besides, this region had also started experiencing the impact of other modernizing influences by the second quarter of the nineteenth century. It, therefore, lay in the logic of history that the winds of change originate in this region. Some abortive attempts to introduce improved devices to produce specialized silk and paper in Ahmedabad during the 1840s were indicative of the new trends. A project promoted by a group of merchants in Surat in 1847, however, seemed to hold much greater promise. Their idea was to set up a joint stock company to produce cotton goods, using modern technology and machines. Some

Englishmen working or living in Gujarat at that time acted as their technical consultants. The project, however, did not go beyond the conception stage, as the promoters developed cold feet even before the first concrete steps were taken. Their nervousness was perfectly understandable as no Indian had ever dreamt of anything like this before.

The message of the changing climate for enterprise, however, was not confined to the narrow circles of mercantile classes alone. For, the man who picked up the thread almost single-handedly from where the Surat merchants had left it off was a civil servant belonging to a family that had no connection with business whatsoever. This was Ranchhodlal Chhotalal, a Nagar Brahman, and a highly educated man for his times—well versed in Persian, English, Sanskrit, and Gujarati. Starting his career as a clerk in the customs department, headed by an Englishman, Ranchhodlal had risen to the highest position in government service to which an Indian could at that time aspire. His position gave Ranchhodlal an opportunity to develop contacts with many English officers including some who had close links with the British textile manufacturers and machinery makers. One of them was Captain George Fulljames, who had earlier secured the technical details for the abortive Surat venture.

As a result of his contacts with the British officialdom in India, coupled with his independent readings about the economic transition in Britain, Ranchhodlal was already nursing dreams of setting up an industrial venture when he heard of the Surat project. He obtained from Fulljames the technical details and cost estimates the latter had secured for the Surat merchants. But he had no money of his own and failed to persuade any of the prominent bankers in Ahmedabad and Baroda to invest in an utterly unfamiliar line of business. Refusing to concede defeat, he later joined hands with an English cotton planter, James Landon, who offered to contribute half the capital required provided the Nagar civil servant arranged for the rest. A couple of Baroda bankers agreed to invest in the proposed venture. But overpowered by an excessive sense of caution, they put forward unreasonable conditions that seemed to betray their mistrust in Landon and thus augured ill for the future. Landon consequently withdrew from the scheme, and a frustrated Ranchhodlal had to shelve his plan once again. Soon after this setback in April 1853, Ranchhodlal was suspended from his job on the charge of bribery, pushing his industrial dream into a limbo.

While risk aversion on the part of the Gujarat merchants held them back from industrial projects, the merchant class of Bombay took the lead in the formation of industrial concerns based on modern technology. To Cowasji Nanabhai Davar, a Parsee merchant of the city, belongs the distinction of being the first Indian to float a cotton mill, the Bombay Spinning and Weaving Company, that turned out to be the first truly successful industrial venture in the country. He had inherited a mercantile business from his father who had connections with prominent British houses in the city. Davar was sufficiently well educated to handle his commercial operations but knew little English. However, the Bombay environment had given him sufficient opportunity to appreciate the value of modern business.

Floated in July 1854, the Bombay Spinning and Weaving Company had a share capital of Rs 500,000 divided into one hundred shares of Rs 5000 each. Davar retained a large chunk of the shares for himself; the rest were taken by other merchants. By a deed of agreement, the shareholders entrusted the management to Davar on certain terms and conditions which clearly anticipated the essential features of the managing agency system. The company earned good profits right from the start, which inspired many other Parsee merchants to emulate Davar's example. So fast was the progress of the Bombay mill industry that by 1860, within a short span of six years of the birth of Davar's firm, the city could boast of at least ten textile companies with 6600 employees. All these were joint stock concerns and the principal promoter in all of these, by virtue of holding the controlling interest, was entrusted with the management responsibility.

Though overtaken by the developments in Bombay, Ranchhodlal in the meantime had not given up his efforts to set up a textile mill in Gujarat. His suspension and failure to get back the government job despite exoneration from the bribery charges undoubtedly blocked his road for sometime, but he never abandoned his cherished dream even while working as a salaried employee of a prominent banking firm of Ahmedabad. The employment brought him in close contact with some of the most powerful merchants of the city who now had first-hand opportunity to appreciate the competence and seriousness of purpose of this erstwhile Nagar civil servant. They now agreed to join hands with him to set up a textile mill. Once the financial hurdle was crossed, Ranchhodlal took little time to complete the procedural formalities, and the Ahmedabad Spinning and Weaving Company was finally registered in 1858—more than ten years after he had first conjured up his dream.

By 1860, thus, both Bombay and Ahmedabad, which would develop into the two major centres of textile production in India, had already witnessed the birth of a modern industry. Machine production of cotton goods has marked the beginnings of industrial transition almost everywhere in the world. This happened in India too. With the end of the administrative control of the East India Company over the country in 1858, following the rebellion of 1857, India became a part of the British Empire. This would further strengthen the forces that had been inexorably leading India and Indian business into a new age.

An Insane Interlude

The process of business transition, however, received a rude jolt from an event in a distant land. This was the Civil War in the United States of America that broke out in 1861. The Confederate States of America, the name the southern states had given to themselves after seceding from the Union, stopped the supplies of raw cotton to Britain. The southern states until then had been the principal supplier of raw material for the British mills, and the southern leaders had hoped that the crisis that their action would cause in British industrial life would force the Government of Great Britain to recognize the independence of the breakaway states. The blackmail, however did not work, as Britain launched vigorous efforts to secure raw cotton from other places—particularly India that promised to be the best alternative source. These efforts, coupled with the rising price of cotton in Lancashire, provided an unprecedented spurt to cotton exports from India.

As Bombay was the principal point of exit for cotton, the British cotton famine brought about a sea change in the business environment of the city. Almost every aspect of the commercial life was now subordinated to the need to export cotton to England. Every commercial establishment, every trading outfit, every businessman was in some way or the other involved in cotton trade. As trading in raw cotton was now more profitable than investing in manufacturing ventures, no new textile mills came into being during those eventful years. Also, as there seemed to be no end to the British famine, many began to indulge in forward trading that set off a speculative trend which seemed to gain strength with every passing day.

All this brought enormous wealth to the city. A small part of the new wealth seems to have been utilized initially for honest trade and laudable schemes directed towards improving the city, but the bulk of it was later used to promote all kinds of companies without any thought to their viability. This set off a senseless speculation the kind of which the city had never witnessed before or since. In the process, persons with no particular qualification or skill became rich overnight. Premchand Roychand, the son of a Surat immigrant, was one of them. With a rather meagre education and working as a mere broker of bank shares before the onset of the share mania, he soon emerged as the lynchpin of the whole operation, with the power over not only ordinary mortals but also the top officials of the Bank of Bombay, controlled by the Bombay government. A nobody in the city's business earlier, he now dominated the stage truly as a colossus. Even though the price of cotton in the Bombay market fell whenever prospects of peace in America appeared bright, the speculators refused to heed the implicit warning, and merrily went on with their share-gambling mania as if the good times would last forever.

The end of the Civil War changed all this. The news of the Confederate defeat reached India on 1 May 1865. The message was clear: Britain would once again turn to America for raw cotton, ending the short-lived glory of the Indian staple. Gripped by unprecedented panic, the city went entirely mad. Investors rushed to dispose of their shares in the bubble companies, for which there were no buyers. The banks and financial institutions that had advanced them funds found themselves in an utterly hopeless situation. The greatly enlarged business community waited helplessly for the doomsday to arrive. And it did arrive on 18 May when the formidable house of Behramji Hormusji Cama, unable to meet its liabilities, fell for Rs 330 lakh. Then followed a succession of failures including many illustrious names. The wreck of Bombay's ephemeral prosperity was complete on 1 July, on which day innumerable 'time bargain' shares matured up but there was no money available to honour the commitments. This caused another wave of failures, sweeping away many more of the neo-rich, the most prominent being Premchand Roychand himself. Sunk deeply in the quagmire of speculation, thanks to the generosity of Premchand, the Bank of Bombay never recovered and eventually closed its doors in February 1866. So did other banking institutions and numerous public firms that had mushroomed during the years of shadowy prosperity.

These developments were a severe setback to Bombay business. For one thing, they delayed the expansion of the nascent cotton textile industry by at least a decade, as not a single new textile mill was set up during the 1860s. It took at least seven long years for normalcy to return to Bombay. In comparison with Bombay, the share mania affected Ahmedabad, another important business centre in the vicinity of cotton-growing regions, to a far lesser degree, perhaps because the city had very little direct connection with England, and also because it was not a port.

In Calcutta

Strangely enough, the speculative fever hit Calcutta too, at the other end of the country, though with less intensity than Bombay. Away from the cotton-producing areas, and exporting practically no cotton, the city was not a direct beneficiary, or victim, of the cotton famine in Britain. Speculation here resulted from an executive order of the Viceroy issued in October 1861, under which wasteland could be acquired on very liberal terms and held in perpetuity. The stated purpose of the order was to encourage Europeans to take to cotton cultivation. This did not happen, but the order gave great impetus to forming joint stock companies for tea plantation, as the bulk of the properties acquired under it lay in the hilly regions, suited to cultivating tea. The result was the emergence of hordes of tea companies almost from nowhere.

There would have been nothing wrong with this rapid expansion, if these were honest ventures. But the fact is that practically all of them had been organized with an eye to quick gains, utilizing the liberal terms on which the wasteland could be acquired, but without much preparation and advance planning. The modus operandi was simple. Someone with money to spare would purchase a piece of wasteland for a pittance, quickly clear it up, plant it with a few tea shrubs, advertise the property as a well-established garden, and then sell it at a price many times over to speculators, who would already have formed a tea company ostensibly for commercial exploitation of the property. The shares of the company would then be sold in Calcutta and London. As the lands in question were far away from the actual places of transaction—Calcutta or London—the buyers of land, the promoters of companies, as well as ordinary investors were very often taken for a ride. There were many instances when even non-existent gardens were sold or a small patch of land with no more than a sprinkling of tea plants on it was advertised as a large garden with excellent quality tea growing on it!

As the hollowness of such claims became clear, the whole operation collapsed like a house of cards by the middle of 1866. The money locked up in unproductive ventures became scarce, and the shareholders sold their holdings at whatever price they could get, with the result that the firms that had mushroomed in the wake of the wasteland order disappeared from the scene by the end of the decade. It would be a few years before the industry would recover from the setback it received during these years.

The tight money situation created by the collapse of the tea industry in 1866 arrested the growth of the jute industry. Before the beginning of the tea boom, Calcutta had only two jute manufacturing firms, both controlled by

Scotsmen. Three more companies were added between 1862 and 1866, all promoted by British traders, but thereafter no jute mill came into existence until 1873.

Madras and other smaller business centres that had little connection with cotton production or trade and tea cultivation remained almost unaffected by the developments in Bombay and Calcutta. As the Indian markets were still relatively unintegrated, developments elsewhere had no impact on the business environment of these places. On balance the years between 1862 and 1866 must be regarded as an interlude of insanity for Indian business.

CHAPTER 6

RISE OF THE INDUSTRIAL ELITE

THE SETBACK THAT THE INDIAN BUSINESS SUFFERED BECAUSE OF THE happenings of the 1860s was only transitory. As the memories of the madness that had engulfed Bombay, and to a lesser extent Calcutta, faded, the forces of change, that had been leading Indian enterprise system into a new direction before the interlude, reasserted themselves. Road construction had received a great deal of fillip during the American Civil War years as the government wanted to facilitate cotton export to the maximum possible extent. The establishment of the telegraph line between India and Europe in 1866 and the opening of the Suez Canal three years later made external communication much easier. The spirit of reform and European liberalism too made further headway, of which the birth of the Prarthana Samaj was the most visible symbol. Founded in Bombay in 1867 by a group of English-educated Indians and Europeans, this organization like the Brahmo Samaj in Bengal, was, to quote a competent authority, 'very much influenced by contemporary English developments', and looked to the West as a model for material progress.

These developments provided fresh reinforcement to the emerging climate for enterprise in favour of industrial transition. The air of despondency, pervading the business climate of the two major centres during the mid-1860s, almost vanished by the beginning of the next decade, yielding place to the kind of optimism that had prevailed before the events in America intervened. This was reflected in the rising number of new entrants into the industrial field in both these urban centres. Also, signs of industrial tendencies began to be seen in areas that had so far remained unaffected by the forces of change.

CONSOLIDATION OF COTTON TEXTILE INDUSTRY

Some statistics would bear this out. While the number of cotton mills in Bombay had remained stationary at ten for more than twelve years after 1860, as many as twelve new factories emerged within a brief span of eighteen months between July 1873 and December 1874; another twenty were added in the next four years. Buoyed by the consolidation of the industry, the leading millowners of the city joined together to set up the Bombay Millowners' Association in 1875 to safeguard their common interests. New factories continued to be set up until 1892 when the city had a total of twenty-eight mills with 445,462 spindles and 4217 looms. The number of mills went up in Ahmedabad too—the only other centre besides Bombay where the industry had made a beginning before the cotton crisis of the mid-1860s—from just two in 1873 to eleven in 1892 with an aggregate of 289,416 spindles and 4485 looms. The Ahmedabad industrialists too set up the Ahmedabad Millowners' Association in 1891, a clear sign of the industry coming of age in this premier commercial centre of Gujarat. Calcutta with two mills and Kanpur with one were the only other places in the country where textile manufacturing had any presence before 1870. By 1892, many other cities such as Surat, Nadiad, Sholapur, Nagpur, Khandesh, Madras, Serampore, and Delhi had cotton mills. A few mills had come into being in south India too. As a result of these developments, the total number of mills in the country had by this time risen to 127 with nearly 33 lakh spindles and 24,700 looms, providing daily employment to nearly 100,000 persons. Bombay and Ahmedabad, however, continued to retain their supremacy.

All these companies were joint stock firms, and the face value of a share in most cases was Rs 5000. Barring a few, these firms were under the control of Indians with mercantile background who simultaneously continued with trading and banking. The managerial structures of practically all these companies were based on the managing agency system, which had by then gained widespread acceptability. Few companies set up during the latter half of the nineteenth century functioned under any other framework. While the joint stock pattern helped the promoter disperse his risk, the managing agency system made it possible for him to enjoy the same kind of unfettered freedom in managing his industrial enterprises to which he had been accustomed in running his trading and moneylending concerns. This was so because the promoter of an industrial undertaking invariably retained the controlling interest in the company and, aided by this privilege, would have a resolution passed by the shareholders at the very outset, appointing his family firm as the managing agent of the new concern on a long-term basis and with almost unlimited powers. A managing agency for all practical purposes, thus, was an organizational fiction, a euphemism for private control over the management of joint stock firms.

In ownership pattern and managerial structure, thus, India did not follow Britain, the principal inspiration behind the rise of modern industries in India, where most textile companies were partnership firms headed by salaried managing directors. While the Indian preference for joint stock pattern was due to the financial conservatism of the promoters, an attribute of trading interests in general, the consolidation of the managing agency system was largely due to the deeply entrenched joint family system. And largely because of the conjunction of these two innovations, clusters of companies engaged in a variety of activities came under the control and management of single families in due course, bringing to the fore the concept of business groups or business houses, identified with respective families. In the technological sphere, however, the promoters of Indian cotton mills blindly and uncritically emulated the British textile industry. Consequently, Britain continued to remain the principal source of industrial machinery for Indian manufacturers.

For the British machinery manufacturers the development of the cotton industry in India meant the opening of a vast market for their products, and many of them opened local offices or agencies in Bombay. Manchester, however, could not view the rise of a potential competitor without serious concern. As the Indian industry consolidated itself, British textile manufacturers stepped up pressure on their home government to take measures to protect their interests against the fast mounting threat from India. Unable to withstand their pressure, the government eventually, in 1882, altogether abolished import duties on all textile goods, justifying its action with reference to the doctrine of free trade—something of a holy cow for British policymakers in those days. Dadabhai Naoroji, generally a sympathizer of the British presence in India, likened the free trade between England and India to 'a race between a starving, exhausted invalid and a strong man with a horse to ride on'. For India's government of the day, however, it was expedient not to get bogged down by such finer points of economic theory.

The enactment of a factory legislation, the first ever in India, around the same time seemed to reduce still further the competitive advantage of the Indian mills. In the absence of any statutory regulation of his working conditions and with no trade union movement worth the name to fight for him, the Indian factory worker was subjected to all those hardships and exploitations that had characterized factory life in England in the early stages of the Industrial Revolution—long hours of work, unhygienic premises, low wages, managerial oppression, etc. Most hard hit were women and children working in the cotton mills. Moved by their plight, a small section of enlightened citizens in Bombay launched a campaign to press for legislative protection to the Indian factory worker. This came as a godsend to the British textile producers whose labour costs were much higher than in India, partly because of the legislative restrictions on exploitation of workers in their country. Similar restrictions in India, they felt, would to some extent offset the vast advantage India had in this respect. Guided essentially by self-interest but wearing a humanitarian mask, the British industry threw its weight behind the demand for a factory legislation in India. The Factory Acts of 1881 and 1892 were the result of these pressures. They provided much-needed relief and protection to the Indian mill worker, but increased the cost of labour to the producer.

Adverse tariff and enhanced cost of labour were not the only hurdles facing the Indian cotton industry. A temporary slump in the industry in 1877 was followed by a glut in the market in 1883. However, the impact of all these setbacks was more than offset by one single favourable development: the conquest of the China market by the Indian producer by the beginning of the 1880s. The rising share of yarn in India's exports to China during these years gave a further push to cotton manufacturing in the country.

A logical outcome of the rapid expansion of the Indian textile industry was that it ceased to be the exclusive preserve of a few enlightened and daring souls. All mills set up before 1870 were entrepreneurial ventures promoted by people who were exposed, directly or indirectly, to the industrial experience in the West. As the industry proceeded on a stable, profitable course, relatively more cautious segments of the business community—general traders, financiers, speculators, moneylenders, etc.—came forward to join the expanding groups of industrialists. More conservative in their business and social outlook, they were probably induced by the demonstration effect of the pioneering ventures. Kutchhi Bhatias were typical of the late entrants. A large number of them had been active in Bombay trade since the early years of the nineteenth century, but they entered the textile industry only after its profitability was firmly established. Morarjee Gokuldas led the way. Others of this community who followed in quick succession were Khatau Makanji, Dwarkadas Vasanji, Damodar Thackersey, and Mulji Jaitha. By

1880, there were six mills controlled by the Bhatias; more were added in the coming decades.

The pattern in Ahmedabad was similar. The Ahmedabad Seths—Jains and Vaishnava banias who had traditionally dominated the commercial life of this city all through its history—took almost two decades after the birth of the first textile mills in Ahmedabad to realize that cotton manufacturing was more profitable than trading. In fact, not they but Bechardas Laskari, a Kanbi, emulated Ranchhodlal's example by setting up the second mill in the city in 1864, and the third mill was not founded until 1876 when Ranchhodlal added another company to his business. Mansukhbhai Bhagubhai, a prominent Jain merchant, was the first member of the mercantile class to join the industry, founding the Gujarat Spinning and Weaving Company in 1877. Another leading Jain merchant, Karamchand Premchand, followed suit with the launching of the Ahmedabad Manufacturing and Calico Company in 1880. The Vaishnava banias waited for another decade. However, once the Jains and Vaishnava banias entered the scene, they left all others far behind, controlling around 64 per cent of the total spinning and 58 per cent of the weaving capacity of all mills in the city, eleven in number, by 1892.

As mentioned earlier, a large majority of the textile mills in India were promoted, financed, and managed by Indians. Ahmedabad had no mill under the control of non-Indians. Bombay had a few by 1892. Strangely enough, the non-Indians too, like the Indian trading interests, entered the industry only after it had already passed the entrepreneurial stage. Perhaps the most prominent of them were the Sassoons who stuck to the safe lines of the family business—multilateral trading and real estate development, particularly foreshore properties—until 1874 when the Sassoon Spinning and Weaving Company was floated. About two decades later, in 1893, the family added the Sassoon and Alliance Silk Mills to its industrial empire. E.D. Sassoon & Co., a splinter branch of the Sassoons founded in 1874 by the founder's younger son Elias following family partition, waited for six years before branching out into the industry with the acquisition in 1880 of Alexandra Mill from Kesowji Naik, a prominent Bhatia millowner and cotton merchant. Naik had earlier bought this mill from the Tatas, the original founders. Within just a few years after entry into the textile industry, E.D. Sassoon & Co. left everybody behind to emerge as the largest employers of factory labour in and around Bombay. James Greaves and George Cotton, two Englishmen, also set up a conglomerate of mills in Bombay in 1877 under the management of their managing agency firm, Greaves Cotton & Co. Bradbury and Brady was another British agency house that controlled several mills in Bombay. The most powerful British agency house in Bombay during this period, Killick Nixon & Co., did not enter the industry until 1896 when it launched Kohinoor Mills. Non-Indian elements in the Bombay textile industry were, on the whole, exceptions. It remained primarily in the hands of Indians, and despite a large number of new entrants belonging to other social groups, the Parsees still held on to their dominant position.

CASE STUDIES

A few case studies would illustrate the processes through which the cotton textile industry consolidated itself in western India during this period. The dogged determination of Ranchhodlal Chhotalal in setting up the first mill at Ahmedabad has already been mentioned. During his life he remained the largest and most successful mill owner and the undisputed leader of the industry in the city. No single cotton manufacturer could claim to have carved out a similar position in Bombay. Sir Dinshaw Petit would come closest to it. His father Maneckji was the founder of the first composite mill in Bombay Presidency. Dinshaw himself floated three mills between 1860 and 1862. Like most people in Bombay, Dinshaw Petit speculated heavily during the Civil War years and lost at least Rs 30 lakh when the crash came. However, still a man of considerable means, he acquired two more mills in 1867 soon after the crash. By 1884, he had six large mills under his management. All his undertakings consistently earned huge profits and made him the richest man and a prominent leader of the mill-owning community in the city—a fact that the British government recognized by knighting him in 1887 and conferring a baronetcy three years later.

Dinshaw Petit had to depend on British technicians like other mill owners, but unlike others, he did not blindly follow their judgement. Once a committee of European engineers diagnosed a breakdown of a steam engine in one of his mills due to defective design and workmanship. Not convinced, Petit asked a young Parsee engineer, Nowrosjee Wadia, to look into the matter afresh. Wadia's enquiry revealed that the damage was due to the inefficiency of the European engineer in charge. Petit, impressed with Wadia, developed an unshakeable faith in his engineering skills and, on his advice, decided to install a steam engine of 4000 horsepower in one of his mills, something that had never been done before by anyone in the industry. Everyone was convinced that the foolhardy venture was doomed to fail. But Wadia proved them all wrong. His success established his reputation as an outstanding engineer, marking the beginning of his rise as a most successful builder of textile mills. Petit's innovative methods, bold approach to business, and leadership qualities won him respect and admiration from his contemporaries.

The hero of the period, however, was Jamsetji Nusserwanji Tata. His father had moved from Navsari to Bombay in the early years of the nineteenth century and established a trading firm. After completing his education at the prestigious Elphinstone College, Jamsetji spent a few years with the family firm before being despatched to China where he stayed for four years. Jamsetji returned to India just before the speculation fever gripped the city. With Premchand Roychand being a partner in his business, Nusserwanji could not have controlled the temptation to speculate. How much money the Tatas made during this period is not known, but it must have been sufficient to justify the decision to send Jamsetji to London to supervise the arrival of consignments of cotton shipped by the firm. Jamsetji left for London with a bunch of securities including a large number of bills on the China market. However, hardly had he set foot on the British soil when the cotton market crashed, rendering worthless all those seemingly precious financial instruments he had brought with him. Without losing his cool in this hour of crisis, Jamsetji convinced his creditors that his problems were entirely due to an abnormal situation and were in no way a reflection of the intrinsic strength of his firm. The experience must have boosted the confidence of the young Tata, just about 26 years of age then. He stayed on in England for a few more months to study the British textile industry and then returned home. Like Dinshaw Petit, the Tatas too recovered rather quickly, and were back to normal operations by 1867 when the profits from a contract for commissariat for the British army fighting in Abyssinia bolstered their financial position.

The Tatas, however, were still a backbencher in the Bombay business world when Jamsetji decided to enter the still small tribe of industrialists. In 1869, he purchased an old and crumbling oil-pressing factory in Bombay, converted it into a textile unit, and called it Alexandra Mills. After two years, he sold off the renovated mill for a handsome profit and left for England to gain first-hand knowledge of textile manufacturing in the world's most developed country. He must have now been fully equipped to re-enter the cotton industry in a big way, for soon after returning home, he launched in 1874 what would remain the flagship company of the Tatas during Jamsetji's lifetime—the Central India Spinning, Weaving, and Manufacturing Company.

His choice of location for the factories anticipated the kind of originality and perceptiveness that would characterize his business decisions throughout his life. Instead of Bombay, the preferred site of cotton producers in general, Jamsetji selected Nagpur to set up the factory. The city was close to the cotton-growing areas of Berar; it had easy access to sources of fuel with the coal deposits of eastern India being not far; being a handloom centre it promised a ready market for the products of the proposed mill; and it was well connected with the rest of the country. Many in the Bombay business circles were sceptical about the future of the enterprise. The critics, however, were proved wrong, and the mill with 14,400 spindles and 450 looms started functioning on 1 January 1877, the date on which Queen Victoria was proclaimed Empress of India. To celebrate the event, the factory was named Empress Mills. He added two more mills during his lifetime—Swadeshi Mills in 1886 in Bombay and Advance Mills in Ahmedabad. Acquired in hopeless condition, both these concerns were converted into profitable and progressive concerns within a short time.

Some features of the management of these companies manifested Jamsetji's propensity for innovation. In Empress Mills, he introduced the ring spindle at a time when the device was yet to come in general use even in the United States where it was invented, and to which Manchester was still indifferent. Simpler to use, and requiring less exacting labour standards, the ring spindles were better suited to Indian conditions. He also introduced in his companies several labour welfare measures and incentive schemes that were ahead of the times. Instead of following the common practice of calculating the managing agents' remuneration on the basis of sales or production, he claimed his commission on the basis of profits, a system that became common in Indian industry much later.

Jamsetji's innovative mind conceived other minor schemes like export of mangoes, the frozen food business, and sericulture. These met with varying degrees of success. He also tried to enter shipping but gave up in the face of a fierce rate war unleashed by powerful British shipping interests. The most successful of his minor ventures was Taj Mahal Hotel established in Bombay, to provide a world-class facility to discerning tourists to the city, just before his death in 1904. All said and done, these accomplishments of Jamsetji were not very different from those of most Indian entrepreneurs of his times. What, however, won him a towering, almost unique, place in the business history of India, are the gigantic industrial projects that were conceived and launched during his lifetime but were completed by his successors. These will be discussed later.

Though nowhere close to Jamsetji Tata in entrepreneurial perception and vision, Morarjee Gokuldas had similar traits in at least one respect. Like Tata, he also set up a cotton mill at a location away from Bombay so that his company could benefit from proximity to the cotton-growing region and availability of cheap labour. Originally from Porbandar, his trading family had settled down in Bombay sometime during the early years of the nineteenth century. Morarjee entered the textile business with the acquisition of a wool spinning and weaving company in an auction in 1869 jointly with three other fellow Bhatias. This was converted into a cotton-manufacturing unit in 1871. Two years later, he bought out the other three partners in the mill and named it the Morarjee Gokuldas Spinning and Weaving Company. The mill consistently earned good profits and developed into a sizeable concern within just three years. He then set up another mill at Sholapur, a city with advantages similar to Nagpur. This mill was still to come out of the woods when Morarjee died in 1880 at the young age of 53. Its operations finally stabilized under the supervision of Morarjee's successors.

After Morarjee's death, Damodar Thackersey Mulji was regarded as the leading Bhatia in Bombay. He had been a piece-goods merchant before entering the mill industry in the early 1870s. By 1882, he had acquired three existing mills and launched a fourth one on his own. Another prominent Bhatia promoter of cotton mills in Bombay was Khatau Makanji, founder of the Khatau Makanji Spinning and Weaving Company. From a modest start, it grew into one of the largest textile companies in Bombay. Setting up its own retail stores to sell its products directly to the consumer was a major innovation attempted by this company. Then and until several decades later, Indian mills usually distributed their products through commission agents. Significantly enough, all the Bhatia promoters of mill companies were persons of progressive views for their times, and the Bhatia community dominated the list of shareholders in the companies promoted by them.

Strangely enough, cotton manufacturing did not attract many Muslims even though a large number of them were involved in commercial pursuits and some had made considerable money in the China trade. Sir Currimbhoy Ebrahim was the only Muslim in the whole of the country who launched a cotton company that grew into a prominent concern. Belonging to a family of shippers who operated between Bombay and Zanzibar, Currimbhoy came to the helm in 1855. China trade became his major interest and his firm, Currimbhoy Ebrahim & Sons, had offices at Hong Kong and Shanghai in China and Kobe in Japan. Extensive trading in opium, cotton yarn, silk, and other merchandise earned him huge profits that provided him the resources to acquire the managing agency of an old mill. A little later, in 1888, he founded a new concern, the Currimbhoy Mills Company. This was the beginning of a cluster of business enterprises that would include, by the end of World War I, six cotton mills in Bombay, a bleaching and dyeing works, and a ginning and pressing company. Seldom, if ever, did Currimbhoy's companies fail to declare dividends, which normally ranged between 15 and 20 per cent. With a cotton mill at Indore, he belonged to a small group of Bombay industrialists whose business vision was not confined to their city alone.

The Calcutta Scene

In Calcutta too, the pattern was more or less similar to that in Bombay. The city had five jute mills and a cotton textile company in 1866, all promoted by British entrepreneurs. No new industrial firms came into being until 1872 when the Champdany Jute Mill was floated in London as a sterling company by an erstwhile Dundee manufacturer. As many as twelve jute mills, all set up by Scotsmen, followed in quick succession, increasing the total loom capacity from 1250 to 3500 by 1875. So swift an expansion proved too much for the market and practically all the mills, both old and new, suffered badly from the recession that inevitably followed. Consequently, between 1876 and 1884, only four jute mills were added.

Something needed to be done urgently to alleviate the hardships of depression, and the formation of Indian Jute Mills Association (IJMA) in 1884 was the answer that the industry leaders devised. A cartel-type organization, IJMA was meant to cope with the problems of overproduction and excess capacity by restricting the time and the number of looms at work. The arrangements never worked very satisfactorily and the industry continued to remain in the doldrums for a long time. Consequently, there were no new floatations between 1884 and 1895. Subsequently, however, the number of mills increased substantially, responding to rising demand, mainly from abroad, with the result that by the turn of the century there were thirty-one jute companies. With a total loom capacity of 15,213, they functioned under seventeen managing agency firms.

The use of coal as fuel by cotton and jute mills as well as the railways provided a great fillip to coal mining. Before 1850, the progress of the industry had remained slow primarily because of limited demand. However, with the vigorous efforts of the Company government, practically all the important coalfields in the country had been discovered by the middle of the nineteenth century. New operators naturally entered the field and by 1860 nearly fifty collieries were operating in the Raniganj area. Coal mining developed at a few other places also, notably the Central Provinces, but eastern India remained the most important centre of the industry.

Like coal and jute, the tea industry remained almost an exclusive British preserve. The industry recovered very fast from the disaster of the mid-1860s. Despite the fact that communication with the tea districts was still not very easy—the hills of Assam continued to be inhospitable—and the price of tea fluctuated dangerously, the number of companies and the capital employed in them registered a continuous rise after 1870. There were, of course, ups and downs. But the industry, on the whole, demonstrated great deal of progress and stability, attracting in the process many new British firms. Practically all these companies had come into existence during the 1860s. The much older Assam Company, however, remained the largest enterprise in the field. Barring a few stray exceptions, all the managing agents (or proprietors in some cases) of the jute, coal, and tea companies were either Englishmen or Scotsmen. Indians remained practically aloof from the scene.

Contrasting with the general trend in eastern India was the role of an Indian in the birth and consolidation of the Calcutta-based Martin & Co. that would grow into a formidable concern by the beginning of the twentieth century. Though usually counted among expatriate firms, this company was set up at the joint initiative of a Bengali civil servant, Rajendra Nath Mookerjee, and an Englishman, Acquin Martin, who represented in Calcutta a London firm dealing in general stores and metals. Both quit their jobs to form Martin & Co. in 1892, which soon grew into a reputable engineering firm. So valuable was Mookerjee's contribution to the development of this enterprise that his holdings in it were only slightly less than Martin's. As Martin's successors had little interest in their Indian enterprise, Mookerjee emerged as the senior partner and its undisputed leader after Martin's death.

Interestingly, the managerial structure of the jute firms, even though under British control, also centred around the managing agency system. Out of all the managing agencies controlling the jute companies, most of which were located along the River Hooghly for obvious reasons, Bird & Co. would have under its management the largest number of firms by the beginning of World War I. Its founder, Sam Bird, had come to India in 1858 and worked as labour contractor for the railways for a few years before forming a partnership with his brother Paul in 1864. The brothers were still labour contractors when the jute industry resumed its progress in the early 1870s after the lull of the previous decade. Looking for new avenues of investment they acquired Burrakur Coal Company originally founded by an American, Richard MacAllister. Following some simple management maxims that MacAllister had neglected, like paying the workers regularly, the Birds turned the company into a profitable concern within a year.

Buoyed by this success, the partnership acquired the managing agency of MacAllister's Oriental Jute Manufacturing Co. in 1880 and re-launched it under a new name, Union Jute Company. Coal and jute would remain the mainstays of the Birds' business, although they also moved into a few other areas around this time. By the end of the century, the Birds were the largest exporter of Indian coal in the East.

Another expatriate firm, Andrew Yule and Company, originated around the same time as Bird and Company. Founded by Scotsman Andrew Yule in 1863 in partnership with his brother George as a trading firm, the partnership was looking after two jute mills, a cotton mill, three tea companies, and an insurance firm by the time the partners retired from management in 1891, leaving the leadership in the hands of their nephew David Yule, who had joined the firm as an employee in 1875. Within a few years of being at the helm, he added a few new concerns so that by the turn of the century Andrew Yule & Co. had under its management as many as thirty-one enterprises in a variety of fields—jute, cotton, coal, tea, railway, and inland navigation. It also had a large landed estate organized as a zamindari company. Like the Birds, Andrew Yule & Co. would continue to grow, though under changing partnership or management, but the foundations of its main business interests had been firmly laid by the end of the nineteenth century.

NORTH, SOUTH, AND NORTH-WEST

As in the east, the credit for starting modern industries in northern and southern India also goes to expatriates. Commercial capitalism had made little headway in these regions, and the native business interests had neither the resources nor the risk-bearing capacity to launch into unfamiliar fields. Elgin Mills at Kanpur was the first cotton company set up in north India. Registered in

1861, the project was conceived by one Hugh Maxwell who later formed a partnership with another British national, David Begg, under the name of Begg Maxwell & Co. (later Begg Sutherland & Co.) to which the management of the mill was entrusted. By 1894, Kanpur had as many as four cotton mills, all started by former employees of Elgin Mills, a sugar mill promoted by Begg Sutherlands, a small engineering works, and a few other industrial firms catering mainly to the needs of the army. With the exception of one of the cotton mills, in the founding of which one Sheo Prasad had played some role, indigenous trading elements would remain aloof from modern industries well until World War I. The involvement of the Marwari banias, who dominated commercial life in the north at this time, was limited to their acting as the sales agents or sellers of the products of these factories, or acquiring a few shares in these companies.

Similar things happened in the south. The Chettiers, the dominant business community around the Madras region, behaved like the Marwaris in the north. They had a reputation for their spirit of adventure and enterprise as also for natural shrewdness and ability. They also had enormous capital at their disposal accumulated through trading and moneylending in Burma, Malaya, and Indo-China. As they continued to thrive in the relatively placid south-east Asian markets, where they had few rivals, the idea of branching out into industrial ventures at home had little attraction for them.

Thomas Parry, the Welsh adventurer, caused the earliest stirrings of industrialization in this region with the establishment of a tannery and an indigo factory in Madras in the first decade of the nineteenth century. But the real advance towards setting up of industrial enterprises was made only after Parry's death. William Dare, the new controlling head of Parry & Co., launched the firm into coffee plantation in 1823 on Wynaad and Bababudan Hills near Mysore. However, the most serious—and pioneering—industrial initiative that Parry's took in 1842 was in the field of sugar manufacturing in South Arcot. Distilleries were added as adjuncts to the sugar factories. Eventually these ventures would develop into East India Distilleries and Sugar Factories Limited by 1897 when all the sugar works and distilleries were merged into a single concern incorporated in London, with Parry & Co. as managing agent. In the meantime Parry had also acquired a bone mill. From the bone mill arose Presidency Manure Works as the finer particles of bones could be used for producing fertilizers, and fertilizers led to the production of sulphuric acid and chemicals. A pottery works was also added to Parry's growing empire with a view to supplying jars and containers for the products of these industries.

By the close of the nineteenth century, the firm, under changing leadership, had its fingers in many pies, although the mainstay of its business was still sugar manufacturing.

Binny & Co. too advanced the cause of industrialization in the south. For more than seventy-five years after its birth Binny had been mainly engaged in agency business and import-export trade. Acquiring the agency of British India Steam Navigation Company (BI) in 1865 was the high watermark of its operations, and by the end of the 1860s, Binny had become one of the three most powerful business groups in the south—Parry and Arbuthnot being the other two.

Perhaps the most significant of all its initiatives was the boost Binny gave to cotton manufacturing in the region. Although the first two cotton mills in Madras were promoted at the initiative of two native entrepreneurs of Bombay, it was Binny's Buckingham Mill Company, set up in 1876, that provided an identity to the textile industry in the region. The company had only spinning operations in the beginning, but weaving was added in 1890. In 1881 Binny founded the Carnatic Mill Company which started as a composite unit. Both the mills began with coarser material but later switched to higher-count goods. In 1886, Binny & Co. acquired the managing agency of a woollen mill founded in 1877 by a British engineer, and reorganized it as the Bangalore Woollen, Cotton and Silk Mills Company Ltd. This company produced, along with cotton goods, blankets and *jhools* (saddle blankets) for the army. Binny also tried to mount a sugar manufacturing concern in 1897 but nothing went right with this venture and it was eventually taken over by its rival—Parry—giving the latter a virtual monopoly over sugar production in south India.

Other British houses that launched industrial enterprises included Harvey Brothers and T. Stains & Co. The former set up Tinnevely Mills at Ambasamudram in 1883, Coral Mills at Tuticorin in 1887, and Madura Mills in 1892, while the latter promoted—in collaboration with Arbuthnot & Co.—the Coimbatore Spinning and Weaving Company in 1888. A few textile companies of relatively smaller size were also set up in the region around this time by Indians. Industrial tendencies, thus, had made some inroads in the south, but trade and not industry remained the defining character of business in the region well until the onset of the next century.

The north-west remained essentially agricultural during this period. All that the region could boast of in the name of industrial enterprises were a few breweries controlled by the Dyer family (linked to General Dyer of Jalianwala

Bagh notoriety), the promoters of the first large-scale brewery at Murree in 1860. Egerton Woollen Mills at Dhariwal set up in 1882, Delhi Cloth and General Mills and Ganesh Flour Mills set up in 1889 and 1891 respectively, both at Delhi, were other industrial concerns. These, however, were exceptions to the general pattern. At the turn of the century, industrial spirit in the real sense of the term was yet to penetrate this region.

REFLECTIONS ON CHANGE

What this broad survey clearly brings out is that in the last quarter of the nineteenth century, India made a convincing leap forward into modern industries. Practically all regions of the country witnessed, though in varying degrees, the rise of machine-based factories, producing a variety of goods. While in the western and eastern parts of the country, cotton, jute, coal, and tea claimed the lion's share of the industrial firms that emerged during this period, companies in the south were by and large concerned with sugar manufacturing, navigation, and shipping. The period also witnessed the birth of a few paper mills, breweries, flour mills, cotton and jute presses, engineering concerns, timber mills, and coffee plantations, apart from the railway companies which were all promoted by entrepreneurs in England and registered as sterling firms. A substantial number of sterling companies were also engaged in jute manufacturing and tea plantation, but the major credit for bringing about a complete transformation in the Indian business scene through the creation of industrial firms must go to Indian entrepreneurs and expatriates.

Surprisingly, both these groups, despite differences in their background, had more or less similar approaches to structures and strategies to achieve their business purposes, with only minor variations. It is somewhat strange that expatriate firms like the Birds and Andrew Yule in Calcutta or Parry and Binny in Madras functioned within the rubric of a managerial system perfected by the Indians. There was, however, a crucial difference between the functioning of the managing agency system in the Indian-controlled concerns and expatriate firms. While in the former, the managing agencies continued to remain with the promoters' families, in the latter, the partnerships controlling the managing agencies went on changing hands as the older generations continued to return home after relinquishing their holdings. There was one more difference: no Indian managing agency firm was ever placed in charge of the management of companies it did not control, while the expatriate managing agencies very often assumed for a fee the responsibility to manage the affairs of sterling companies operating in India.

How much the Indian business scene had changed during this period is clear from the fact that by the end of the nineteenth century as many as 627 firms with a total paid-up capital of over Rs 2500 lakh were engaged in some kind of manufacturing activities. Just about two decades earlier, the number had been 264 companies with a total paid-up capital of a little less than Rs 1100 lakh. If we also take into account the companies in service industries such as banking, insurance, navigation, warehousing, and land and building, the number in 1900 was 1366 with a paid-up capital of over Rs 3700 lakh as against 505 with a total paid-up capital of less than Rs 1500 lakh in 1882. The industrial development, without question, was uneven, lopsided, and location specific. But that is beside the point. It was now joint stock industrial enterprises and not proprietory trading concerns that set the tone of business in India. Trading firms, of course, did not disappear; they still remained an important part of the business scene. But they were, by and large, adjuncts to the industrial concerns—distributing the goods produced by manufactories.

SOURCES OF FINANCE

Strangely enough, the sources of finance underwent little change. Before the dawn of the industrial era, family and clan network and shroffs and sahukars (generally referred to as indigenous bankers) used to provide capital for starting or sustaining an enterprise. The rise of industries and joint stock firms made little difference, as industrial finance, by and large, continued to come from similar sources. For those industrialists who came from a commercial background, it was natural to fall back on family resources and their business linkages. But even those who were not so happily placed, those who made their debut in business with industrial enterprises, depended primarily on shroffs, sahukars, and other moneyed classes for funds.

The very fact that the nominal value of a share of the early cotton mills normally ranged between Rs 2500 and 5000 indicates that the promoters were obviously targeting rich merchants and moneyed individuals as prospective investors. True, in later years, particularly after the mid-1870s, shares of lower value began to be issued with a view to attracting persons of more modest means. Still never during this period was the new issue priced less than Rs 100—not a very small amount then; in most cases it ranged between Rs 500 and Rs 1000. The paid-up capital of most of the early cotton mills was rather small—Rs 500,000 to 1,000,000 in Bombay and never above Rs 500,000 in Ahmedabad. The mill owners also raised part of their working capital through the system of public deposits. These too could only have come from relatively well-to-do people.

A high rate of interest was a natural corollary of the prevailing sources of industrial finance. For, expectation of quick returns is integral to the business calculation of trading interests. Little attention was given to developing clear and consistent norms with regard to reserve and depreciation as they would eat into the funds available for dividends. Some enlightened managements like Greaves Cotton & Co. had a clear-cut policy of building up a dividend equalization fund that enabled them to declare dividends at a uniform rate of 10 per cent every year, and J.N. Tata was probably the first mill owner to allow for depreciation while calculating the net profits. But these were isolated cases. Since the prevailing company law imposed no discipline in these respects, it took some time for these practices to gain general acceptance.

The tight hold of mercantile interests on the sources of industrial finance could have been loosened had there been an efficiently functioning stock market and an alternative source of credit, such as banks organized on modern lines. But such institutions were still woefully underdeveloped at the turn of the century. In the middle of the nineteenth century, when industrial transition began to take shape, there was nothing even distantly similar to a stock exchange in India. As business picked up, brokers in the two major centres took the first, albeit feeble, steps to create a more organized instrument to regulate their profession. But the birth in 1875 of the Native Share and Stock Brokers Association in Bombay, the first stock exchange ever set up in an Asian country, and the establishment of the Calcutta Stock Exchange in 1908 did not bring about a material change in the situation, as these institutions continued to suffer from many disabilities.

The situation with regard to banking was somewhat better but still woefully unsatisfactory. Even though modern banking institutions began to emerge as early as the last quarter of the eighteenth century—as mentioned earlier, the agency house of Alexander & Co. launched the first European-type bank in 1770—modern banks were still extremely limited in number and size as well as in the range and quality of services provided. Such institutions around the end of the nineteenth century were of two types: banks promoted by private parties and institutions sponsored by the state.

While each of the three Presidencies had a government-controlled bank—known collectively as Presidency Banks—the number of private banks of any consequence in the entire country was limited to four. Of these, three were under European control, including Bank of Allahabad founded in 1865.

Only one private bank—Punjab National Bank founded in 1894—was in Indian hands.

The state-backed institutions were specifically prohibited from granting any loan for a period longer than three months; they were prohibited from accepting immovable property as security; and they could open cash credit facility against negotiable instruments only if such instruments satisfied certain highly stringent conditions. Such institutions could hardly be of much help to industries, requiring long-term accommodation. As for the private banks, they were still too small to provide the long-term finance that industrial projects by their very nature required.

The Indian branches of foreign banks constituted yet another category of banking institutions in India at the turn of the twentieth century. These included the Chartered Bank of Asia, Chartered Bank of India, Australia, and China, London and Eastern Banking Corporation, National Bank of India, (the forerunner of Grindlays Bank), and Bank of Hindustan, China, and Japan. Comptoir D'Escompte of Paris, and First National City Bank of New York also had branches in India. All these, however, focused mainly on the exchange business. The conditions, thus, were hardly conducive for the modern institutions to make a dent in the age-old sources of credit in India.

With their dependence for funds on conventional sources, Indian industrialists had inevitably to pursue strategies characterized by relatively low investment, short gestation period, and quick returns. Their dependence on the traditional sources of business finance also provided continued reinforcement to the management structure of their industrial concerns. If family dominance remained a salient feature of the management of industrial enterprises, even though the enterprises themselves were organized as joint stocks, it was at least partly because community and family linkages continued to remain the principal source of industrial finance.

CHAPTER 7

DEVELOPING AN IDENTITY

THE RISE OF MODERN INDUSTRIES DID NOT IMMEDIATELY DISTURB THE harmony and cooperation between Indian and European business interests that had been a characteristic feature of their relationship during the pre-industrial period. As long as trade and commerce constituted the whole of Indian business, both these elements needed each other in many ways. This generated a sense of interdependence between them. The Indo-British partnerships formed during the 1830s and 1840s were the most visible manifestation of such interdependence. Although the Indian and European promoters of industries in India were much less dependent on each other, there were few signs of conflict between them during the early phase of industrialization.

This was so because the areas of operations of the two groups of industrialists were by and large separate and, therefore, scope for direct competition was limited. Almost until the end of the nineteenth century, the only industry in which the Indian industrial entrepreneurship had expressed itself was cotton textiles, where European presence was extremely limited. On the other hand, jute textiles, coal mining, steam shipping, inland navigation, and tea and coffee plantations remained almost European preserves. Under these conditions, the hangover of the decades-long close business interaction between the Indian and British commercial interests was too strong to vanish quickly.

EARLY MANIFESTATIONS

Below the surface, however, the Indian industrial class was becoming increasingly conscious of its own distinct identity during the last quarter of the nineteenth century. Manchester's growing hostility towards the Indian textile industry proved to be the first visible assault on the Indian sensitivities. Most educated Indians condemned the government decision to abolish, under Manchester's pressure, all import duties on textile goods in 1882. Many Indian industrialists also saw in the Factory Act of 1892 a Manchester ploy to snatch away their competitive advantage. If these measures created serious doubts about the bonafides of the alien government in the mind of the Indian industrial class, another measure caused its near alienation from the government. This was the imposition of a countervailing excise duty in 1894 on the production of textile goods in India to offset the duty on imports, that had to be re-imposed in search of new sources of revenue.

This decision evoked widespread protest from all sections of Indian industrialists. The leader of the Ahmedabad mill owners, Ranchhodlal, and J.N. Tata, not given to joining bandwagons of protest, unequivocally condemned the decision. Their views were in tune with a vast section of the informed population in the country. This happened at a time when the emerging middle class, for a variety of reasons, had already started developing a sense of disillusionment with the Crown government, to which powerful publicists like Dadabhai Naoroji, Mahadev Govind Ranade, and Romesh Chandra Dutt gave expression in their writings. They eloquently pointed to the exploitation of Indian resources for the benefit of Great Britain and to the racial biases in the administration of the colony. They were not against the imperial connection but wanted Indians to be treated on a par with the British subjects of the Crown. The Indian National Congress founded in 1885 was an organized expression of these proto-nationalist sentiments.

It was, therefore, natural for the industrialists to have close ties with the Congress. Apart from supporting the Congress, Indian business interests also began to form their own pressure groups around this time, with the result that a number of chambers of commerce representing native business at local or regional levels came to the fore after 1880. Until then all chambers of commerce in India, including those in the three Presidency cities (set up as early as the mid-1830s) were almost exclusively European affairs.

The growing sense of identity in Indian business interests, particularly the industrialists, and the rising nationalistic tendencies in society as a whole provided a great deal of impetus to the idea of *swadeshi*—economic autonomy. The idea was not new. A few scattered advocates of it existed as early as the mid-nineteenth century. For a faction of the Arya Samaj, a reformist Hindu sect founded by Swami Dayanand in 1873, swadeshi was an article of faith.

That the advocates of swadeshi had some impact on the counsels of business circles is clear from the fact that J.N. Tata named one of his textile companies, set up in 1886, Swadeshi Mills, and the Parsee founder of Godrej and Boyce Manufacturing Company, Ardeshir Burjorji Godrej, launched his enterprise to produce security material in 1897 at Bombay under the belief that in order to attain self-rule, India must reduce its dependence for manufactured goods on the West.

By the last quarter of the century, the swadeshi spirit had a much greater impact on the Delhi-Punjab region, where the Arya Samaj movement had made considerable headway, than any other part of the country. Agriculture was still the main occupation in this region. As the swadeshi propaganda gained momentum, the importance of modern industries for the economic progress of the region was increasingly realized by the contemporary opinion leaders, particularly those exposed to the outside world either through education or contact or both. The establishment of Punjab National Bank in 1894 was a result of this belief.

All the founders of the Bank were highly educated, active in reform movements and Congress organization, and firm believers in the benefits of industrialization. One of them, Harkishan Lal, even translated his belief into action by launching a series of joint stock companies—insurance firms, flour mills, a spinning and weaving mill, a cotton press company, an oil pressing concern, a timber works, a match factory, soap factories, brick kilns, saw mills, ice factories, laundries, banks, etc. The most important of these were Bharat Insurance Company, probably the first Indian enterprise of this kind, and Peoples' Bank of India. Practically all his enterprises failed because of lack of systematic procedures and careful planning. But this should not devalue his contribution to the process of generating industrial interest in the Punjabi middle class, traditionally oriented to commercial and trading pursuits.

THE BATTLECRY OF SWADESHI

With the exception of Harkishan Lal's companies, no other enterprise founded in Punjab or elsewhere at the turn of century identified itself with swadeshi as explicitly as Punjab National Bank. But the spirit continued to simmer until 1905 when Lord Curzon's decision to divide Bengal into East and West metamorphosed it into a full-fledged movement. Comprising Bengal, Bihar, Orissa, and Assam then, the province, the Viceroy believed, was too unwieldy for efficient governance. His scheme envisaged the division of the province into Eastern Bengal and Assam with its capital at Dacca, and West Bengal with its capital at Calcutta. Whatever its justification, the plan created deep resentment among the Bengali intelligentsia. A call to boycott foreign goods and patronize swadeshi (indigenously produced) goods was their answer to the Viceroy's ill-conceived measure. Rising from Bengal, the battlecry of swadeshi reverberated through the entire length and breadth of the land. This created additional demand for the products of Indian mills, representing the only organized industry in the country under native control. As the market for the Manchester goods in India declined, as many as thirty-nine mills with 36,304 looms and 982,327 spindles were floated between 1904 and 1910, and the production capacity of many units set up earlier was expanded. Ahmedabad witnessed the rise of the largest number of companies—eighteen.

The swadeshi agitation being much more strident in Bengal than elsewhere, its impact on the province was naturally much greater. As stated earlier, the disastrous experiences of the 1840s had practically killed the Bengali enthusiasm for business. The swadeshi movement revived it. The result was the birth of a number of enterprises promoted by Bengalis. As a traditional industry like cotton textile did not hold much attraction for the Bengalis, most of these new ventures focused on more sophisticated manufacturing lines. The most important among these were the Bengal Chemical and Pharmaceutical Company, Calcutta Chemicals, Bengal Lamps, Calcutta (later Bengal) Pottery Works, Oriental Match Factory, and Bande Match Factory. Bengal Chemicals was the brainchild of a scientist, Prafulla Chandra Ray, who had a Ph.D. degree in Chemistry from the University of Edinburgh. Calcutta Chemicals, Bengal Lamps, and Calcutta Pottery were founded by similar nationalist-minded persons.

If the push factor of swadeshi was responsible for rekindling the spirit of enterprise among the Bengali bourgeoisie—*bhadralok* in popular parlance—it was the pull factor of demand that sustained their undertakings. For, the products that the swadeshi enterprises offered were becoming quite popular with the urban middle class, and they were not produced in India until then.

Firms to produce goods that involved more intricate manufacturing processes than cotton textiles arose in western India too, though in lesser number. One of these was the Alembic Chemical Works at Baroda. Like Ray's Bengal Chemicals, this undertaking grew out of the experimental endeavours of a professor of Chemistry at Baroda College, Tribhuvandas Kalyandas Gajjar, in collaboration with one of his students, A.S. Kotibhaskar. Their experiments caught the notice of a rich and educated landholder, B.D. Amin, who joined hands with the two scientists to form a public limited company, Alembic Chemical Works, to undertake industrial application of the formulations developed by these scientists. At the time of its registration in 1907, Alembic was one of the four chemical companies in the entire country, and the only one in western India.

Around the same time, Laxmanrao K. Kirloskar was struggling, in another part of western India, to create an enterprise based on his own technical expertise. Belonging to a Maharashtrian Brahman family of petty civil servants, he had been trained as a technical draughtsman. While working as a teacher of mechanical drawing at Victoria Jubilee Technical Institute, Bombay, he acquired a good knowledge of mechanical engineering through self-study. Denied a well-deserved promotion at the Institute, he quit the teaching job in protest and decided to earn a living through self-employment. After a series of trials and errors, spanning a decade, Laxmanrao eventually hit upon the idea of producing a better variety of plough to replace the traditional implement normally used by India's farmers—an idea that would eventually lead to the establishment of Kirloskar Brothers, his managing agency firm, from whose womb would emerge several enterprises of all-India standing. On a more modest level was the Paisa Fund Glass Works set up at Talegaon near Poona in 1905. The company was so named because the start-up capital was raised through small contributions from a large number of persons.

Perhaps the most visible beneficiary of the swadeshi sentiments was the Tatas' steel venture, though the swadeshi movement had nothing to do with its origin. In fact, J.N. Tata's dream of promoting steel manufacturing in India preceded the swadeshi movement by several decades. It had started taking shape in Tata's mind as early as 1882 when he chanced to see the copy of a report on the financial prospects of iron-working in Chanda district prepared by a German expert. According to this report, the Chanda deposits in Bombay Presidency could yield ore suitable for conversion into iron and steel, using charcoal as fuel for smelting. However, in the face of the ludicrous prospecting laws then in force, Tata could do nothing concrete. It would have been foolhardy indeed to make a large investment in prospecting when he was not sure about how long the concessions would be allowed to last and whether the mining rights would continue to remain with him after the area had been explored. Under these conditions, Tata had no alternative but to wait for more favourable times.

And he waited for nearly twenty years—until 1899 when the irksome, archaic regulations were replaced by a new set of rules that granted much greater security to prospectors to reap the fruits of their labour. Jamsetji took the fullest advantage of the altered situation to revive his dream. He acquired the prospecting licence for selected areas of Chanda district, but it was soon discovered that the Chanda deposits were unsuitable for smelting. Jamsetji, however, did not give up despite his failing health, and entrusted the project to his forty-four-year-old son Dorabji who had worked closely with him since 1884 and thus fully imbibed the founder's values, aspirations, and ideals. Dorabji and his associates identified an alternative area with rich deposits of iron ore, lying in the neighbourhood of Durg district in the present-day Chhatisgarh state. The exploration was in full swing when Jamsetji passed away in Germany in 1904.

The Durg exploration yielded highly satisfactory results. The Tata team now got busy with logistic arrangements to launch the steel company at a site selected near a village in Bihar, known as Sakchi. Nobody knew how and from where the huge start-up capital for the project would come. Dorabji tried to interest the London money market which responded coldly to his proposal. Returning to India empty-handed in 1907, when the swadeshi spirit was at its height, he issued an appeal to Indians for funds, along with a prospectus. So overwhelming was the response to the appeal that within barely three weeks the entire capital required for the project was secured. With the financial hurdle crossed, Tata Iron and Steel Company (TISCO) was finally registered in 1907. With a plant capacity of 100,000 ingots, the company went into operation in 1911. This was the first steel firm in India in the real sense of the term.

IMPACT ON THE SOUTH AND ELSEWHERE

The south did not remain unaffected by the inducement provided by the swadeshi movement. However, business life in the region was still too heavily dominated by the British agency houses at the turn of the century, to leave much room for the Indian-promoted manufacturing enterprises to emerge and flourish. The swadeshi spirit, therefore, manifested itself in the establishment of a number of modern banks. These, however, were undertakings of modest size which offered no challenge to the well-entrenched foreign interests in the region. And they had little chance to grow as all the three principal agency houses operating in the region—Parry, Binny, and Arbuthnot—had banking departments that together controlled a large chunk of business in this sphere.

An unexpected development in 1906 brought about a radical change in the situation. This was the failure of Arbuthnot & Co., which had by this time developed into a formidable concern having business links with firms in Calcutta, Bombay, London, Liverpool, and Manchester. Sir George Gough Arbuthnot, the head of the firm at the turn of the century, had a very high standing in the business and social life of Madras. The people of Madras had immense faith in the house and felt entirely safe in investing their savings in its banking department. They, however, had no inkling that behind its seemingly solid facade, the house was tottering at its very foundation. Sir George was a respectable figure in Madras, but his understanding of business matters left much to be desired. Perhaps without realizing the consequences and misled by some of his unscrupulous associates based in London, he started using a part of the deposits placed with the house for investment in a host of speculative ventures in India, Britain, the United States, South Africa, and the West Indies. In this fashion, the firm's deposits were completely wiped out by 1906, and Arbuthnot & Co. had to declare itself bankrupt. Sir George tried to wriggle out of the mess he had created, but was tried for cheating and sentenced to rigorous imprisonment for eighteen months.

The Arbuthnot crisis shattered the credibility of the other two agency houses in the region. While Parry, owing about Rs 24 lakh to the public, could honour its liabilities by arranging a quick loan from a London firm, Binny, with claims against it amounting to more than Rs 40 lakh, was not so lucky. It had to suspend payment for a short while during which time Sir James Lyle Mackay (later Earl of Inchcape), the head of British India Navigation Company (BI), acquired the firm with arrangement to honour the depositors' claims in full. A new Binny & Co., registered in London as a sterling firm, now became a part of Sir James's growing empire.

With the public trust in the banking system of the agency houses eroded for ever, the ground was now cleared for the Indian-controlled and Indian-managed banks to emerge. The swadeshi groundswell gave an added impetus to the process. The establishment of Indian Bank in 1907 was the result. Though Indian Bank was the most visible example of swadeshi-inspired enterprises in the south, a few more business units came into being under the influence of the new spirit. These included United India Life Assurance Company, Madras, floated by an Indian trading firm, Lingam Brothers, and Swadeshi Steam Navigation Company, Tuticorin, promoted by V.O. Chidambaram Pillai, a radical nationalist, and his associates. Swadeshi Steam, however, could not survive long in the face of dirty machinations against it by the British shipping interests.

Banking firms were established in other parts of the country as well around this time. The most important among these were Bank of India (1907), Punjab and Sind Bank (1908), Central Bank of India (1911), and Bank of Baroda (1908), the last being the first major banking institution set up in princely India. Their rise, however, cannot be attributed primarily to the swadeshi spirit which had lost much of its vigour by the end of 1907. The Tatas' hydroelectric power project, as a consequence, could not benefit from the swadeshi upsurge in the manner in which their steel venture had done. Like the steel company, this project too was the brainchild of J.N. Tata who, during the closing years of his life, was increasingly drawn to the idea of generating power from the waterfalls in the Lonavala section of the Western Ghats. His idea was to feed the mills in Bombay that used coal, an expensive and polluting material, for fuel.

Jamsetji had already completed many preliminaries before he died, leaving the project to the care of Dorabji. Busy placing their steel company on an even keel, Jamsetji's successors had to leave their hydroelectric project on the shelf until TISCO commenced operations. Once this was accomplished, the Tatas turned their attention to the hydroelectric scheme. A public limited concern, Tata Hydro-Electric Power Supply Company, was registered in 1910. The money market was tight and Indian investors, who had made it possible for the Tatas' steel dream to become a reality not very long ago, were very cold in their response. Thanks to the backing of Lord Sydenham, the Governor of Bombay, and the untiring efforts of Dorabji, Indian princes and other investors came forward with their subscriptions, to enable the company to commence power generation by 1915.

EFFECTS OF THE FIRST WORLD WAR

By this time, the outbreak of World War I had already created an extremely favourable environment for the Indian business and industry. As the war disrupted imports, domestic demand for India-made goods went up. This naturally pushed up the energy requirements of the Bombay mills. The Tatas responded by expanding their hydroelectric system. As a part of a well-thought-out perspective plan, two more companies, Andhra Valley Power Supply Company and Tata Power Company came up in quick succession. By the end of World War I, the Tata hydroelectric system, complete in all respects, was capable of satisfying the entire power needs of the region.

The war period also witnessed the consolidation of TISCO. Before the war, British steel manufacturers looked upon the Tata venture with suspicion, and their Indian distributors carried on ceaseless, derisive propaganda against Tata steel; it was as perishable as wood and as weak as bamboo, they would often remark. Official circles too had nothing but contempt for the TISCO product. During the war, however, it was TISCO that supplied most of the government requirements, while imports remained disrupted. 'I can hardly imagine,' a grateful Viceroy conceded unhesitatingly after the war, 'what we should have done during these four years, if Tata company had not been able to give us steel rails.' TISCO was now a respectable firm with a rightful claim on government gratitude and support. More importantly, it developed around it an aura of a national enterprise and the Tatas were now looked upon as a 'national house'.

Shortly before the war, the Tatas had moved into a new line—cement production—with the establishment of their Indian Cement Company at Porbandar in Kathiawar. This was the first successful attempt to produce cement in the country. Shortly after the outbreak of the war, Dorabji and his associates added another cement unit in Bihar. As the business conditions became increasingly buoyant with no end to the hostilities in sight, they founded a series of other enterprises embracing a variety of fields: engineering, electrochemicals, construction, sugar, and soap and toiletries. They also promoted an industrial bank, the first of its kind in India, and an insurance company. With the exception of their New India Assurance Company, all these enterprises were set up with an eye on short-term gains and without adequate planning and preparation. The Tatas would later rue their decisions to float these concerns, but as long as the war and its after-effects lasted, they earned handsome profits.

The business behaviour of the Tatas during the boom years was typical of Indian business in general. Few, if any, prominent business houses could control the temptation to float new concerns without due regard for their core competencies. The industrial sector on the whole gained enormously during the war with rising demand and prices. The cotton industry benefited the most from the wartime boom. The profit that the industry earned during this period was ten to fifteen times more than the pre-war average.

The greatest gainers were the companies that catered to the domestic demand for cloth. With constantly falling exports of Indian yarn to China since the closing years of the nineteenth century—resulting eventually in the loss of the Chinese market altogether by 1913—most of the mills controlled by Indians had already restructured their production plans to concentrate primarily on weaving. This was a major factor in the business success of such mills under the changed market conditions. In contrast, most European-controlled mills, whose production strategy centred primarily around export, found themselves in deep waters during the war. Such mills could reap little benefit from the wartime boom and some actually suffered heavily. Perhaps the best example of the plight of export-oriented companies was Greaves Cotton and Co., one of the largest producers of textile goods, controlling as many as seven spinning mills in Bombay. Unable to reorganize its operations so as to switch over to weaving on time, and therefore ill-equipped to bear the strains of the changed environment, it was forced to dispose of its mills by 1915. In contrast, only a few—probably only one—Indian-controlled companies changed hands between 1913 and 1917.

European industrialists in eastern India, though engaged mostly in export-oriented industries, earned phenomenal profits during the war. For, out of the three industries in which expatriates had major interests, the war created difficulties only for tea mainly because of shipment difficulties. While the military requirements for an ever-increasing quantity of gunnies, hessians, sandbags, and corn sacks came as a boon to the jute industry, the growing need for energy for cotton and jute mills, now working overtime to meet the war-generated demand, helped the coal mines. The jute firms benefited the most and declared consistently high dividends.

The wartime performance of Bird & Co. was typical of the firms engaged in these industries. The company had been thoroughly reorganized during the decade preceding the war under the leadership of Earnest Cable, now senior partner after the retirement of the Bird brothers, and the company was in a trim shape to take full advantage of the profitable situation that the war created. Consequently, practically all the branches of its business prospered during the war. It also launched a few new companies heralding its entry into fields in which it had no interest until then. Of all the wartime initiatives of Bird, by far the most important was the purchase of F.W. Heilgers & Co., until then one of its chief rivals in Calcutta. The company had been founded as early as 1872 by a German–British partnership. Apart from coal and jute, Heilgers had interests in industries Bird had not yet touched, such as paper (Titaghur Paper Mills established in 1882), lubricating oil, shipping, and forestry.

Most of the wartime promotions and acquisitions were consistent with Bird's core competencies. But like the Tatas, it also entered some other lines during the war in which it had little or no experience. These included trade in hides, leather manufacturing, footwear production, wood products, manufacture of railway sleepers, sugar, and mica mining. These 'war babies', to use a phrase used by a high official of the company, would start causing sleepless nights to the parent firm within just a few years after peace returned, but for the moment everything was hunky-dory.

The boom conditions that favoured industrial firms, whether under Indian or European control, during the war also benefited the commercial sector as traders, both big and small and scattered throughout the land, earned substantial profits in the process of distributing industrial goods or agricultural products. The financial sector, in contrast, went through its worst phase. This was a natural consequence of the reckless expansion of banking firms during the decade preceding the war. Only a handful of the banks founded between 1900 and 1913 were sound institutions. Most of them had emerged in response to the mounting demand for money, but without sufficient back-up capital. The absence of a central regulatory authority made matters worse. On top of it all, the directors and officers of these institutions indulged in gross and fraudulent misuse of funds to feather their own nests. They ran modern banks like traditional *pedhi*s. This was bound to lead to disaster, and this is what happened. During a short period of five years from 1913 to 1917 as many as eighty-seven banks with a total paid-up capital of nearly Rs 200 lakh failed.

In the ordinary course of things, the prosperity of the industrial and commercial sectors should have had a spillover effect on the banking sector. If it did not happen during the war, it was simply because the two sectors were completely divorced from each other, so much so that the Company Law of 1913, which introduced many salutary reforms in the industrial and commercial sectors, did not even attempt to define a bank, much less regulate it. As things remained much the same for the banking sector even after the war, the fortunes of the Indian joint stock banks continued to fluctuate until 1936 when a new company law coupled with the establishment of a central banking authority, Reserve Bank of India, brought about a semblance of order in this area. The traditional sector naturally continued to be the principal source of industrial finance, with inevitable consequences for the managerial structure and the policies relating to dividend and reserve.

THE MARWARI ENTRY INTO INDUSTRY

Amidst the rejoicings of the industrialists and the wailings of the bankers, a momentous development, taking place during the war years, went almost unnoticed. This was a quiet entry of the Marwaris—Rajasthani émigrés engaged in business pursuits away from their native region—into the modern sector. By the turn of the century practically every major urban centre in the country had a sizeable Marwari population engaged mainly in trading, moneylending, brokerage, and speculation, although a few industrial undertakings promoted by the Marwaris had also come into being in Hyderabad, Poona, Bombay, Jabalpur, Nagpur, and Indore before the outbreak of the war. Sarupchand Hukumchand, who had made his money through cotton and opium speculation, was by far the most prominent of early Marwari industrialists; he had two mills at Indore, his headquarters—one founded in 1909 and the other in 1914. Among the non-textile ventures was Perfect Pottery Works founded at Jabalpur in 1905 by the Sevaram Khushalchand family.

These, however, were stray, sporadic cases. Established at places where industrial activities had not made much headway, and where the Marwari presence was still limited, they did not set a noticeable trend. It was during the war that the process of transition gained sufficient momentum in Bengal, particularly Calcutta, where the Marwaris had the most emphatic presence. By the turn of the century, their dominance of the internal trade in raw jute was almost complete and they also claimed a sizeable share of the export trade. As banians of European managing agencies, they had close links with them. It was a common practice among the European agency firms to allot to their partners, managers, and officers a certain number of shares in the companies under their management. With the share prices rocketing sky high during the war, the holders of a large number of such shares found it advantageous to dispose of their holdings. And the Marwaris, with their proximity to the European firms and therefore their employees, found it easy to acquire these shares. The profits earned through trade during the war stood them in good stead in this regard. It was, however, just the beginning of a process that would unfold fully somewhat later. For the time being, no Marwari presented a convincing evidence of the community's inclination to move away from purely commercial lines—with two exceptions.

One of them was Ghanshyamdas Birla, whose family symbolized more than any other Marwari, the transition of the community from trade to industry. Maheshwari Bania by caste, the Birlas originated from Pilani in the Shekhavati region of Rajasthan, which had been the original homeland of the early Marwari migrants. The first Birla to leave Pilani in search of better commercial opportunities was Sheo Narain, who moved to Bombay shortly after the rebellion of 1857 and made a small fortune during the speculation mania of the mid-1860s. His son Baldev Das joined him to take care of the expanding business. Dealing in opium, silver, sugar, and cotton, they established themselves comfortably in trade but were forced to move to Calcutta when Bombay was threatened by the plague epidemic around the turn of the century. Here the Birlas got associated with the influential Marwari firm of Tarachand Ghanshyamdas, and a little later became the banian of the powerful European house of Andrew Yule & Co.

These associations helped them understand the dynamics of the Calcutta business. Making good profits in opium, jute, and hessian trade, they set up a firm of their own—Baldeodas Jugalkishore—named after Ghanshyamdas's father and elder brother. By the time the war broke out, the Birlas were firmly settled in Calcutta; their fortunes received a further boost from the wartime boom. Jute export claimed their major attention during these years and they opened an export office in London in 1917—this being the first case of a Calcutta-based Indian firm doing so. According to a rough estimate, their total worth during these years quadrupled—from Rs 20 lakh to nearly Rs 80 lakh. And in this achievement the role of Ghanshyamdas, just about twenty years old when the war broke out, was considerable.

By this time, Ghanshyamdas had also emerged as a prominent leader of an influential group of Marwaris who wanted the community to develop a modern, progressive outlook, shed off its traditional conservative image, and forge closer links with the emerging forces of Indian nationalism. In the course of his commercial dealings with his English clients, he had been subjected, on many occasions, to overt or covert racial discrimination which had left a bitter taste in his mouth. At the same time, he had also developed a grudging respect for the European superiority in business methods, their organizing capacity, and their many other qualities. These experiences at an impressionable age, coupled with the augmented financial power that came in the wake of the war, were an important factor in Ghanshyamdas's decision to enter modern industries. Acquisition of a sick cotton mill in Delhi in 1916 marked the beginning of his industrial career. Although his elder brother Rameshwardas, looking after the family business in Bombay, had already joined two other parties to float a cotton mill there about two years before, Ghanshyamdas's venture was the first industrial undertaking of the family over which the Birlas had complete control. Barely four years later, they set up Birla Jute Mill in Calcutta in blatant defiance of the Scottish monopoly.

The other exception was Sarupchand Hukumchand who had already founded two cotton mills in Indore before the war and added a third one in the same city shortly after the war broke out. Finding the business opportunities in central India a little too restricted for his ambition, he opened an office in Calcutta in 1915. Sarupchand's reputation must have preceded him in the eastern metropolis, for his new office is reported to have done brisk business on the very first day. Within just a few years, he became sufficiently powerful to found Hukumchand Jute Mill. He would remain the most formidable Indian competitor of the Birlas in the area of jute manufacturing until 1939 when he decided to sell off his mills to the Birlas and fade into insignificance.

Sarupchand and Ghanshyamdas were not the only Marwaris to branch out into the modern sector during or soon after the war. Hargovind Dalmia acquired Mathuradas Mills in Calcutta in 1921. Baijnath Juggilal, the forerunners of the House of Singhanias who had been active in trade and banking for generations in Kanpur, also branched out into cotton manufacturing. Lakshmichand Jaipuria partnered with Sardar Shobha Singh to set up Khalsa Mills in Delhi in 1923. The family of Nandlal, managing a textile mill at Indore also emerged as a major Marwari house in 1922. And Anandilal Poddar of Bombay joined hands with a Japanese to set up Toyo-Poddar Cotton Mills in Bombay in 1924. These initiatives, however, represented only the beginning of the transformation of this community. It would be almost another decade before the Marwari presence on the industrial horizon of India would become conspicuous.

NO LONGER SECOND FIDDLE

In many ways the prosperous years of World War I reinforced the trends that were developing during the swadeshi period. New enterprises sprang up in the wake of rising opportunities created by the war; apart from the Marwaris, new social collectivities or caste groups, hitherto aloof from the industrial scene, were drawn to the modern sector; and industries to which Indians had so far remained indifferent began to attract them. The commercial sector too began to draw individuals and groups hitherto uninvolved in business at the lower levels of the spectrum. The growing interest of Indians in the business profession was reflected among other things in the emergence of a growing number of trade associations, controlled either exclusively by Indian interests or dominated by them, in various parts of the country.

Larger in number, engaged in a variety of businesses, and varied in social composition, native Indian business had become quite conscious of its distinct identity by the end of World War I and was no longer prepared to play second fiddle to the British business interests in India. The days of the comprador were definitely over.

CHAPTER 8

TOWARDS MATURITY

WHILE THE INDIAN BUSINESS WORLD BECAME INCREASINGLY CONSCIOUS of its distinct identity, the attitude of the government towards it underwent a drastic change. Instead of giving it a stepmotherly treatment, as had been the case previously, the government was now keen to placate it—or at least not alienate it. A major factor behind this change of heart was the critical support the native business had provided to the war effort. Also the government was keen to prevent the alienation of the burgeoning class of industrialists at a time when the forces of Indian nationalism were becoming more and more assertive.

NEW CLIMATE, NEW TRENDS

The most visible evidence of the new stance of the government was the appointment of the Indian Industrial Commission, the first of its kind in British India, to examine what the government could do to provide an impetus to industrialization. The Commission recommended the appointment of a Fiscal Commission to go into the question of tariff protection to Indian industries. The Fiscal Commission refrained from recommending general tariff protection to Indian industries, but favoured a case-by-case scrutiny. The Indian Tariff Board, set up soon after for the task, ushered in what is generally known as the policy of discriminating protection. The new industrial policy was much less than what the Indian industrialists would have liked, but it was definitely better than the hands-off approach, pursued until then, that often worked to the advantage of British manufacturers and the detriment of the Indian interests.

Manchester could not have liked even the mild pro-native stance that the policy of discriminating protection implied. The expatriate firms in India, on the other hand, acquiesced in the new policy because they hoped that some of the industries in which they were interested might also benefit from the policy. They, however, felt deeply concerned when the Government of India Act of 1919, promising greater devolution of powers to Indians, provided for the representation of native business interests in the legislative councils of the provinces as well as in the proposed Central Legislative Assembly. For, never before until then had an Indian national represented India's business interests in the legislatures. The European interests would outnumber Indians in the legislatures even under the new dispensation, but the message of providing for separate representation of native business could not have been lost on the expatriates.

All this was happening while the political climate of India was undergoing a remarkable change, thanks to the arrival of Mohandas Karamchand (later Mahatma) Gandhi on the scene. With his pacific militancy, with his stress on peace and non-violence, with his saintly demeanour, and with his religious idiom of discourse, he made a deep impression on the Indian business interests, as these virtues seemed to conform to their own cultural orientation. Never in the history of the Indian National Congress did any of its leaders establish such close personal bonds with the captains of Indian industry and commerce as Gandhi did. Their relationship with the nationalist movement during the first thirty years of its history was purely institutional, but it became intimately personal after 1915, thanks to the spell that Gandhi cast on them. This further widened the gulf between the native and the expatriate business interests. The European business community had so far remained more or less disinterested in political developments. Under the changed situation, they began to feel, as a prominent member of the Bengal Chamber of Commerce put it in 1920, that without meaningful political participation, 'European Commerce will not only suffer but its continuance may prove quite impossible'.

Developments in the next two decades did nothing to reduce their anxiety. For, the native industrial sector made substantial progress during this period despite ups and downs caused by changes in the general economic environment. The European interests too advanced, but their gains were less impressive than those of the natives, with the result that their shares in the capital employed in the Indian companies fell from about 72 per cent in 1918 to 40 per cent by 1939, while native shares registered a rise from 13 per cent to 34 per cent. These aggregates, significant though they are, hide a very important new trend.

The Indian investments were no longer confined to just a few industries such as cotton textiles and cotton gins and presses, in which they had established a competitive advantage before the war, but had also expanded into new lines such as sugar, paper, starch, shipping, engineering, chemicals, air transport, and many others. In fact, the native investments in these new lines were growing at a much faster pace than in the more traditional industries. Also, the Indian challenge to the British monopoly in industries such as jute and coal had become much more pervasive and determined. Investments in the relatively new lines as well as in more established industries by Indians and non-Indians alike led to a considerable expansion of the country's industrial base. Simultaneously, the social composition of the Indian business class also expanded, and modern industries made some inroads in new, hitherto untouched, regions and areas.

The industrial scene was still undeniably lopsided; modern industries were still localized to a few regions, mainly cities; India was still dependent on imports for most industrial products, even for finer varieties of textiles despite almost a century of progress in cotton manufacturing; and trade was still the backbone of Indian business on the eve of World War II. But there is little doubt that because of the developments between the two World Wars, it was now industry that defined the contours of Indian business. These contours were generally identified with certain families or groups—thanks to the managing agency structure governing the formation and management of industrial enterprises—even if they were joint stock concerns in the eyes of the law. Most of the families that had already entered the industrial field before the end of the war now carved deeper niches for themselves—some were also consigned to oblivion—while the new entrants gained in strength and vitality. These were the principal constituents of the private corporate sector that free India would inherit from the colonial regime, and these had already come to the fore before the end of the 1930s.

EXPANSION OF OLDER HOUSES

At the top of the Indian business world when World War I ended were unquestionably the Tatas. Imbued with confidence and hope, thanks to their wartime performance, the management of the house had to contend with new realities, coming in the wake of recessionary trends that set in after 1922. The textile companies in the group came under a great deal of strain in the face of shrinking profits, but they weathered the storm because of the vast domestic market for their products, coupled with the fact that they were among the best managed mills in the industry. All the cotton companies in the group, with the exception of Tata Mills set up during the war, continued to pay reasonably good dividends during the 1920s—sometimes as high as 50 per cent—and set aside sufficient amounts of reserve.

The Tatas, however, had trouble with their 'war babies'—the companies set up during the war without regard for the core competencies of the house—which found it difficult to stand on their feet once war-created demand disappeared with the arrival of peace. Consequently, they were all wound up or otherwise disposed of one by one with the exception of Tata Oil Mills and Tata Mills, which too maintained a precarious existence. While Tata Industrial Bank was merged with Central Bank of India, Tata Construction was acquired by Walchand Hirachand, and the cement companies merged with Associated Cement Companies (ACC) formed in 1936 with the merger of ten out of the twelve cement companies in the entire country. The formation of ACC had become necessary to tackle the problem of overproduction—a consequence of mushrooming of cement units during the war.

The problems of the post-war plight of the 'war babies' were nothing in comparison with the difficulties in which the Tatas' most prestigious undertaking, Tata Iron and Steel Company (TISCO), found itself soon after the war. The genesis of the problem lay in an ambitious plan of expansion launched while the war was still on. This should have been completed by 1921 but was delayed primarily because of the shortage of equipment, with the result that a large amount of capital remained locked in facilities producing nothing. By the time the expanded plant became operational, the Tata steel had lost its competitive advantage, thanks to a rise in imports of steel products—cheaper in price and preferred by consumers. Consequently, while TISCO now produced more steel, it sold less of it. The result was that the profits of the company plummetted and its cash balances touched rock bottom.

The Tata management took three major steps to save the most prized legacy of the founder. First, the company borrowed two million pounds on the London market. Second, Dorabji pledged his personal fortunes to obtain a loan of Rs 100 lakh from Imperial Bank of India (set up by amalgamating the three Presidency banks in 1921). An additional loan of Rs 100 lakh was raised from the princely state of Gwalior. And third, the management stepped up its efforts to secure protection for the steel industry. With the nationalist elements in the Central Legislative Assembly, constituted under the Reform Act of 1919, supporting the Tatas with one voice, protective duties were finally levied on imported steel. Incidentally, steel was the first industry to benefit from the new industrial policy. Government orders and a vigorous drive to cut costs also helped the company stabilize its position. The company also captured a large market for steel in India and for pig iron abroad which could be produced more economically in the country. Buoyed by its success in placing its affairs on an even keel, the company launched another modernization programme to raise the capacity of the plant to one million tonnes shortly before World War II began.

While the Tatas demonstrated exemplary patience and fortitude in handling the affairs of their steel company during these years of crisis, they took recourse to a rather soft option to alleviate the post-war agonies of their electric companies. These companies had emerged from the war much less consolidated than TISCO, and conditions became still worse as the Depression hit the Bombay mill industry, the main users of power from the Tata electric system. Unable to reverse the process, the Tatas sold 50 per cent of their holdings in the managing agency firm to American & Foreign Power, a syndicate based in the United States, in 1930. The decision invited a great deal of flak from the Indian industrial circles, but given the ground realities, the Tatas had few options. Consequently, their hydroelectric system would remain under a joint control until 1951.

Soon after the hydroelectric system was placed under joint Indo-American management, the second-generation leadership of the house came to an end with the death of Dorabji Tata in 1932. His younger brother, Ratan, had already died as early as 1918, and Jamsetji's sons left no issues. Jamsetji's nephew, Nowroji B. Saklatvala, who had worked closely with the founder, succeeded Dorabji as the head of the Tata empire and remained in this position until his death. The reversal of TISCO fortunes and many other developments took place under his leadership. A part of the credit, however, must go to his key associates, among whom were his brother Sohrab D. Saklatvala, and a much younger man, Jehangir Ratanji Dadabhoy (J.R.D.) Tata. The son of R.D. Tata (Jamsetji's wife's brother) and his French wife, J.R.D. was educated in France and had thoroughly imbibed European values and ethos before returning to India in 1924 at the age of 21. An eight-year-long apprenticeship with the steel company provided him with a great deal of insight into the intricacies of business. During the post-Dorab regime, he was treated as a critical partner in most of the decision-making and was thus fully prepared to take over the leadership of the group when Saklatvala suddenly passed away in 1938. J.R.D. was then 35 years old. His fellow directors elected him as chairman of the group in a fit of absentmindedness, he often jocularly used to say.

Leading the house into air transport was J.R.D.'s major contribution. Civil aviation had already developed into an industry in Western countries, but even as late as 1932, India had no air services. While a student in France, J.R.D. had been fascinated by the flying device partly because of his friendship with the son of Louis Bleriot, the first individual to fly across the English Channel. Returning to India, he secured a pilot's licence, and successfully undertook a solo flight between Bombay and Karachi to demonstrate his capabilities. He then persuaded Dorabji to start an airmail service between these two major cities of the Presidency. This marked the beginning of the age of air transport in the country and also of Air India, which started as a division of Tata and Sons.

The Tatas' aviation venture, however, was yet to stabilize when World War II broke out. So was the case with another ambitious project launched by them after J.R.D. came to the helm. This was Tata Chemicals, reputed to be the biggest chemical works in the country at the time of its birth in 1939. India produced no industrial chemicals then; consequently the country was wholly dependent on imports for even basic inputs such as caustic soda, soda ash, and other soda compounds that textiles, glass, paper, soap, and many other industries required. Searching for an appropriate location, the Tata management accepted a proposal from the Maharaja of Baroda to set up their chemical factory at Mithapur situated near Dwarka on the sea coast in his state. The site selected was ideal because salt, the basic raw material, was available in plenty at Mithapur, which literally means 'the city of salt'. But hardly had the first move towards launching the project been made, when the outbreak of World War II disrupted all the calculations of the promoters.

By this time, the Tatas had as many as fourteen major companies under their control with combined sales of Rs 280 crore. No one in Indian industry was anywhere close to it. A still more impressive testimony to the quality of their entrepreneurship was the fact that most of their companies were engaged in basic industries, requiring large investment and involving long gestation. The Tatas, without question, had become the 'first family' of Indian business by the end of the 1930s.

The Birlas who would later emerge as the Tatas' most formidable rival for supremacy in the Indian business world, were still far behind. Late entry was only one of the reasons; the post-war environment was another and perhaps more important. The fortunes of their jute and cotton mills projected or acquired soon after World War I continued to fluctuate during the 1920s. And yet the Birlas decided to set up a brand new cotton mill in Gwalior, lured by the offer of important concessions by Maharaja Scindia of the princely state. Jiyajirao Cotton Mills, floated in 1921, was the result. Production started a year later. The post-war boom was still continuing, which encouraged the Birlas to add one more cotton mill to their expanding empire by acquiring the old Kesoram Mill, founded in 1877, from Andrew Yule and Company.

The economic environment was already showing signs of turning hostile at the time of the Kesoram acquisition. It became worse subsequently because of, among other things, the rising imports of cotton goods from England and Japan. Admittedly, there were some favourable signs in the wind as well for Indian cotton manufacturer—for example, the abolition in 1924 of the universally despised excise duty on the production of Indian mills, the imposition of protective import duty on selective textile products in 1930, and a new swadeshi wave that swept the nation in 1930–1 in response to Gandhi's renewed call to boycott foreign goods. The overall economic environment after 1923, however, was confusing and remained so until the outbreak of World War II.

With short and limited experience in the industry, and with all their companies still relatively young and not very stable, the Birlas must have felt it imprudent to risk expansion of their industrial net under these conditions. There were no new Birla floatations for almost a decade after 1922, Kesoram Mills being the sole acquisition. Trading and speculation were the preferred focus of the house until 1932, when a statutory change in the government policy, granting tariff protection to the Indian sugar industry, stirred them once again into organizing new industrial concerns.

Although a few sugar mills had come into existence earlier, it was this change in government policy that gave a real boost to the Indian sugar industry. Within no time new mills sprang up. New floatations came so fast that within a span of seven years between 1929–30 and 1936–7 the number of factories increased from 27 to 150, and by 1938–9 the industry ranked third in the Indian organized sector in terms of total capital employed. The Birlas were among the first to seize the opportunity provided by the new policy. They set up one after the other as many as five sugar plants within a short period of just two years in eastern UP and western Bihar where sugarcane was grown in abundance. By the close of the 1930s, the Birlas were the third largest producer of sugar in the country. Only Begg Sutherland with nine plants and the Delhi-based Punjabi house of Gokulchand Narang with eight plants were ahead of the Birlas.

Their rising sugar fortune seems to have whetted the Birlas' appetite for industrial floatations. Sutlej Cotton Mills in Lahore set up in 1934 was one of these. But the most ambitious Birla venture of the decade was Orient Paper Mill, registered in 1936, which breached what until then was a European monopoly. Titaghur Paper of Bird & Heilgers and Bengal Paper Mills of Balmer Lawrie were the only companies in the field. The Thapars and the Bajorias were the other native groups that followed the Birla lead, but their units had much smaller capacity. Although the Birlas' paper company was yet to start production when the outbreak of World War II changed the entire business scene, the machinery from Germany had already arrived, which would stand the company in good stead during the war. Another, and far more important, initiative taken by the Birlas on the eve of the war, Textile Machinery Corporation (TEXMACO), too had to wait until the end of the war to achieve its objective. This was the first company ever floated in this field. However, the Birlas' plant in Calcutta was requisitioned by the government for war purposes shortly after it became operational. Textile machinery manufacturing, therefore, would start only after peace returned.

With the exception of TEXMACO, all the other companies of the Birlas were in consumer goods industries that required relatively low investment. So, even though they were not far behind the Tatas in respect of the total number of companies under their management on the eve of the war, in terms of the capital invested in these companies, they still had a long way to go. And yet it was G.D. Birla, and not a Tata, who emerged as the most dominant voice of Indian business during this period. This was largely due to his efforts to organize the disparate indigenous elements in the Indian business world under a common platform and the close links he forged with the leaders of the freedom movement, especially Gandhi. He, however, pursued a very balanced course to make sure that he did not unduly offend the expatriates or alienate the government.

G.D. Birla's contemporary Walchand Hirachand's nationalism had little regard for such sophistication, perhaps because he had come under the influence of nationalist propaganda while a student at Bombay and Poona. Belonging to a Gujarati Jain family, he had grown up in Sholapur where his father, Hirachand, had selling agencies of a few textile mills. Walchand, however, decided to explore other possibilities. In the process he, in partnership with one Laxman Phatak, developed a highly successful business in railway construction by 1912. World War I created more jobs for them and brought greater prosperity. By the time the war ended, Walchand had in his own right become a man of some means and had built up a sizeable business. With the new experience and self-made capital, he was ready to exploit new opportunities.

He decided to launch into shipping, an unusual line for an Indian at that time. He must have been aware of the monopoly of British shipping interests in the Eastern waters and of the use of all means, fair or foul, by them to maintain it—fierce rate cutting being the most common weapon used. These warnings from the past apparently meant nothing to Walchand. For, having accidentally learnt in 1919 that SS Loyalty, a steamer owned by Maharaja Scindia of Gwalior, was up for sale, he decided on the spur of the moment to purchase her as the first step towards starting a shipping concern. With absolutely no experience of the shipping industry, he persuaded some hard-headed business luminaries of Bombay to join him in the adventure. These included Narottam Morarjee (son of Morarjee Gokuldas) who took a 50 per cent interest, Kilachand Devchand, a prominent cotton trader, and Lallubhai Samaldas, a merchant statesman who had business connections with the Tatas and Killick Nixon. They joined hands to purchase the vessel and form a company. Thus was born Scindia Steam Navigation Company in 1919 with a nominal capital of Rs 450 lakh—barely three months after Walchand had taken the first fateful step. Surprisingly, the investors responded with great enthusiasm and the shares issued were oversubscribed.

But running a shipping line was not easy. The most formidable hurdle to contend with was the awesome power of British India Navigation Company (BI), which after its merger with the mighty Pacific and Orient (P&O) Steamship Company in 1914, had emerged as the virtual master of the Indian Ocean. The head of this concern, James Lyle Mackay (now Earl of Inchcape), had accumulated enormous business power in India controlling five of the most prominent expatriate firms—Kilburn & Co., Macneill & Co., Barry & Co., Mackinon Mackenzie & Co., and Binny & Co. To kill the nascent enterprise he used every conceivable weapon in his armoury. A determined Walchand somehow repulsed his assaults to enable Scindia to commence its passenger and cargo services between India and Europe. But the India-Europe sector failed to generate sufficient profit. The Scindia management explored many other possibilities to generate more revenue, but without much success. And yet the Scindia Board, largely because of Walchand's persuasion, spurned Lord Inchcape's offer to buy off their company.

Scindia retained its identity but under Inchcape's pressure its management had to agree to confine its operations to the Indian coasts and its fleet to seven ships during the next ten years. Walchand described Inchcape's terms as a 'slave bond' but Scindia's options were limited. With some minor modifications, this agreement remained the basis of Scindia's operations until the end of the British rule, during which period the company barely managed to stay afloat. Undeterred by these adversities, its management pushed forward the idea to develop a modern shipyard. But this was still at a planning stage when the company was forced to review all its activities in view of the outbreak of World War II.

Though Scindia received Walchand's best attention during the inter-war years, he never neglected his original construction business nor shut his eyes to other possibilities. Soon after the end of World War I, he joined hands with the Tatas to float Tata Construction Company. By the mid-1920s the Tatas, preoccupied with the affairs of their steel and hydroelectric companies, sold off their interest to Walchand, who renamed the company Premier Construction Company. In the meantime, he had also diversified into sugar production, taking advantage of the protection granted to the industry in 1932. His Ravalgaon Sugar Farm Limited had its factories in a village of the same name in Nashik district. After launching into sugar production, Walchand and his two brothers, Lalchand and Gulabchand, developed it into what has been described as 'one of the best equipped and most efficient sugar farm in India'. The complex was later renamed Walchandnagar by Lalchand, Walchand's brother.

Walchand was a dreamer and some of the manufacturing projects he dreamt of during the 1930s must have appeared sheer foolhardiness to most other businessmen of his times. Laxmanrao Kirloskar, his contemporary and like him imbued with nationalist pride, was more down to earth. Although he had already established an integrated, modern factory complex at what is now Kirloskarwadi in Maharahtra state before the outbreak of World War I, his product lines still consisted of mainly two items—improved iron plough and shaft cutter when the war came. Though the Kirloskars made only modest profit during World War I, they nevertheless, were in a much better shape at the end of the war, which encouraged them to convert their partnership firm, Kirloskar Brothers, into a public limited company in 1920.

The new-found confidence of the firm was also reflected in a vigorous programme of expansion and diversification launched soon after peace returned. A number of new products were put in the market in the 1920s, of which the most important were a diesel engine and centrifugal pump to facilitate the drawing of well water for irrigation. After 1926, the founder had his eldest son Shantanu, with an engineering degree from the prestigious Massachusetts Institute of Technology (MIT), to help him. He used his knowledge and skill to develop new products as well as to streamline the operations of the company. The Great Depression, however, destabilized the Kirloskars once again for, their main customers, the farmers, were particularly hit by it. Producing odds and ends, Laxmanrao and Shantanu just managed to keep the house afloat during those difficult years.

The Kirloskars' problems during the depressed conditions of the 1930s stemmed partly from the fact that their product portfolio was much too limited. However, even business groups that had their fingers in a variety of industrial pies, like the one headed by Lala Shri Ram, found it difficult to weather the storm. The emergence of this house was a post-war phenomenon. In fact, Shri Ram's father, Madan Mohan Lal, was still a paid secretary of Delhi Cloth Mills (DCM) founded by a group of Punjabi promoters in 1889, when the war came. The war proved to be a godsend to the father-son duo who improved their fortunes severalfold by supplying tents to the army and government, produced by a separate 'tent company' in which DCM had a 50 per cent stake; the remaining 50 per cent was shared between Shri Ram and a contractor with very close links with the government. Shri Ram emerged from the war a man of some means and with a great reputation for his business acumen. More importantly, with the money earned through the army contract, Shri Ram and his father increased their holdings in DCM to 16 per cent by 1921, which was sufficient to give them the control of the company. Thirty-two years after its birth, DCM thus became a fiefdom of its paid secretaries.

The production facilities were expanded before the post-war boom ended. This along with the fact that DCM was the only textile producer in the Delhi–Punjab region, enabled the company to increase its sales more than three times between 1923 and 1929. After the Great Depression set in, DCM like other companies, did feel the pinch. Still, both sales and profits of the company registered a net rise between 1931 and 1939 because of three factors: accent on production of coarser and cheaper varieties of cloth; Gandhi's call for boycotting foreign goods during the early 1930s; and a number of incentives, including bonus on sales given to the sales agents. Encouraged by these results, the DCM management set up another textile mill in 1935, Lyallpur Cotton Mills, away from Delhi in western Punjab where cotton was grown in abundance but no textile mill existed. The house had in the meantime set up Daurala Sugar Works near Delhi in response to the protection granted to the industry.

Sugar, being a processing industry like cotton textiles, was not far removed from DCM's main business; pottery and light engineering definitely were. Shri Ram's entry into these lines was through acquiring existing firms both in Calcutta and on the initiative of experts known to Lala Shri Ram. Bengal Pottery Works, acquired in 1934, was an old company set up during the swadeshi movement of the early twentieth century. It remained beset with problems even after it came under the new management. Just before the outbreak of World War II, however, a new and up-to-date plant had been installed which would stand the company in good stead to meet the augmented demand for its goods during the war. The other acquired firm, Jay Engineering Works (JEW) was only two years old when it became part of the DCM group. The sewing machine developed by the company's engineer founder was the only item the company produced at the time of the takeover. The new management decided to add many other items to its portfolio such as electric fans, cooking ranges, pressure gauges, railway signalling apparatuses, and water meters. Factories were planned and machinery installed, keeping in view the needs of these product lines. But the company was still running in loss when it had to divert its resources to produce goods required by the government to meet the exigencies of World War II.

Diversification did not help DCM in the short run. However, the production infrastructure developed in the course of diversification would contribute in no small measure to the prosperity of the group later. In contrast, the textile manufacturers in western India showed little enthusiasm for diversification. This was particularly true of Ahmedabad where the industry had made phenomenal progress since the beginning of the century—growing from merely twenty-nine mills in 1900 to seventy-two by 1929. During this period, the families of the old leaders like Ranchhodlal Chhotalal and Manusukhbhai Bhagubhai had been relegated to insignificance mainly because of the incompetence of the founders' successors, and new ones like Mangaldas Girdhardas Parekh and Amratlal Shodhan had come to the forefront, both rising from the position of small traders.

The Depression did not change the overall situation. The relative positions of the families controlling the industry, however, changed drastically. The Shodhan family, the industry leader in 1929, unable to withstand the pressure of family feuds and mismanagement, had to dispose off most of its companies to others. The Parekhs somehow held their own, but remained more or less stagnant, and Ambalal Sarabhai, who had a high status among Ahmedabad mill owners, refused to expand even though his Ahmedabad Manufacturing and Calico Printing Company (Calico Mills)—the largest single unit in the industry—made handsome profits. In contrast, the Lalbhais, who had only a token presence on the Ahmedabad industrial scene at the end of World War I, attempted major expansion between 1929 and 1931—just before the Great Depression set in so as to emerge as the largest group in the industry by the middle of the decade.

The credit for building this group almost from scratch belongs to Kasturbhai Lalbhai who had only one mill under his control in 1920. By 1936 the number of his units had gone up to seven including Arvind Mills, the only other company in the city, besides Sarabhai's Calico, to produce finer counts. While expanding his textile empire, Kasturbhai, like other Ahmedabad industrialists, gave little thought to diversification. Just before the outbreak of World War II, however, he launched production of starch, a basic material for processing textile goods, which no one in India produced then. It was a minor venture requiring little technological sophistication. Ahmedabad, by and large, remained a one-industry city, earning for itself the sobriquet 'Manchester of India'.

The Ahmedabad mill owners remained confined not only to a single industry, but also to a single city. For some inexplicable reason, they exhibited practically no interest in setting up industrial firms elsewhere in the country or even at other places in the Gujarat region. Perhaps the only exception was Mafatlal, who had entered the industry with the establishment of a cotton mill at Ahmedabad during the swadeshi movement of 1904–5. However, his next two mills were set up elsewhere in Gujarat, and Bombay became his virtual headquarters soon after the war.

By the time Mafatlal moved to Bombay, the textile industry in the metropolis was already in a crisis situation and the Great Depression made it infinitely worse. It is not surprising under these conditions that the number of Bombay mills that stopped working during the 1930s was far larger than elsewhere—twenty-two out of seventy-five. The most distinguished casualty was the Currimbhoy group, the second largest managing agents in the city controlling as many as twelve companies, and the only Muslim among the prominent industrialists of the city. Most other houses somehow escaped such a cruel fate but few, if any, remained unaffected by the blasts of the Depression. The depressed state of business gave an opportunity to some trading families to enter industry by acquiring cheaply the distressed mills. These included the Marwari firms of Ramnarain Ramnivas Ruia and Chaturbhuj Piramal. The former took over the managing agency of the Bradbury and Phoenix Mills and the latter of the Morarjee Gokuldas Mills. The Morarjee Gokuldas family also lost its Sholapur Spinning and Weaving Company to another Marwari family, the Jhajharias, and practically lost its place in the cotton textile industry.

Mafatlal's response to the business climate prevailing during the two World Wars was quite different from that of textile manufacturers in Ahmedabad as well as Bombay. On the one hand, he continued to consolidate his textile operations by acquiring and floating new companies, keeping abreast of the shift in demand pattern. On the other hand, a number of enterprises both in related and unrelated areas were set up with a view to reducing undue dependence on a single industry. The establishment of Mafatlal Fine Spinning and Manufacturing Company in 1930 was his most impressive achievement in the realm of cotton textiles, while a number of ginneries set up in the cotton-growing regions of Gujarat were intended to supply clean cotton to his own as well others' mills. He also set up a few ginneries in Uganda in partnership with the Gujarati settlers in that British colony, and acquired Bombay Uganda Company at Bombay from the Bradburys to market the output of his African ginneries.

These initiatives of the Mafatlal group, though not very common among the textile magnates of western India, were still within the confines of an industry that was closely identified with that region and with native Indian entrepreneurship. The establishment of Gagalbhai Jute Mills, named after Mafatlal's father, in Calcutta in 1929 was a clear manifestation of Mafatlal's desire to explore other possibilities. It was also a bold challenge to the firmly entrenched foreign interests in jute manufacturing. The mill soon established a reputation for quality and proved the wisdom of a move that might have seemed rash to others. Sugar and shipping were other non-textile lines that claimed Mafatlal's attention during the 1930s. He had indeed come a long way since he used to hawk around the streets of Ahmedabad, carrying cotton goods on his back.

New Entrants

What the foregoing discussion brings out is that despite the vicissitudes in the business environment of the inter-war period, most of the Indian entrepreneurs who had already achieved some degree of stability before World War I, consolidated their position. The period also brought new entrants into the industrial field. Juggilal Singhania of Kanpur, who had set up a small cotton mill in 1921, and his son Kamlapat added several new enterprises during the 1920s and the 1930s, including a jute mill, two cotton mills, two sugar mills, and a small light engineering firm under the name of J.K. Iron and Steel Company. Another Marwari trader who branched out into industry during this period was Jamanlal Bajaj of Wardha who founded Hindustan Sugar Mills at Golgokarnanath in the United Provinces in 1932 and acquired a steel rolling mill, Mukund Iron and Steel Works at Lahore in 1937 jointly with Jeewanlal Motichand, a Gujarati friend of his who was then based in Calcutta. The credit for nursing these companies to health, however, goes to Rameshwar Prasad Nevatia, Bajaj's son-in-law, as the founder had wholly dedicated his life to the causes dear to Gandhi, and had practically disassociated himself from the management of his business.

Perhaps the most notable among the new entrants was Ramkrishna Dalmia, a Marwari from Rohtak in Punjab, who would have a meteoric rise in Indian industry during and after World War II. Having made a fortune in Calcutta through trading and speculation during the 1920s, he entered the industrial sector during the 1930s with the establishment of five sugar mills in Bihar. He later set up Dalmia Cement Company with factories in Bihar, Punjab, Sind, and Madras, all functioning as part of a diversified group known as Rohtas Industries. Highly individualistic in temperament, he kept his companies out of the selling syndicates formed to meet the problem of overproduction in sugar and cement, and refused to merge his cement enterprise with Associated Cement Companies (ACC), to which he gave a stiff competition. He was among the first Indians to start manufacturing paper.

Another Punjabi who entered the industrial field during the inter-war years and would rise to great heights later, was Karamchand Thapar of Ludhiana. With a smattering of a college education, he operated as a small trader in Calcutta for some time jointly with some of his relatives before founding his own independent trading firm, Karamchand Thapar & Brothers, in 1929. The Thapars, however, soon entered the industrial field and registered their presence in three different sectors in which they would develop a dominant interest later. The first was sugar manufacturing that commenced in 1932 with the acquisition of a tottering concern located at Baitalpur in Gorakhpur district of the United Provinces, a sugarcane producing area. This was followed by Deoria Sugar Mills established three years later in the neighbourhood of the Baitalpur factory. The opening of their first colliery in 1933 marked the

Thapars' entry into coal mining, a field that had been attracting many Indians, particularly Marwaris, Gujaratis, and Punjabis since the beginning of the twentieth century. On the eve of the outbreak of World War II, the Thapars had no less than five coal concerns under their control. The third major sector the house entered in the 1930s was paper manufacturing with the setting up of Shree Gopal Mills in 1936 at Jamuna Nagar in Ambala district of Punjab. With their stakes in these three sectors, the Thapars had become a fairly diversified group by the end of the 1930s.

Gujarmal Modi, whose trading family had a long tradition of supplying provisions to the army, was another Punjabi Hindu to take to manufacturing during the 1930s. Originally from Patiala, he first organized a sugar mill in 1933 at Begamabad near Delhi, and then promoted a vegetable oil producing concern, Modi Vanaspati Manufacturing Company, just before the war broke out. These two units would later develop into the highly diversified Modi Industries Ltd, with its headquarters at the sprawling industrial township of Modinagar near Delhi. A few cotton mills of modest size, most of them promoted by Marwari traders, also sprang up in central India.

Perhaps the most spectacular development during the inter-war years took place in south India, that had just a few Indians on its industrial horizon until well after World War I. Coimbatore in Madras Presidency had a solitary cotton company until the beginning of the 1920s. Though this enterprise had been jointly promoted by two Chettier families as early as 1906, the real credit for developing Coimbatore as the principal cotton textile centre in the south goes to Naidu or Kamma entrepreneurs, belonging to the landholding classes. They started off by setting up, like many entrepreneurs in the west and north, ginning factories and then went on to promote a number of cotton mills in the immediate post-war period. The major role in this development was played by three Naidu families—G. Kuppuswami Naidu, V. Rangaswami Naidu, and P.S.G. Naidu. They were all large landholders cultivating cotton, who took to cotton trading around the turn of the century. The profits made during the war years enabled them to promote cotton companies, all spinning units of modest size. Among the factors that contributed to the success of their enterprises were ready access to the raw material produced in nearby regions, the presence of a large number of handloom weavers in Madras, and availability of cheap electric power.

The Chettiers, the southern counterparts of the Marwaris, remained by and large aloof from the modern sector. Though three Chettier-promoted mills did come into existence between 1921 and 1925, not until after 1930 did the Chettiers begin to look seriously upon modern industry as an avenue of prudent investment. A number of Chettier moneylenders in Burma suffered colossal losses around this time, as the bulk of their money loaned against the security of agricultural land became unrecoverable during the Depression. This was among the most important reasons that induced them to turn to the textile industry at home. On the eve of World War II, however, their presence on the industrial horizon of the south was still very limited.

In fact, families belonging to social groups, not commonly associated with business-type occupations were much more visible in the industrial arena of the south at this time. The emergence of one of the most prominent industrial houses in the region during the inter-war years was the outcome of the enterprising initiatives of the Seshasayee Brothers. Brahman by caste, and trained as electrical engineers, R. Seshasayee and his brother-in-law, V. Seshasayee, started with a road transport service around Trichinopoly in Madras Presidency. They later moved into servicing and sale of buses, cars, and motorcycles and then into design, supply, and erection of electrical installations in south Madras during the 1920s, in which field the partners established an enviable reputation. The success encouraged them to form three public limited companies between 1924 and 1937 to cater to the need of three different regions of the Presidency. On the eve of World War II, thus, the Seshasayee Brothers had already laid a strong foundation for future expansion and growth.

Another Brahman business house in the south also began to take shape during the 1930s. Its origin lay in a commercial concern, India Trading Company Limited, dealing in steel. Founded by C. Rajan Iyer around the beginning of World War I, the company earned handsome profits during the war. With his improved financial position and some valuable experience gained in this line, he made a debut in industry with the promotion of Indian Steel Rolling Mills Limited in 1934. This was the first enterprise in this field in south India.

TRADE–INDUSTRY NEXUS

The inter-War years thus witnessed the emergence of industrial enterprises in many parts of the country that had remained hitherto unaffected by industrial stirrings. These resulted from the initiatives and accomplishments of new entrants into industry or of those who were still on the peripheries when World War I ended. Trading and moneylending, however, continued to remain an important element in the overall scheme of Indian business. In fact, private funds still remained the main source of industrial finance, as the Indian banking system never entirely recovered from the crisis that had overtaken it after 1913, despite the amalgamation in 1921 of the three Presidency Banks into a single institution—Imperial Bank of India—and the establishment in 1934 of Reserve Bank of India to regulate the operations of private banking companies. Stock markets too remained as weak and disorganized as ever before even though many cities, apart from Bombay and Calcutta, had stock exchanges by 1939.

It was hardly surprising under these conditions that there continued to exist, despite the progress of industrialization, a very close nexus between traders and industrialists. Most of the industrial houses still kept their family pedhis and trading establishments intact, and the number of traders serving on the boards of industrial firms was by no means small. In many groups, transition from trade to industry was not yet complete; so their trading and industrial operations were not fully divorced from each other.

Besides, there were some traders whose position in the Indian business world was no less important than that of some of the prominent industrialists. Purshotamdas Thakurdas in Bombay, Badridas Goenka in Calcutta, and T.V. Sundaram Iyengar in Madras weilded the kind of influence in their respective regions and even at national level, that many industrialists might have envied. Known as the 'cotton king' because of his dominant position in cotton trade, Thakurdas served on the boards of as many as twenty-one industrial companies without having a controlling interest in any. A director in many Tata companies and a close confidant of Dorabji Tata, he was in constant personal contact with G.D. Birla. One of the key founders of the Indian Merchants' Chamber and East India Cotton Association, that regulated cotton trade at national level, he played, as we shall see later, a critical role in the creation of the Federation of Indian Chambers of Commerce and Industry (FICCI). Goenka enjoyed a similar position in eastern India. Though a graduate—few Marwaris of his generation could claim such an achievement— he was the leader of the conservative section of the Marwari community in Calcutta that confronted the reformist group led by G.D. Birla. He too, like Purshotamdas, served on the boards of many companies, including Imperial Bank of India (he became its chairman in 1933, the first Indian to hold this position) and Reserve Bank of India.

While both Thakurdas and Badridas hailed from the business castes (Thakurdas was a Gujarati Bania and Badridas a Marwari), T.V. Sundaram

Iyengar was a high-caste Tamil Brahman. Starting his business career with trading in timber in a small way, he moved into road transport shortly before World War I. During the 1920s he added distribution of imported cars to his operations, and acquired during the 1930s the sole selling agency of General Motors Corporation, the American automobile giant. Through the sale and servicing of imported cars, under the auspices of his family firm, T.V. Sundaram and Sons, he carved out a formidable position in the trading world of south India by the end of the decade to emerge as the head of a prominent group in the region later.

The important place of traders in the total scheme of things was also reflected in the process through which an apex organization representing purely Indian interests came into being. Despite the fact that a large number of local chambers of commerce—some dominated by Europeans, some by natives, and a handful by mixed interests—had come into being before World War I, there was still no organization of all-India character. Whenever the occasion demanded, the representatives of these bodies assembled together to discuss specific matters of common interest. The Associated Chambers of Commerce (ASSOCHAM) founded in 1921 was the first pressure group ever formed in the country that claimed to represent the whole of Indian business, native as well as European. It came into being at the initiative of Bengal Chamber of Commerce and, like Bengal Chamber, was heavily dominated by the European interests.

The birth of ASSOCHAM was received with great deal of misgiving in Indian business circles. G.D. Birla, who was fast emerging as a prominent leader of the native interests, was probably the first to suspect, as he wrote to Purshotamdas Thakurdas, that 'the organization will be very detrimental to Indian interests, if steps are not taken immediately to organize a similar institution of the Indians'. He, therefore, suggested to him as early as 1923 to take a lead to bring 'the merchants from all parts of India' on one platform so as to put forward 'their well-considered and combined views before the Government with a force which will carry greater weight than those of the combined European institutions'. Thakurdas was sceptical in the beginning, but ASSOCHAM's opposition to the grant of protection to the Indian steel industry (which in effect meant TISCO of which Thakurdas was a director) coupled with the continued opposition of the representatives of the European interests in the Central Legislative Assembly to measures aimed at helping native interests, eventually brought him around.

Things now moved much faster and the Federation of Indian Chambers of Commerce finally came into being in 1927 with Thakurdas as its first president. Among the eleven members of the first executive committee, not more than three had substantial industrial interests. It is also significant that 'Industry' was not a part of the original name of the organization; the word was added a year after its birth.

The birth of FICCI symbolized, among other things, the growing maturity of Indian business during the inter-war years.

CHAPTER 9

EXPATRIATES AND MULTINATIONALS

DESPITE THE GREAT STRIDES THEY HAD MADE DURING THE INTER-WAR years, the Indian interests were still far from a position of supremacy in the business world of their own country. For, out of the 57 largest groups in 1939, only 19 were Indian, with a total of 196 companies under their management whose paid-up share capital aggregated to Rs 55.10 crore. The remaining ones—all British, except the Swedish Match Company—accounted for 713 companies which together had a paid-up share capital of Rs 198 crore. Moreover, except cotton textiles, iron and steel, sugar, cement, and paper, the Indian presence in most other industrial sectors was either peripheral or far less impressive than the British. Even in service sectors such as insurance and finance, the British groups were ahead of the Indians in terms of the number of companies controlled. While tea plantations and jute textiles were almost exclusively in the hands of the foreigners, Indian stakes in coal mining, light engineering, and chemicals were none too high either. Though the Tatas were the largest of all business groups, native and foreign, in the country and their steel company, TISCO, was the largest industrial undertaking, it was the British house of E.D. Sassoon that was ahead of everyone else in the cotton textile industry over which the Indians exercised overall dominance.

The apparent supremacy of the non-Indian interests in the world of Indian business concealed a significant trend. While the Indian interests were gaining in strength, the British interests were either stagnant or declining. Even the sectors that were virtual British preserves at the end of World War I, such as jute textiles and tea plantation, were not free of the signs of British retreat or stagnation, and the stirrings of Indian challenge. It seems that the British interests were now less keen to invest in Indian trade and industry than before. In fact, there was, according to a well-regarded authority, a sudden, massive, and persistent withdrawl of capital from India in the 1930s due, among other things, to the repatriation of profits by expatriate firms, instead of reinvestment in Indian trade and industry. This may or may not be correct, but there is no dispute that private foreign investment in Indian business had reached some sort of a plateau by 1939, while native investment was on the ascendant. Just about twenty years earlier few could have imagined such a reversal.

Two sets of explanations have been advanced to explain this phenomenon. One would have us believe that feeling uncertain about their future in India in the wake of mounting nationalism after 1919, the expatriates considered it imprudent to increase their stakes in the Indian economy. While according to the other, the phenomenon had more to do with the problem of capital. Neither of these explanations, however, is satisfactory. To accept the first, we will have to believe that the investment decisions of the expatriates after 1919 were guided by their apprehensions about something that was still some thirty years away, and nowhere clearly in sight. The second explanation, on the other hand, does not tell us why few expatriate houses of any significance (as distinct from multinationals, which, as we shall see later, spread their tentacles into India around this time) came into being during the inter-war years—the years that witnessed the emergence or consolidation of a number of native business groups—even if it may offer some clue to understanding why existing firms did not grow.

The available histories of expatriate firms, even though small in number, point to a different possibility.

EMPIRICAL BASE—EASTERN INDIA

Let us start with Bird and Heilgers, one of the most prominent of expatriate firms, that gained enormously during the years of World War I, as did practically every business house. Troubles for the firm came with the return of peace. The 'war babies', the companies set up without much foresight and planning during the war, now became difficult to handle. Consequently all these—Assam Sugar Estate and Factories, Concrete Products, Chhotanagpur Mica Company, India Leather Manufacturing Company, Indian Graphite Company, and Surma Valley Saw Mills—had to be closed down one by one within barely six years after the end of the war. And yet the core of the Birds' business remained sound and continued to show on the whole good results. According to figures compiled at the end of 1928, jute manufacturing and trading yielded the best operating results, followed by coal and paper in that order.

Then came the onslaught of the Great Depression. Prices of all the products in which the firm had interests fell. Coal and jute, the mainstays of the Birds' business, were hit particularly hard. Coal was depressed even before the global slump. Things became worse after 1930. Jute mills too had to cut production to avoid holding a large inventory of unsold goods. In the field of minerals, some concerns were on the verge of closing down. Among the major industries in which the firm was interested, only paper presented a refreshing exception to a generally depressing state. To make matters worse, the Marwaris were around this time acquiring shares in the European-owned concerns and thus entering their boards. Under these conditions, it was necessary for the European managing agency firms to guard against the possible loss of the companies under their management to others. With their 'protective holdings' in the companies under their management being 'astonishingly small', as Edward (Tom) Benthall, the head of the firm, noted, the Birds were quite exposed to the danger. Though their empire remained untouched, they had to be vigilant. Under these conditions, consolidation instead of expansion was what sound business calculations demanded.

Despite the hard times, the Birds did not altogether stop exploring new avenues. All through the Depression, prospecting for new coalfields proceeded apace. An organization engaged in gunny export was taken over from the Inchcape group. And when the clouds of the Depression became a little less dense, new and modern spinning frames were installed in one of the jute mills, taking advantage of the fall in machinery prices. The Birds also floated an investment company in 1936. This, along with three other investment companies that the firm already controlled, provided a protective shield against the possible threat from clandestine corporate raiders. The investment companies could also become a source of attracting Indian funds into the group companies at a time of sagging profits of the manufacturing concerns.

Given this backdrop, the Birds' failure to carry out a major plan of diversification was quite understandable. This related to steel making. Realizing that the companies under their control produced practically all the essential inputs for manufacturing steel—coal, coke, iron ore, limestone, power, refractory bricks, etc.—the firm had promoted as early as 1921, The United Steel Corporation of Asia Limited (TUSCAL), requiring an outlay of Rs 20 crore, in conjunction with a famous British steel firm. The sagging market for steel had stalled the project then, but it was never wholly abandoned by the Bird management. By the mid-1930s, conditions seemed favourable for reviving the scheme as Tata Steel, which had a virtual monopoly on steel manufacturing in India, could not meet the entire demand. In fact, around this time, one Charles Perin, an American expert who had earlier worked with TISCO, was projecting a steel company with the help of British and American capital. To realize an old and dormant dream as also to ward off the threat from the American intruder, the Bird management formed a joint front with the Tatas and Martin & Co. The latter had grown into a gigantic managing agency since its birth in 1892, and developed substantial interest in iron manufacturing as a result of acquiring Burn & Co., formed originally in 1781, that had under its umbrella two pig iron undertakings—Bengal Iron and Steel Co. (BISCO) and Indian Iron and Steel Co. (IISCO). Although technically both the firms remained separate, they now had a common identification as Martin Burn & Co.

The Tatas, Martin Burn, and Birds decided to collaborate to promote a new steel mill. According to the plan the Tatas were to supply 50 per cent of the capital while the other two parties were to share the other half equally. However, the plan ran into difficulties very soon because, among other things, Sir Biren Mukherjee, the dominant voice in Martin Burn's management after the death of his father Sir Rajendra Nath in 1936, felt unhappy with the prospects of the Tatas having majority control. The Tatas and the Birds were still hopeful of being able to salvage the project with the Tatas supplying 60 per cent of the capital, but the Birds found it difficult to raise the necessary funds to meet their share of the projected cost. In the meantime the birth of Steel Corporation of Bengal promoted by Martin Burn in 1939, pre-empted them.

Thus if the Birds did not expand during the inter-war years, it was not due to the lack of will but because of the conspiracy of circumstances. As far as the core areas of their operations were concerned, business prudence demanded a strategy of 'keeping going', to use a phrase of the company historian. Formidable entry barriers prevented diversification into related lines, while the disastrous outcome of experiments with unrelated diversification during the 1920s remained a stern warning against indiscriminate adventure.

Andrew Yule & Co., another large expatriate group, showed no signs of its interest in India sagging during the inter-war years either. In fact, every indication was to the contrary. David Yule, the head of the managing agency firm since 1892, reorganized what until then was a partnership firm into a private limited company soon after the war, Andrew Yule & Co. Ltd, in which his friend Thomas Catto was a principal shareholder. As David himself spent all his time in England after 1920, Catto as vice chairman was now the real helmsman in Calcutta.

Although Andrew Yule, with jute, coal, and tea, as the mainstay of its operations, had to contend with the vagaries of fortunes in these lines after World War I, this did not discourage it from launching new companies as ancillaries to its main businesses. Port Engineering Works had been established in 1917, while the war was still on, to meet the needs of jute mills and shipping companies. Dishergarh Power Supply Company and Associated Power Company were formed in 1919 to supply power to the collieries in the Raniganj field. Perhaps the most noteworthy of the post-war floatations was India Paper Pulp Company, set up in 1919 to manufacture paper from bamboo pulp instead of imported wood pulp. The management's determination overcame a host of difficulties, mechanical and otherwise, and by 1933, India Paper Pulp Company was sufficiently established to be converted into a public limited company. Another significant undertaking that came into being at the initiative of Andrew Yule was Concord of India Insurance Company, formed in 1931. The firm also took over the management of Tide Water Oil Company and Hooghly Printing Company, while business conditions were still depressed.

All these enterprises were related to the main lines of Yule's operations. The firm's attempt to diversify into unrelated lines met a similar fate as Bird's initiatives of this kind. Perhaps the most illustrative of failure to manage unrelated diversification was the attempt to undertake production of tobacco suitable for use in high-grade cigars. Tobacco Industrial (India) Limited was formed in 1931 for this purpose. It was, however, soon found that the leaf produced in the company's tobacco fields took longer to mature than the experiments had indicated. Consequently, the company had to be wound up. The group also relinquished the management of a number of other enterprises during the 1930s, for which the firm had become managing agents soon after the war. These included companies for making soda, sugar and *gur*, potteries, and aerating gas. It washed its hands off these enterprises because it belatedly realized that these were beyond its core competencies.

The experience of these two largest expatriate firms in Calcutta seems to indicate that while they had reached the limits of their growth in areas that were consistent with their intrinsic expertise, expansion into other fields was blocked either by their lack of experience or because of formidable entry barriers. The same thing seems true of other Calcutta-based houses about whom we have some information.

Between its birth in 1886 and the end of World War I, Shaw Wallace and Company had developed substantial interests in tea, coal, shipping, insurance, and exports of Indian produce. The firm also held the Burmah Shell distribution agency for kerosene and a number of insurance and shipping agencies. Between the two World Wars, all these lines registered substantial expansion, so that by 1939 Shaw Wallace held the managing agencies of at least seventeen tea estates and had risen to be the fourth largest coal producer in India. To its flourishing export trade in Indian produce, it added the imports of fertilizers and piece-goods. It also took to manufacturing sulphuric acid and superphosphate with a plant at Madras and collaborated with the Tatas in the formation of Indian Tinplate Company at Jamshedpur. Although the firm's Karachi branch was closed in 1934, and the trade in imported piece-goods was discontinued in 1939, there is no doubt that Shaw Wallace on the whole registered expansion and growth during the two World Wars.

Duncan Brothers too had a similar career. Founded in Calcutta in 1859, the firm had risen to the position of one of the largest tea producers in the country by 1919, controlling as many as fifty-four gardens in Assam. Duncans also had four jute mills under their management, besides handling the exports of country produce. In 1924, the firm, a partnership until then, became a private limited company. During the inter-war years, the Duncans expanded much less than Shaw Wallace, but still acquired two large tea estates in the princely state of Travancore. There is no evidence of any contraction in their Indian operations during the inter-war years.

THE NORTH, WEST, AND SOUTH

The expatriates in northern and western India too either expanded during the inter-war years or at least held on to their existing possessions. Begg Sutherland & Co., the pioneer of textile and sugar industries in the north, was still among the largest firms in the region, while Mohan Meakins, born in 1854, was still a premier brewery. E.D. Sassoon & Co. not only held its own but also expanded its textile empire through buying off mills in distress. Its United Mills comprising nine cotton mills, one woollen mill, one oil mill, and a trading company, was the largest single textile undertaking of this kind in the country in 1939. Sassoon also had extensive interests in shipping and insurance. Harvey Brothers, who had entered the Bombay textile industry in its expansionist phase and played a pioneering role in the development of the industry in the south, more or less held on in 1939 to the position they were holding in 1919. Bradbury and Brady, however, could not stand the rigours of the Depression and sold off its mills in Bombay to a Marwari family, Ramnarain Ramnivas Ruia. Forbes, Forbes & Co., which had become a formidable concern with the amalgamation of two major agency houses, Leckie & Co. and Ritchie Steuart & Co. with it, before the beginning of World War I and was now known as Forbes, Forbes Campbell & Co., continued to remain a formidable trading concern with some interest in the textile industry. Likewise, Killick Nixon & Co. with its extensive interest in railways, shipping, insurance, and textiles had no reason to feel insecure.

James Finlay & Co. of Glasgow, though not an expatriate house in the strict sense of the term, had developed extensive interests in India between 1862, when it opened its first Indian branch at Bombay, and 1919. Starting with general trade and marine insurance, Finlay went into jute manufacturing in a big way in 1873 with the floating of a mill on the Hooghly, built a huge network of tea estates in Assam, Travancore, and Ceylon, floated three cotton mills in Bombay, and opened three more branches in India—Calcutta in 1870, Karachi in 1890, and Chittagong in 1901. During the inter-war years it took to sugar manufacturing with the establishment of a company in Bihar, and opened a branch at Vizagapatnam, and its cotton mills changed over to the production of finer goods to beat the hardships of post-war Depression. Despite the ups and downs of its Indian operations during these years, natural in an era of economic turbulence, it held on to fourth rank among all the business houses operating in India in 1939—the rank it was occupying before the beginning of the Great Depression.

The situation in the south was no different if we go by the experience of the two dominant expatriate firms operating in the region—Parry and Binny. Right from the start Parry had developed a tradition of exploiting every possible opportunity without much thought for its basic expertise. For more than a century since its birth, it functioned more like an adventurer than a stable business organization. By the end of the nineteenth century, however, it had developed some measure of distinctiveness. It still operated in multifarious fields, but sugar and distillery along with banking and trading had become the mainstays of Parry's business. Its interests in this area were further augmented by the acquisition of another sugar concern—Deccan Sugar and Abkari Company (DSA), operating in Godavari district of Madras—from Binny. It felt that by bringing all the sugar interests in the Presidency under a single banner it would benefit from the economies of scale. Business results, however, belied these expectations. Overburdened by a huge debenture account, the company incurred a massive loss in 1902. The Arbuthnot crisis of 1906, referred to in an earlier chapter, further aggravated the situation. However, by the time World War I broke out, the affairs of the firm had been placed on a sound footing through a judicious mix of strategies, and Parry was in a much better shape than at any time before in its history.

Parry gained from the war, as did most other companies. Its confectionery and distilling companies were the main profit makers, thanks to the disruption in imports of chocolates and alcoholic drinks. The firm also profited from managing the Calcutta branch of a German firm, Orenstein and Koppel (O&K), that distributed all sorts of light railway material from rolling stock to fish plates. Things changed for the worse soon after peace returned, particularly because its trading operations could not stand the rigours of the post-war slump. Its usual gambling tendency was also responsible for some of its problems. After 150 years of business experience, Parry still seemed to suffer, as Sir Edgar Wood, the head of the firm in 1929, put it, from the 'ignorance of what constitutes an economic unit'.

Parry would have found it difficult to survive the post-war setbacks, had it not been for the cushion provided by the old staples—sugar, confectionery, and distilling. EID and DSA continued to do well during the inter-war years partly because of the protection granted to the sugar industry and partly because Parry had effected a thorough reorganization of all its sugar factories even before the grant of protection. To expand its business in these lines, the firm added one more company, Travancore Sugar and Chemicals Limited in 1937. This emerged from amalgamating three separate companies—one each in sugar, distillery, and pharmaceutical—that Parry had taken over from the government of the princely state of Travancore and Cochin.

Parry thus, like most other expatriates, had mixed fortunes during the inter-war years. But the question of withdrawing from India or reducing its stakes in the country was never considered by the management. Sir William Wright, who played the dominant part in Parry's affairs during the inter-war years, was basically a cautious and conservative leader. To his colleagues, who occasionally felt disheartened by the unevenness of the firm's fortunes, his stock advice was: 'Fear not! We shall rise again.'

Binny, though somewhat less adventurous than its rival, started the twentieth century in a less stable position than Parry and thus could not withstand the Arbuthnot crisis, as we have seen in a previous chapter. The firm's takeover by the British India Navigation group and its re-emergence in 1906 as a sterling company registered in Britain changed little. The new company inherited all the agencies and retained all business connections of the defunct partnership. The organization of the new company represented a remarkable continuity, and caused little dilution in the gambling spirit that seemed to be a characteristic feature of the business attitude of practically all expatriate firms operating in south India around this time. The general health of the firm, however, continued to be sound as both the cotton mills at Madras as well as the cotton department of the Bangalore mills continued to do well. Some of the agencies acquired a few years before the war were also reasonably profitable.

On the eve of the outbreak of World War I, thus, Binny's position, like that of Parry, was much better than at the turn of the century. But it was the war that brought to Binny a real taste of prosperity, and the textile mills were again the principal contributors. The firm's mills had already established themselves as undisputed leaders in producing khaki drill through mineral-dyeing process. Not surprisingly, it was asked by the Army Clothing Department to supply the requirements of the allied army in West Asia. To meet its obligation to the army, Binny installed Northrop automatic looms in its Madras mills. The Northrop loom was the most efficient and modern weaving device developed until then and Binny had the distinction of introducing it in India, and remained for a long time the only company in the country to use it. The mill in Bangalore, producing only yarn until then, started weaving operations for the first time. Diversification was hardly possible during the war, and yet the Binny management, true to the adventurous tradition of the firm, did initiate a move in 1915 that would eventually lead it into a new field soon after the war—jute textiles.

The firm underwent another reorganization soon after the war. As a part of this reorganization, the London company while retaining the old name, divested itself of all businesses that were now taken over by a new organization, Binny and Company (Madras) Limited, in which the London firm held the majority shares. This happened in 1920. A few months later, the two Madras-based cotton mills, and all the cotton-pressing companies were amalgamated into one company—Buckingham and Carnatic Mills, which now became the largest cotton company in the whole of south India. Producing finer varieties of goods by using a superior variety of short-staple cotton grown in India, the mills made consistently good profits throughout the inter-war period. One of the major factors in their success was the use of automatic looms—the Binny mills were the only ones in India to use this weaving equipment at this time—for which they received high approbation from experts.

The strategy adopted for distributing goods also helped the mills to weather the storm of the Depression. Instead of depending on traditional commission agents for this purpose, as most Indian mills did, Binny had started building up a marketing network of its own as early as the mid-1920s, the lynchpin of which were the indentors in various regions—something similar to a strategy that Arvind Mills of Ahmedabad later adopted. The indentors were the ears and eyes of the management, who stood guarantee for the wholesalers' and retailers' commitment to adhere to the price and other norms fixed by the management. As the Depression became more severe, other devices to boost sales were resorted to, such as opening showrooms at Calcutta and Madras and reaching out to the rural markets through mobile sales vans. The company, in the meantime, continued to introduce new products in the market, such as anti-crease suiting which the Binny mills were the first to manufacture in India.

In the meantime Binny's old agencies in trading, shipping, insurance, and transport functioned normally, which encouraged the management to expand this side of operations substantially. In fact, never in its entire history had Binny taken so many sales agencies as it did during the 1930s. By all indications, Binny in 1939 was looking forward to a long innings for itself in India.

An Alternative Explanation

These few examples are sufficient to cast serious doubts on the validity of the existing explanations of why the expatriates grew at a slower pace in comparison with the Indian houses or demonstrated stagnating trends during the inter-war years. To understand the business behaviour of the firms discussed in the preceding section—and others like them that had had a long history in India and were firmly settled before the end of World War I—it is necessary to keep in mind that the growth of firms normally slows down after they attain a certain size, and their entrepreneurial manifestations become relatively less aggressive. This apart, the industries for which these firms had honed their core competencies had reached a stage in their development that precluded further investments. Industries like jute manufacturing, coal mining, tea plantation, and even cotton textiles had reached more or less a saturation point, and plans to expand in these areas at a time when the economic environment was none too benign would have been counterproductive indeed. And the expatriate firms had no particular competitive advantage over Indian entrepreneurs in the new industries that were rising behind tariff walls. The entry barriers in these fields were relatively low and the Indians had the benefit of community linkages to raise finances. They also possessed a better understanding of the needs and tastes of the domestic consumer for whom they largely produced.

The reluctance of the established expatriate houses to enter the new lines is, thus, fairly understandable. So even if there was no contraction in their business interests in India or no retreat from the lines in which they were firmly entrenched, they could not have contributed to the expansion of the British presence on India's business scene. The new industries could not have attracted fresh British entrants either, for apart from the competitive disabilities from which the old houses suffered, the fresh entrants could not have had the advantage that normally comes with being pioneers, and which had been one of the most important factors in the rise and consolidation of the old expatriate houses. This was a sufficiently strong disincentive against new groups of British entrepreneurs floating new firms in India to exploit the opportunities that were unfolding themselves as a consequence of the government at long last, proppping up the process of Indian industrialization in whatsoever limited measure.

India, however, offered vast opportunities for investment in fields other than industries that had reached an optimum point of development or those in which the native industrialists had a dominant presence or competitive advantage. The country's industrial horizon was still full of large gaps, as there were many fields where the ground had been barely scratched or whose development was still woefully inadequate in comparison with the needs of the country. For instance, India had no chemical industry worth the name until well after Independence. Although a few concerns to produce sulphuric acid and chemicals based on it had come into being before World War I, their output was very small, and there were absolutely no producers of the alkali group of chemicals, entailing much higher investment and more complicated processes. Consequently, Imperial Chemical Industries of Britain and I.G. Farben of Germany had a virtual monopoly on the supply of almost every variety of chemicals to India.

Aluminium presented a similar picture. Although a Calcutta-based unit, Aluminium Manufacturing Company, catered to the growing need of aluminium for utensils, no one produced aluminium sheets. The Singhanias'

Aluminium Corporation of India, projected in 1937, was yet to start production when the war came. In the realm of machine tools, the situation was only slightly better as there were three small producers—P.N. Dutta and Co. of Calcutta, Cooper Engineering Works, Satara, and Indian Machinery Company—but their combined production hardly exceeded one hundred tools per year.

Surprisingly, indigenous production of cotton textile machinery, despite the preponderant position of the cotton textile industry, had made very little headway, as the Birlas' Textile Machinery Corporation (TEXMACO) was the only company in the field. Likewise, Lala Shri Ram's Jay Engineering Works was the only producer of sewing machines. In the field of glass manufacturing too, India could hardly boast of indigenous development of any great consequence until the end of the 1930s, although the beginnings of the industry can be traced back to the swadeshi days of 1904–5. The industry did receive a fillip from the disruption of imports during World War I, but progress was slow during the inter-war years in the face of imports and Depression. Consequently, there was nothing like an indigenous glass industry in India in 1939 and for a large part of its needs, particularly for more sophisticated products, India was still almost wholly dependent on imports.

A similar situation prevailed in a host of other fields. For instance, despite the fact that match manufacturing in the country had started as early as 1894 and received a great deal of impetus during the swadeshi movement, Indian enterprises could hardly stand up to the challenge from Swedish Match Company, the unquestioned world leader in this field, which supplied practically the entire need of the country. Fields such as electrical engineering, railway equipment, paints and varnishes, rubber products, metal manufacturing, industrial gases, and a number of other lines had no producers at all on the Indian soil. Thus the staple industries of the old expatriates and the consumer goods industries, which the native entrepreneurs were in a better position to exploit, by no means exhausted all avenues of investment.

Native entrepreneurs had neither the means nor the technical expertise to exploit these avenues. Fresh British entrants could have been lured to launch enterprises in these fields, but their entry was blocked by the multinationals who were much better equipped to exploit these opportunities. Multinationals' interest in India did not erupt suddenly during the inter-war years; some of them had established selling agencies for their products as early as the last quarter of the nineteenth century and a few, like British American Tobacco Company and General Electric Corporation, had even set up Indian subsidiaries during the first decade of the twentieth century. It was during the inter-war years, however, that they registered an impressive presence in India when about forty subsidiaries, either wholly owned or substantially controlled by well-known multinationals, were set up. Significantly, these subsidiaries had nothing to do with the fields in which the expatriates or native interests were active; they operated in areas that had been left, by and large, unexplored such as those mentioned earlier.

A large number of multinationals had maintained marketing branches in India for several years before establishing their subsidiaries. Some, like Lever Brothers, preferred to utilize existing British firms or Indian agents to distribute their goods. Obviously, they wanted to be reasonably sure that sufficient demand for their products existed to justify undertaking production in India itself. Lever Brothers took more than a decade to decide, while others took a much shorter time. A few firms decided to launch production in India with a view to jumping the tariff walls. Swedish Match Company, for instance, set up Western India Match Company (WIMCO) within a year after the government imposed high revenue duty, which gave a competitive advantage to match producers in India. Similarly, Imperial Tobacco, that had started manufacturing operations in India before World War I, stepped up production substantially during the early 1920s after the duty on imported cigars and cigarettes had gone up to 75 per cent *ad valorem*. Firms engaged in producing equipment became sure of the adequacy of demand in India only after the government decided in 1930 to purchase railway stores in India itself, instead of in Britain as was the case before.

The spread of multinationals to India—and most of them were British— thus blocked the space that might otherwise have been available for autonomous British enterprises to multiply and take root. The slower growth of foreign-owned companies in comparison with those under the control of Indian houses was due to this fact and not because of the decline or stagnation of old expatriates, which, as we have seen, were weathering the challenges of the inter-war years to the extent the climate for business permitted. There is no evidence of the rising wave of nationalism having any effect on their future plans. The rapid rise of multinational undertakings during this period also shows that political turmoil and uncertainty about the future constitutional set-up had very little impact on the evaluation of business opportunities in India by the parent firms. So confident were these multinationals about their future in India that many of them established more than one factory in different parts of the country. WIMCO, for instance, set up as many five factories between 1923, the year of its birth, and 1930, and the parent firm founded another subsidiary, Assam Match Company (AMCO), in 1926. Likewise, the Indian subsidiary of Dunlop Rubber Company had an extensive network of distributors in practically all major cities in India.

It is beyond the scope of this volume to examine the impact of the multinationals' subsidiaries on the Indian economy. One thing, however, is certain. They played a pioneering role in introducing and developing those industries for which neither the Indian houses nor the expatriates showed much enthusiasm. But for their initiatives, the beginning of these industries would have definitely been delayed. They also introduced modern technologies, capable of large-scale production, in their respective fields. Whenever necessary and appropriate, they also made use of managerial practices and devices prevailing in the countries of the parent firms. To promote the sale of its products Imperial Tobacco, for instance, took resort to several methods almost unknown in India then, such as giving away free samples of cigarettes, advertising its wares through decorative visual displays in village markets, and organizing special events to publicize the products. These activities were normally organized by the company's salesmen themselves. But occasionally the task was entrusted to an advertising firm— a rare phenomenon in those days.

Like Imperial Tobacco, most of the subsidiaries were satisfying existing demand as well as trying to create new demand, as the products they offered were used only by a limited circle of consumers. The multinationals' investments in their Indian operations consequently must have been relatively modest. The British holdings in the firms controlled by the old expatriates were in the meantime going down. For, with the rise in the number of shareholders in their firms there was no threat to their control over their companies, even if they reduced their protective holdings in them. In this fashion, they could release additional funds for investment elsewhere. Native Indian interests too usually diluted their protective holdings in their companies with the rise of the number of shareholders. The very fact that the multinationals looked upon investment in India as a safe and wise proposition, and were keen to expand their operations—there can be no other reason behind their efforts to promote demand for their products—suggests that they saw a long future for themselves in the country.

There were, of course, individuals who perceived things differently. Sir Victor Sassoon, the head of E.D. Sassoon & Co., for instance, shifted his headquarters from Bombay to Shanghai, the nerve centre of its operations in East and South East Asia, as early as 1931. He explained his decision in the following words: 'There will be less scope in India for a foreigner in the future because of the cut-throat competition with Indian firms, which have less overhead charges, and because of the anti-foreign prejudice. It looks as if India under Swaraj will have a great deal of internal trouble.' Sir Victor hated Gandhi from the core of his heart and dismissed the freedom movement as undisputable proof of the Communist conspiracy. China in his view offered a better field for foreigners. Few expatriates held such extreme views about political developments or their future in India, and Sir Victor himself would later rue his judgement of China after the Communist takeover forced him out of that country. More significantly, his Indian operations continued to flourish for more than a decade even after he shifted base to China. Not until 1943 did the company sell out its interest in the United Mills to a group of Marwaris. The prevailing high price of the shares rather than a sense of insecurity seems to have been a major factor behind this decision. In fact, it was not until 1950 that the family disbanded its Indian operations altogether. On the eve of World War II, British expatriates and multinationals, by all accounts, felt as secure in India as their Indian counterparts.

CHAPTER 10

DURING THE WAR
AND AFTER

TO INDIAN BUSINESS, WORLD WAR II CAME AS A GODSEND. THE CLOUDS of Depression, though somewhat less dense than during the first half of the decade, still seemed quite intimidating in most sectors of the economy in 1939. Despondency still befogged the view of the future. The producers did not have an effective answer to the problems created by falling or stagnant demand and the distributors did not know how to attract customers. The Great Depression was not as severe in India as in the developed economies; it was nevertheless severe enough. The coming of the war in September of 1939 brought about a complete transformation in the situation.

RETURN OF PROSPERITY

As during World War I, imports were disrupted, demand for indigenously produced goods went up, and with it the prices. Capacity utilization in industrial firms was stretched to the extreme limit, and the producers as well as the distributors made handsome gains. Scope for reinvesting the profits earned was, however, limited because of the difficulties in importing capital equipment that India did not produce. This in itself was sufficient to constrain the supplies; the ever-escalating purchases of Indian products by the British government to meet the needs of the Allied Forces made it worse. This naturally pushed up the prices of everything from foodstuffs to coal and steel. The government was forced to fix the prices for government procurements and thus protect itself against the offensive of the market forces. Moreover, to pay for its Indian purchases, Britain resorted to what amounted to a system of deferred payments—through the printing of paper money against India's sterling reserves deposited with Bank of England. India was not allowed to touch these reserves during the war. This completed the ingredients for inflation which hit the common consumer hard.

The producer, however, continued to ride the crest of profitability in practically all sectors, though the rates of profit understandably varied. To ensure maximum production, the government offered a series of incentives to manufacturers and invoked the infamous Defence of India Rules to ban strikes and lockouts. Several provisions of the Factory Act were relaxed, and all necessary steps were taken to ensure unhindered supply of raw material to the production centres. While Japan's swift military advances in South Asia and the Quit India Movement launched by Gandhi in August 1942 caused some concern in the Indian industrial circles, the war years on the whole were a period of uninterrupted prosperity for Indian business in general.

On the eve of the war, three major groups of players dominated the Indian business scene. One was of the native business houses, dominant in consumer goods industries for which there was a large domestic market, such as cotton, sugar, and cement. The old expatriate firms constituted the second group. They were mostly concerned with export-oriented industries such as jute, coal, and tea. The third group consisted of the subsidiaries of multinational firms that focused on what may be called new industries, such as chemicals, engineering, and stores. Subserving these three groups, directly or indirectly, were a large number of traders, scattered all over the country, whose operations varied in size, complexity, and reach.

The division is somewhat unreal in the sense that these groups were not watertight compartments. Indian holdings in companies controlled by the expatriates were substantial, and in many Indian companies British nationals and even firms held a large number of shares. Enterprises under the Indian control produced goods that were inputs for companies controlled by the British and vice versa, and the distributors of industrial products, the traders, had substantial financial stakes in industrial undertakings—both Indian and non-Indian. In a very real sense, thus, these various groups were the constituents of an integrated business system. For the sake of convenience, however, the state of Indian business during the last phase of British rule, including the years of World War II, will be reviewed in the following discussion with reference to these three categories.

PERFORMANCE OF THE ESTABLISHED GROUPS

The Tatas occupied a commanding position among all business groups, Indian or foreign, operating in India when the war began. They retained this position when the war ended. The enterprises the house controlled in 1939 included TISCO, which was almost synonymous with the steel industry of India, four cotton mills, an oil mill, a chemical company, and an airline. All these, with the exception of Tata Airlines and Tata Chemicals, prospered. The chemical company at Mithapur could not start production until 1944 because of the difficulties in importing plant and machinery, and Tata Airlines had to halt operations because all air services were commandeered by the government.

The textile mills were perhaps the greatest gainers, as the textile industry in general registered unprecedented growth during the period, thanks to the high prices the cotton goods commanded, some varieties registering as high as 400 per cent rise in prices. Particularly lucky were the producers of coarse and medium varieties of goods, the worst victims of the Depression of the 1930s. The government, a major buyer of textile products during the war, was in greater need of such goods than of the finer varieties. The agriculturist, now with an improved purchasing power consequent upon high prices of foodgrains, also patronized these varieties. Things began to look up for the industry soon after the war began. Thanks to the entry of Japan into the fray in 1942, a major source of competition to domestic producers was completely eliminated, reducing imports to insignificance. Indian mills now held an undisputed sway over the domestic market; more importantly, the neighbouring countries, whose needs were previously met through imports from Western countries and Japan, now increasingly turned to India for supplies. For the first time since its inception, the Indian textile industry emerged as a force to reckon with in the markets beyond India's borders. The product mix of the Tatas' four textile mills was such that they together could cater to almost every segment of the market. They naturally profited from the rising demand for every variety of goods.

Textiles, however, had ceased to be the main business of the Tatas by the end of the 1930s; they were identified primarily with the steel industry, which received a great boost from the war. As the government needed every ounce of steel the company could produce, TISCO's production went up from 0.8 million tonnes in 1939 to 1.1 million tonnes in 1943. If it did not rise further, it was only because the existing capacity of the plant did not permit it to do so. Even though the company had to sell its products on prices fixed by the government under the Steel Control and Distribution Order, and thus could not reap the full benefit of the demand-supply gap, the profits earned during these years were still substantial. TISCO's good performance was partly due to the contribution of its Research and Control Laboratory, set up in 1937, which was probably the first case of an Indian business group taking a concrete step to promote research and development (R&D). Taking advantage of the disruption in imports, the laboratory tried to develop a number of new products such as shear blades, machine tools, service helmets, parachute harness, and even razor blades. Referring to these aspects of the war-time operations, J.R.D. Tata later remarked with some satisfaction: 'As a result of elaborate researches conducted at our works, we have been able to manufacture and supply, in addition to large quantities of carbon steel, an extensive variety of special steels, representing nearly 112 specifications.'

Of particular significance were two special varieties of steel developed by the Tatas' researchers during these years. One was a high-tensile alloy steel known as TISCROM which would be later used in building the famous Howrah Bridge in Calcutta. And the other, TISCOR, was a corrosion-resistant, extra strong steel used for building all-metal coaches for the Indian railways. Another Tata product, developed during the war that became very popular with soldiers, was a light armoured car known as Tatanagar. Remarkably sturdy and completely safe against bomber raids, the vehicle was used extensively by the British Indian army engaged on the North African front. According to J.R.D. Tata, TISCO 'provided approximately three million tonnes of steel for purposes connected directly or indirectly with the war'. To achieve these results, however, the company had to pay a heavy cost. Excessive use told heavily on its plant and machinery with the result that production had come down to about 750,000 tonnes by the time the war ended. There was no doubt that TISCO emerged from the war with its productive capacity greatly impaired.

But the house of Tatas itself emerged many times bigger and stronger and started expanding into new directions soon after the war. Tata Chemicals, at long last, started production, marking what according to an authority was 'a decisive phase in the development of the Indian chemical industry' and the beginning of 'the foundations of a heavy chemical industry in India'. Although the initial results were disastrous, prompting some well-wishers to advise J.R.D. Tata to abandon the project, he decided to persevere in the face of heavy odds saying: 'When we go to a place, we arouse hopes in people.' The group chairman also picked up the thread again of his airlines plan which the war had disrupted. Air India, registered as a public limited company in 1946 as a part of the Tata empire, was the first enterprise ever launched in the country to promote air transport.

Unlike the chemical and airlines companies, Tata Locomotive and Engineering Company, launched in 1945, was an entirely post-war initiative. In due course this would develop into the biggest undertaking of the Tatas. Initially, however, the company produced locomotives, wagons, boilers, and other components for Indian railways. Providing an outlet for the steel produced by TISCO, this company was in the nature of a forward integration, consistent with a strategy that for various reasons did not fully succeed during the 1920s. The full potential of these initiatives was yet to unfold when Independence came, introducing an entirely new element in the business climate of India.

The Birlas, the second largest native business house, prospered during the war much more than the Tatas in relative terms. This was so primarily because of two reasons. One, the rise in prices of most of the goods the companies under their control produced was much higher than in case of the Tata firms. Second, as the government needed only a part of these products, which had to be delivered at the prices fixed by respective government departments, a large portion of their output could derive greater benefit from the demand–supply gap. With the exception of jute, all other industries in which the house had interest maintained high profitability throughout the war, thanks to the domestic demand always outstripping the supply. Although Birla Jute's rate of profit during the war never reached the level earned by the sugar, textile, and paper companies in the group, it nevertheless reached an impressive figure of 68 per cent by 1943 through continuous rise. Before the war began, the company's profits were limited to merely 13 per cent. As a result, the Birlas' net worth went up many times over—by more than six times, according to one estimate—between 1939 and 1945.

The profits earned during the war gave a tremendous boost to the activities of the house. Though it was not easy to float new concerns, acquiring existing ones was not difficult. According to G.D. Birla's biographer, as many as twenty-two 'big factories' were taken over 'for an investment of only rupees twenty crores' and a large number of new companies were floated. What motive inspired which acquisition or floatation is not easy to determine, but the available details about a few may provide some understanding.

The Birlas acquired New Swadeshi Mills at Ahmedabad in 1944, obviously to strengthen their textile operations at a time when the textile industry was enjoying an unprecedented boom. Founded in 1906 during the heyday of the swadeshi movement, it was a large undertaking with 35,000 spindles,

800 looms, and 2000 employees, but had suffered continual neglect and mismanagement coupled with frequent changes in ownership. The acquisition did not cost the Birlas very much but it gave them a foothold in the second largest textile centre in the country, besides expanding their textile operations. The mill made a quick recovery under the Birla management.

Among the new floatations were an insurance company, a cycle manufacturing concern, a bank, and an engineering company. Hind Cycles Limited, planned before the war, started functioning in 1940, but was never rated highly for its products, and would wither away soon after the war in the face of rising domestic competition. United Commercial Bank was founded in 1943 to provide finances for the growing empire of the group, and an engineering undertaking, Central India Machinery Manufacturing Corporation (CIMMCO), was set up at Gwalior in 1945 at the fag end of the war to manufacture various kinds of machinery, specially cotton textile machinery. Hindustan Motors Ltd was registered in 1942 with a paid-up capital of nearly Rs 5 crore, and a small assembly plant in the princely state of Baroda was acquired. However, it was only after the war that the Birlas took the project in right earnest, entered into collaboration with Morris Motors of the United Kingdom, set up their assembly line at Uttarpara near Calcutta, and produced their first vehicle in 1950 with the brand name of Hindustan. While G.D. Birla was the guiding spirit behind all these developments, his two brothers Rameshwar Das and Braj Mohan (Jugal Kishore the eldest of the four brothers had practically withdrawn from business by this time to devote himself almost wholly to religious and social activities) shared a substantial part of the workload. Some of the these projects, in fact, were conceived by them.

While the Birlas went about quietly building a strong base on which would rise a colossal business edifice after Independence, Walchand Hirachand continued in his old adventurous ways. He had been actively pursuing two gigantic projects when the war began. One was shipbuilding while the other was concerned with producing passenger cars. He had not gone very far with these projects when the war broke out. Yet, he added a third capital-intensive project. This was to manufacture aircraft. Walchand could not have been unaware of the difficulties in mounting such gigantic projects during the war, and yet he continued to pursue them with the relentless vigour characteristic of him.

The world was already nearly two years into the war when the foundation stone of Scindia Shipyard was laid by the-then President of the Indian National

Congress, Rajendra Prasad, underlining the nationalist identity of the enterprise. To implement the car-manufacturing project he secured the support of Dharmsey Mulraj Khatau, the well-known mill-owning family in Bombay, and Tulsidas Kilachand, a prominent cotton trader in the city. The trio formed a managing agency firm, in which Walchand and Kilachand had equal holdings and Khatau a minority interest, to manage Premier Automobiles, registered as a public limited company in 1944. Land for the proposed factory was taken on lease in a Bombay suburb, and an old firm, Bombay Cycle and Motor Agency, was acquired to provide marketing support to the planned enterprise. Also acquired was Cooper Engineering Limited, in existence since 1932, which specialized in the production of internal combustion engines for various applications in industry. The two acquisitions were intended to provide forward and backward support to the car-manufacturing operations.

Similar preparations were made to operationalize the aircraft plan. Walchand got the idea to launch aircraft production in the course of a casual conversation with the head of an aircraft-manufacturing company in America, engaged in building an aircraft factory in China. Walchand immediately plunged into a flurry of activity. The princely state of Mysore promised to provide land for the factory site in Bangalore at a concessional rate along with a liberal subsidy, while Walchand and his old friends, Khatau and Kilachand, formed a managing agency firm on equal partnership basis. Factory buildings for Hindustan Aircraft Company, registered in 1940, were completed in record time by Walchand's construction network, and production started in 1941. Everything was going well for the new venture, when Japan's swift advance into South East Asia changed the entire picture. Alarmed at the prospects of the aircraft company falling into enemy hands if the Japanese forces stormed into India, the government asked the management to be ready to blow up the factory if such an eventuality arose. On Walchand's prevarication, the government decided to take over Hindustan Aircraft in 1942 under war powers. Thus ended Walchand's dream of pioneering the production of aircraft in the country.

The shipyard and the passenger car projects also could not get off the ground because of the exigencies of the war. The shipyard was completed in 1946, while the first vehicle did not roll off the assembly line of Premier Automobiles until March 1947—in collaboration with Chrysler Corporation of the United States. Another venture promoted during the war also did not become operational until peace returned. This was Air Services of India, an old air transport company, acquired by Scindia Shipping in 1943. As if the burden of these quasi-born enterprises was not enough to test the mettle of the management, Scindia Steam Navigation, the most glittering emblem of Walchand's agressive entrepreneurship, had to surrender as many as sixteen steamers out of its fleet of nineteen to the government to help in the war effort. Eight of these were lost in the war. The vessels that survived needed a complete overhaul. To build new steamers was not easy as the cost after the war was three times higher. Soon after the war ended, however, the company started building two vessels at its Vizagapatnam shipyard and ordered three more to be built in England.

Walchand did not have complete control over these enterprises. They have been discussed in connection with his business activities simply because he was the moving spirit behind them and the dominant voice in their managements. In contrast to these enterprises, Walchand's own concerns, those which he and his brothers controlled, made handsome profits during the war. Premier Construction had more business than it could handle during the war. Ravalgaon Farm did still better because of the escalating demand for its basic product—sugar. Also plants were installed for refining cooking oil and producing vegetable ghee under the brand name of 'Walda', rhyming with Lever Brothers' popular product Dalda. Oil and *vanaspati* took the company into the production of soap and tin containers. By the end of World War II, thus, Walchandnagar had developed into a highly diversified complex of agriculture-based industries. On the whole, however, the war brought less benefits to the Walchand business empire than to the Tatas, Birlas, and many other Indian business houses. And yet, by the time India won Independence, the Walchand group had established itself as one of the top ten native business groups in India.

More down to earth, the Kirloskar Brothers fully utilized the opportunities provided by the war to pull themselves out of the hardships created by the Depression of the 1930s. Large orders were received from the government for machine tools, hospital furniture, and pumps. One of the new lines stimulated by the exigencies of the war was the manufacture of iron springs for hand grenades. About 500,000 iron cots and a much larger number of springs for hand grenades were sold at highly profitable rates during the war years. The facilities at Kirloskarwadi proved inadequate, and expansion became necessary. The princely state of Mysore provided about 100 acres of land at Harihar on the banks of River Tungabhadra where Mysore Kirloskar Limited set up its factory in 1941 to produce machine tools—the first significant venture in the country in this sector. Laxmanrao's second son, Rajarampant, who like his brother had an engineering degree, was placed in charge of this concern—the first Kirloskar enterprise set up away from Kirloskarwadi. The venture yielded great profits right from the start.

The wartime gains not only revived the confidence of the Kirloskars, but also gave new direction to their production plans. Except during the war, agricultural implements had always remained at the top of the manufacturing priorities of the house. The management had no intention of abandoning the farmer whose patronage had nursed the house to maturity, but the stability of wartime operations encouraged the Kirloskars to move out of the narrow range of their product lines and do something to cater to the needs of Indian industries as well. The result was the birth of two companies soon after the war. One would produce electric machinery for Indian factories and the other would specialize in the production of oil engines.

Established in Bangalore in 1946, Kirloskar Electric Company was among the first firms to manufacture electric motors in India. An increasingly large number of industrial establishments were switching over from coal to electricity for power, but they were totally dependent on imports for the machinery necessary for the changeover. The Kirloskars had been making some tentative experiments to develop an electric motor since 1939, which received a real boost when Ravindra Kirloskar, Laxmanrao's youngest son, joined the team in 1942 with a degree in electrical engineering from the United States. The registration of the new company was a culmination of these early steps. It would specialize in the production of electric motors, transformers, generators, and other items needed in railway workshops, textile mills, and irrigation and agricultural projects.

The establishment of Kirloskar Oil Engines at Kirkee near Poona, likewise, was not a fresh initiative. The Kirloskars had been producing a humble version of diesel engines since the mid-1920s to provide motive force to the centrifugal pumps used for pulling water from wells for irrigation purposes. The reason for establishing a separate company was to expand the product range in this line to include internal combustion engines of the industrial and marine types and thin-walled bearings for automobile engines. There were only two other companies in the entire country—Orient Engineering Works, a small undertaking in Punjab, and Walchand's Cooper Engineering at Satara near Bombay—that produced diesel engines.

Despite all their experience and experimentation, the Kirloskars still did not possess the technology to enable them to compete with imported products.

They, therefore, decided to enter into technical collaboration with well-known British firms whose products had already gained a foothold in India. During those years of aggressive nationalism, few, if any, native Indian business groups had entered into collaboration with foreign companies until then. No one under these conditions could clearly foresee the course of the Kirloskars' alliance with the British firms. The future, however, would vindicate their decision when foreign collaboration would become the most preferred route to technology acquisition for Indian business houses after Independence.

Most of the textile-producing groups, or those who were primarily engaged in textile production, did nothing other than earning huge profits during the war. Lala Shri Ram's DCM did a little more. Concentrating on the production of the coarsest varieties of yarn and cloth—the varieties that sold at the highest profits in the textile sector—DCM added a chemical division in 1940 to produce hydrochloric, sulphuric, and other acids required for bleaching, dyeing, and other purposes. Another initiative taken by the group during the war years was DCM Tent and Garment Factory set up in 1941, marking the first ever attempt to promote garment manufacturing in the organized sector. It failed primarily because of the cheap and unimaginative designs of the garments produced. The opening of retail stores in different parts of the country to market DCM products did not succeed either. For the expenses involved in maintaining the outlets turned out to be much higher than expected. Nothing very exciting happened to Shri Ram's other enterprises. The sugar factory added a power alcohol plant at its Daurala premises to produce hard liquor for the army. While this turned out to be a profitable operation, a sugar company, acquired in 1940 in a dilapidated condition, remained a source of loss for several years. Bengal Potteries and Jay Engineering, whose future was still uncertain before the war, gained substantially by switching over to the production of goods required by the army.

Other textile producers were less clear about their post-war plans. Out of the three largest mill owners of Ahmedabad, only Ambalal Sarabhai took some feeble steps to diversify into other lines by setting up Sarabhai Chemicals at Baroda, but had no idea where else to invest his wartime profits. Kasturbhai Lalbhai, who had already diversified into starch production before the war, started thinking about further diversification only after peace returned. Consequently, his Atul Products Limited, marking 'the beginning of the full-fledged dyestuffs industry in the country', to quote an expert, did not come into being for more than two years after the war. And Mangaldas Parekh made no attempt to move away from the safety of the textile sector. The mill owners of Bombay, such as the Khataus, the Mafatlas, and the Thackerseys, as well as of the south such as K.Thyagraja Chettier, G.V.Naidu, and V.R. Naidu too preferred to stick to their traditional sector until much after the advent of freedom. As the industry had brought great benefit to them during their long association with it, most of the textile manufacturers felt too secure to explore other profitable fields.

PERFORMANCE OF THE YOUNGER GROUPS

In contrast, the relatively later entrants into the industrial sector demonstrated much greater propensity to add new lines to their undertakings. The Singhanias, for instance, developed into a huge organization during the war under the leadership of Padampat, the founder's grandson. Having acquired National Insurance Company at Calcutta and set up Hindustan Commercial Bank with its headquarters at Bombay, the group was now no longer confined to Kanpur. The Modis, likewise, set up a washing soap factory in 1940 to utilize the waste from their vanaspati factory. Production of toilet soap was taken up a little later. Two more concerns came into being in the wake of the growing success of the vanaspati operations—Modi Tin Factory to supply containers to the vanaspati unit and Modi Oil Mills to provide cottonseed and groundnut oil. Apart from these undertakings, the Modis also made large profits through supplying provisions to the armed forces; they also set up a company to manufacture biscuits and confectionery. These, however, were undertakings of modest size by way of preparation, as it were, for the launch of Modi Spinning and Weaving Mills—the biggest Modi enterprise until then. This company was projected soon after the war but could not start production until 1949.

Entry into the textile sector, it seems, was still a source of prestige for the backbenchers, like the Modis in Indian business. For the Thapars too, another backbencher who had established themselves firmly in jute, coal, and paper before the war, entered the textile industry soon after the war. Their Jagajit Textile Mills was set up in 1946 in Punjab, the province to which they belonged. The Dalmias set up a number of cement plants to expand their operations in this area and also floated Bharat Bank and Bharat Airways in 1943 and 1946 respectively. They formed a combine with Ramkrishna Dalmia's son-in-law, Shanti Prasad Jain, to emerge as the formidable Dalmia–Sahu Jain group just before Independence.

For groups rooted in less traditional sectors and facing stiff competition from the entry of multinationals, the war came as a blessing. Alembic Chemicals in Baroda, for instance, which had hard time keeping its head above water during the Depression, started producing India-made foreign liquor in 1942 to take advantage of the disruption in supplies from abroad; and this remained the mainstay of their operations during the war. Liquor took the company into glass manufacturing to supply bottles, and an engineering unit to produce tools, equipment and spare parts for the distilling and pharmaceutical plants. On a more modest scale, the Alembic management also set up a subsidiary to produce vegetable oil at the fag end of the war, and also a container factory to supply packaging material for its products. From a single-level firm with modest-sized operations, Alembic emerged from the war a diversified business group. At the other end of the country, Bengal Chemicals, struggling for existence during the Depression, stabilized its position to some extent but still remained modest in size and much less diversified in operations.

Out of all the southern new entrants into industry during the inter-war years, the Seshasayees made the most spectacular progress during World War II. Their power generation and distribution operations, still confined to the urban centres until the end of the 1930s, expanded into rural areas soon after the war broke out, and in 1940, their South Madras Electric Company, formed by merging their three existing units, emerged as an undertaking of substantial proportions. They were by now sufficiently strong to take over control of Mettur Chemical and Industrial Corporation, a state undertaking formed in the wake of the development of hydroelectricity in the south. The most daring example of their entrepreneurial spirit was the launching of Fertilizer and Chemicals Travancore Limited. Fertilizer production had hardly begun in India in 1943 when the company came into being. Soon after the war, the Seshasayee Brothers also assumed responsibility for the management of state-owned companies concerned with electro-chemicals in the princely state of Travancore Cochin. A distinguishing feature of their management was that they held relatively small blocks of shares in the companies they managed, retaining the shareholders' trust because of sheer efficiency and performance.

Unlike the groups whose exploits have been described in the preceding pages, Associated Cement Companies (ACC) was not under family control. It was the only professionally managed native Indian business group, or close to it, during the period under review. When the war came, it was still struggling with the problems of integration that the merger, hardly two years old, of the companies belonging to as many as four family groups had inevitably created. ACC also had no answer to a fierce rate war unleashed by the Dalmia cement companies. Concerned about the impact of their feud on the war effort, the government hammered out an agreement in 1941 between them and thus enabled ACC to take full advantage of the rising demand. As it was virtually impossible to import machinery or spares, ACC set up a workshop to fabricate spares and rehabilitation machinery to meet the immediate needs. From this germinated the idea of a Central Research Laboratory that would develop later. The company also attempted to produce new varieties of cement during the war. But for the war, ACC would have found it difficult to stabilize its business affairs so quickly after its birth.

RISE OF THE OBSCURE

The war also provided an opportunity for a few business families, still relatively obscure in the Indian business world in 1939, to emerge as the nuclei of new business groups. Perhaps the most prominent were the Bangurs, tracing their origin to one Mangeeram Bangur of Didwana in Rajasthan. Mangeeram had established himself as a trader, property dealer, and share broker in Calcutta during the 1920s, and made a fortune through these operations. The Bangurs did not show much interest in industrial ventures before the war except for the acquisition of a small cotton mill in Bombay in 1934 and contributing financially to a few modest ventures promoted by another Marwari family, the Somanys. Large profits earned by the producers of textile goods and cement during the war, however, prompted the Bangurs to set up Maharaja Shree Umaid Cotton Mill in Rajputana in 1944 and Shree Digvijai Cement in Saurashtra the same year. This was the limit of their industrial interest when the war ended. But they had already created a sufficiently strong base to emerge as one of the most prominent groups soon after Independence.

Unlike the Bangurs, Indra Singh (whose son Baldeo Singh would later become the first Defence Minister of free India) had no trading background. He belonged to a Jat Sikh family of Ropar in Punjab, possessing large landed property. An engineer by training, he left his job with Indian Railways to settle down in business at Jamshedpur on the eve of the war. This was a time when the Tatas were keen to support the establishment of steel-consuming ventures in or around the steel town as a part of their strategy to bolster TISCO. With their active encouragement, Indra Singh took over two existing companies, struggling for survival, in 1939. These were Indian Steel and Wire Products, making nails, rods, wires, etc., and Jamshedupr Engineering and Manufacturing Company producing casting for jute mills. He made huge profits during the war, which enabled him to acquire two cotton mills, one in Khandesh and the other in Madras, and a cement company in Sylhet (now in Bangladesh). A newspaper-publishing concern was added soon after the war.

The boom conditions prevailing during the war prompted a few trading families in the south to move into industry. These included S.N.N. Sankaralinga Iyer, whose participation in the modern sector was still confined to banking and investment concerns until the end of the 1930s. He promoted a few small-scale manufacturing units during the war, and then floated two cement companies soon after the war. The entry into industry of the illustrious Raja Sir Group (Annamalai and Muthiah Chetty) also dates from the early 1940s when they acquired Lotus Mills in Coimbatore. Another family belonging to this community, M.C.T. Chidambaram Chetty, moved into industry a little more convincingly. Like the Raja Sir Group, this group too had its major interests in financial institutions and insurance companies until well after the beginning of the war. The war years, however, witnessed a significant departure when they, jointly with a Bhatia partner, took control of Elphinston Mills in Bombay in the early 1940s and established Travancore Rayon and Pudukottai Textiles soon after the war. A.M.M. Chetty or the Murugappa group, another banking family belonging to the Chettier community, moved into industry with the promotion of a light engineering concern, Ajax Products, producing office and security equipment and coated abrasives. On the whole, however, the Chettiers, with enormous capital at their command, still remained focused on trading, banking, and speculation. One of them, R.M. Alagappa Chetty, became a victim of the deeply entrenched speculative tendencies of his community. A powerful champion of industrialization in the south, he made substantial investment in textiles in the princely state of Travancore and Cochin. But overtrading and speculation led to the complete obliteration of his group from the business map of the region shortly after the war.

While all these groups originated before the war, the emergence of Mahindra and Mahindra, which would develop into one of the most prominent business houses after Independence, was an entirely post-war phenomenon. What is more, the connection of the founders of this group with the world of business was at best tenuous. The scions of a landholding Khatri famly of Ludhiana in Punjab, Kailash Chandra Mahindra and his brother Jagdish Chandra, after completing their education at Cambridge and Oxford respectively, worked for some time with two large houses in India connected with the steel industry—Kailash with Martin Burn and Jagdish with the Tatas. By the late 1930s, however, they left the corporate world to join high positions in government. While the war was coming to a close, the brothers, getting disillusioned with salaried jobs once again, decided to launch a company of their own. The result was the birth of Mahindra and Muhammad in 1945 in partnership with Ghulam Muhammad, a Muslim friend of the brothers. Import of steel was the main business of the partnership, although it also promoted and acted as managing agents of Machinery Manufacturer Organization (MMC) registered in Bombay in 1946. A large part of the share capital of MMC was provided by the Ranas of Nepal with whom the brothers had established close contact. All this was going on well when the division of the subcontinent disrupted the promoters' plans. Ghulam Muhammad decided to migrate to Pakistan (where he would later become Governor General) and withdrew from the partnership. The name of the firm was consequently changed to Mahindra and Mahindra.

With the launching of their firm, the two Mahindra brothers joined a very small class of highly trained professionals who chose consciously and deliberately to be industrial entrepreneurs. Most educated Indians preferred the security of salaried jobs, leaving the task of promoting industrial firms to the scions of trading families. With huge profits made during the war, many trading families would make the transition to industry after Independence, with the result that industry would continue to be dominated by erstwhile traders. But the Mahindra brothers', and before them Indra Singh's, choice of occupation was a pointer, howsoever feeble, to a new trend.

Expatriates and Multinationals

The expatriate groups in the meantime betrayed no signs of weakening—at least outwardly. Martin and Burn, the largest of them with twenty companies in 1939, in fact improved its position by 1945, adding five more companies to its empire. The Martin family continued to hold the largest controlling block in the managing agency firm, followed by the Mukherjees, who remained the most powerful voice in the management. Like most others, the companies controlled by the group reaped huge profit and at the end of the war, the two unincorporated firms, Martin & Co. and Burn & Co., which had retained their separate legal existence, amalgamated to form Martin Burn & Co., a public limited concern. Andrew Yule, too, held on to its pre-war position. As before the war, it held the largest number of companies under a single managing agency when peace returned. And it held on to this position when Independence came.

Our knowledge of the wartime career of Bird and Hielgers, the third largest expatriate group is somewhat more detailed. Many products produced by Bird's companies—coal, paper, gunny bags, and various inputs for making steel—were essential for the war effort. Companies producing these items naturally had their hands full. New methods were employed to increase production besides working the plants overtime to meet the insatiable wartime demand. A few new products were also introduced, the most important of these being 'parajutes'—parachutes made of sacking cloth. Titaghur Paper Company made huge profits through supplying to the government with paper of several varieties, including paper for one-rupee currency notes issued for the first time during the war.

In contrast to the coal, jute, and paper companies, Bird's limestone, dolomite, and, manganese dioxide companies had mixed fortunes. Although their supplies to the steel-producing companies increased substantially, they encountered great difficulty in exploiting the export market. They also had difficulty in transporting their products within the country because of the shortage of railway wagons. Selling agencies engaged in the distribution of cement, vegetable oil, and sugar, however, benefited a great deal as these products were always in short supply. With the resources accumulated during the war, the capacities of many of Bird's companies were increased when peace returned. Also, the shipping department was greatly expanded so as to handle resumed exports of manganese ore and jute goods to Norway, Sweden, the United States, Australia, and other countries. The management was naturally full of hope for Bird's post-war prospects, encouraging Benthall to declare soon after Independence that 'we have been an Indian entity and intend to remain so'.

Others also must have thought along these lines, for no major expatriate firm packed up during the interregnum between the end of the war and the advent of freedom. Shaw Wallace, Begg Sutherland, Harveys, Assam Company, James Finlay, Killick Nixon, Forbes, Forbes Campbell all seemed to be more concerned with the reorganization of their affairs during this period than preparing to bid farewell to India.

The same was the case with the two major expatriate firms in the south—Parry and Binny. Both underwent considerable expansion during and after the war. While the war was still on, the Parry management started the process of Indianizing the workforce. Within a year after Independence, the seat of management and control was shifted from London to Madras with the conversion of the firm into a public limited company, registered under Indian law, making it possible for Indians to subscribe to the firm's share capital. Binny went through a similar process. Production of its mills went up by 84 per cent during the war. New products inspired by the war needs were introduced, the plants had to be overworked to meet the ever-escalating demand; and new agencies were added. The firm even opened a branch at Cochin, the first ever away from Madras, to meet the demand of the expanded business. All this was reflected in the rise of Binny's profits—from an average of Rs 5 lakh annually between 1930 and 1939 to more than Rs 10 lakh per year by the end of the war.

These details about major expatriates seem to suggest that they, like the native houses, emerged from the war much stronger. It is possible—though it is very difficult to come to a firm conclusion—that the European holdings in aggregate terms in firms controlled by the expatriates went down during the period because of the Indian interests, particularly Marwaris, acquiring shares in them. This, however, proves nothing. For no expatriate firm ever lost control over any of its companies through this process, or suffered diminution in terms of the number of companies. Michael Kidron, who has made a special study of the subject, has rightly pointed out: 'Indian investment did not by and large upset foreign control in its traditional fields until after the Second World War.'

The overall impact of the war on the Indian operations of multinationals was along similar lines. The existing ones consolidated their positions, and new ones entered the scene. Imperial Chemical Industries (ICI), the biggest of them all, in fact, started production during the war. Until then, it only had marketing operations in India. Imperial Tobacco, another large enterprise, expanded its production facilities to meet the growing demand for cigarettes. The company also joined hands with other concerns to produce many inputs that it could not produce by itself and set up a couple of subsidiaries for this purpose. These initiatives helped the company reduce its dependence on imports for inputs. Efforts to develop substitutes for imported items continued to receive the utmost attention even after the end of the war with the result that imports of inputs (other than tobacco) registered a continuous fall from the pre-war level of about 80 per cent. Import substitution had already become an integral part of the long-term strategy of the company by the time the British rule ended.

Like ICI and Imperial Tobacco, all multinational subsidiaries engaged in producing goods for which India depended largely on imports expanded their operations during the period. Except in a few cases, like Swedish Match, no parent firm loosened its control over its Indian subsidiary during or soon after the war, and all, including those who diluted their holdings, remained the largest single shareholders in their Indian affiliates. A few, like Bata Shoe Company that had made a modest beginning just a few years before the war broke out, became household names. What is still more revealing is the fact that at least seven more subsidiaries either wholly owned or controlled by multinationals came into being during the interregnum between the beginning of the war and the eclipse of the British rule, as many as five in the year of Independence itself, and more were in the offing when India became independent. In aggregate terms, the Indian subsidiaries of the British multinationals at the time of India's independence constituted, according to a well-regarded authority, about 6 per cent of all subsidiaries set up by them throughout the world, and their number was still increasing.

This survey of the Indian business scene points to three major conclusions. First, business houses and establishments in general, whether controlled by foreign or Indian interests, were much stronger and more prosperous on the eve of India's Independence than they were before the war. Second, while the emergence of new expatriate firms had practically stopped, the old firms in this category were still holding their own without any sign of losing interest in India. It has been suggested in certain quarters that the expatriates' position in India was on the decline during the late 1930s and 1940s. The micro-level experiences of those firms about whom we know do not bear this out. The expatriate decline, as will be argued later, was a post-Independence phenomenon, attributable to the new climate of enterprise. And last, multinationals operating in sectors in which there was relatively less indigenous interest, saw new opportunity for themselves in India at the dawn of freedom.

The impending end of colonialism was bound to generate uncertainties about the future among the non-Indian actors in Indian business, but few looked upon it as the end of the road.

CHAPTER 11

INDEPENDENCE:
A NEW BUSINESS CLIMATE

INDEPENDENCE FOR INDIA OPENED UP A WHOLE NEW VISTA OF opportunities that would benefit Indian business in the long run. In the short run, however, it created a gamut of problems calling for readjustment. The communal holocaust that greeted the division of what until 15 August 1947 had been one unified country into two sovereign nations was hardly conducive to a wholesome business climate. This, however, was only a temporary setback. The contraction of the size of domestic market, consequent upon the emergence of Pakistan, was a permanent loss. The creation of Pakistan also meant the loss of some finest cotton-growing tracts and most of the jute-growing areas that supplied raw materials to India's two largest industries. Also lost to the country were a few manufacturing units that belonged to Indian business groups, such as Sutlej Cotton Mills of the Birlas in Lahore, Lyallpur Cotton Mills of Lala Shri Ram in Lyallpur, and Mukund Iron and Steel Company of the Bajaj group in Lahore. And the budding Mahindras had to contend with the loss of their Muslim partner to the new state.

At the end of the colonial era, the business scene in what would henceforward be known as India presented a remarkable mix of continuity and change. Trading and moneylending no longer covered the entire canvas, as it did when the process of colonization began. But it was still an important constituent. Though the so called business communities, reminiscent of the age of caste-based occupational choices and fragmented markets, had not yet disappeared from the scene, an all-embracing business class was already taking definite shape, thanks to the emergence of a national market and growing occupational mobility. Modern industries had made considerable headway investing India with the distinction of being the most industrialized country in Asia except Japan. But the managerial structure of the industrial undertakings, represented by the managing agency system, was no less family-centric than the management of trading concerns. Moreover, industrialization had touched only the fringes of the Indian economy as the country could boast of only a few industries, while some of the critical areas showed only a bare beginning or relatively poor progress. And as the industrial firms were entirely dependent on imported technology, they were sadly ill-equipped to embark on major innovations—an indispensable instrument of sustained industrialization. Despite the fact that modern industries had made their appearance almost a century before the end of the colonial era, India at Independence was still a proto-industrial society.

There was a great deal of uncertainty about the policy approaches that the new Government of India, headed by Jawaharlal Nehru, would adopt to ensure accelerated economic development of such a society—the approaches that would inevitably impinge on the functioning of business enterprise under the new political set-up. The colonial regime, pursuing by and large a policy of the least possible interference with private enterprise, had constricted but little the freedom to conceive, organize, and implement business plans. With the coming of freedom the Indian business community was certain that it would now be subjected to much greater surveillance and control. In fact, the so-called Bombay Plan, jointly produced by some of the most prominent figures in Indian business in 1944, stated it in so many words. Underlining the authors' faith in the concept of economic planning, this document was meant to project the direction for the country's future development. There was, at the same time, a widespread belief that a national government would on the whole be much more supportive of the legitimate goals and objectives of private enterprise than a colonial system could have ever been. What, however, was not at all clear was how much of the cake of new opportunities the private business would be allowed to partake of, and how much of its freedom of action would be curbed under the new dispensation.

This was so because the Congress had failed to evolve a clear-cut, coherent approach to economic reconstruction before it assumed power. True, the economic policy resolution adopted by the Congress at its Karachi session in 1931 contained some ingredients of a development strategy, and the appointment of National Planning Committee (NPC) under the chairmanship of Jawaharlal Nehru in 1938 was a pointer of some significance to future direction. The

Karachi resolution as well as the NPC deliberations had hinted at the possibility of public ownership of basic industries and the regulation of the economy in general. Also, an influential section of the Congress leadership including Nehru himself, professed socialism of some variety or the other. Nobody, however, could be sure about how far left the free India would go. The Indian business world, by and large, had supported the freedom movement with funds and in many other ways. The Congress could not easily disregard it after coming to power. Also, an influential section in the ruling party led by Sardar Vallabhbhai Patel, tilted towards a more capitalistic system and would not agree to regulating business activities beyond a point. In between these two extremes, were many shades of opinions about the role and place of big business in the nation's life. During its long career, the Congress had basically remained a broad coalition of conflicting interest groups whose only reason for being together under the same banner was a common quest for political freedom. Constituted as it was on the eve of Independence, such a coalition was hardly in a position to project a coherent economic philosophy.

Yet no one with even an elementary understanding of the situation prevailing at the dawn of India's freedom had the slightest doubt that any attempt to restructure its economy on classical capitalistic lines would run counter to the general mood of the young nation. The colonial exploitation perpetrated by a prominent capitalistic power had left an unsavoury image of the capitalistic system itself. In fact, in the popular mind in all countries subjected to colonial domination at that time, colonialism and capitalism were synonymous. The wartime conduct of a section of Indian business had tarnished the image of private enterprise still further. D.R. Gadgil, a highly perceptive and respected observer of the times has left a vivid account of this phenomenon:

The standard of social behaviour maintained by them [Indian business interests] during the war and after...have not been high. These standards have been revealed in a variety of ways: general avoidance of controls and extensive black marketing in all directions, evasion of income tax on a very large scale, hoarding and speculative operations even in times of public distress, hoodwinking and misleading official authorities and defeating public ends. A specially distressing feature of the situation has been that the standards of the richest and most influential do not appear to have been any different from those of others.

There were many people in the Indian business world to whom these remarks did not apply, but the dominant mood in the country in 1947 was one of antipathy, if not downright hostility, towards the business class as a whole.

Policy Parameters

The Industrial Policy Resolution of 1948, the first major pronouncement of the new government on the nation's future direction, reflected all the pulls and pressures of the times. While stressing progressively greater participation of the state in economic activities, the document recognized the role played by private capital in the industrial development of the country, and assured it of a significant place in the future endeavours directed to the nation's economic development, though within a framework of regulation and control. Under the new policy, the state would have exclusive right to establish new undertakings in certain specified fields, pertaining primarily to basic industries, but the private sector was left free to operate in the remaining spheres. Admittedly, the state was not expressly debarred from participating in the residual fields as well, but in view of the fact that the task of accelerating the pace of development was stupendous, the state was expected to concentrate on developing mainly such industries that required relatively large outlay and in which private enterprise was unable or unwilling to invest. Visualizing a mixed economy, as the Bombay Plan drafted by the industrialists had done just a few years ago, the document did not mark a radical departure from the past. There is no denying the fact, however, that the economic order it projected for the future was significantly different from that which prevailed during the colonial regime.

Lest the young nation's energies and resources were frittered away in haphazard and uncoordinated efforts, the government decided to take recourse to the instrument of economic planning within a framework of a mixed economy. The idea was to make sure that all economic activities, falling within the purview of the public sector or private sector, were undertaken on the basis of periodic projections of national need as defined by the nation's Planning Commission, and completed according to the set targets. The First Five-Year Plan (1951–6), though hurriedly put together, was a clear indication of the importance the government attached to the idea of economic planning. This document, being very similar to the Bombay Plan, created no misgiving about the government's attitude to free enterprise. History offered no precedent of economic planning and liberal democracy going hand in hand, but few among the policymakers believed that there was inherent contradiction between the two.

The system of industrial licencing was the second instrument devised by the new government to achieve the objectives of industrial policy. Under this system, introduced under the Industries (Development and Regulation) Act of 1951, the existing undertakings engaged in scheduled industries had to be registered with the government, and no new industrial undertaking could be established nor any substantial expansion to existing plants effected, without the prior procurement of licence from the central government. The existing as well as new undertakings were also required to secure permits from the government to procure the goods and equipment they required to implement their business plans. The principal purpose behind these requirements was to ensure that industrial investments adhered to the objectives and targets of the plans, and made for balanced economic development of various regions. The licencing requirements obviously placed serious restrictions on the freedom of private enterprise, but the fact remains that planning without some regulation would have been a misnomer. The requirement, thus, was a natural corollary of the concept of planning.

Apart from investing the government with the powers to determine how much the scheduled industries would produce and where they would have their production facilities, the Act also conferred on the government the powers to control the price and distribution of their products. Subsequent legislations armed the government with similar powers with respect to a host of other industries. As domestic production in the areas brought under the control mechanism lagged behind the existing demand, the decision had a reasonable basis. Also the control system was not invented by the new government; it had first been introduced by the colonial government during World War II to ensure unhampered support for the war effort. The new government, however, spread its application much wider though in gradual stages, so that in the ultimate analysis only a few industries remained out of the control network.

This was also true of the import and tariff policies pursued by the new government. Although the colonial regime had resorted to import controls during World War II, the post-war years had witnessed a substantial relaxation in this respect. However, with the balance-of-payments situation turning progressively adverse from 1947, conserving scarce foreign exchange became the driving force of the import and tariff policies. Without going into specific details of these policies, which evolved in gradual stages and were marked by brief intervals of liberalization, it will be sufficient to state that restriction on import of consumer goods, emphasis on import substitution, protection to embryonic industries, facilitating inflow of plant and machinery for priority sectors, and preferential treatment to small and medium sector were the dominant themes that formed the overall approach in these matters. It would have been possible for the government to be less stringent in its tariff and import policies if the nation's record on the export front had been more encouraging. But except for the first couple of years after Independence, when it held its own, India's share in world exports registered a progressive decline.

All these measures cumulatively brought about a sea change in the nation's business environment. Independent India did not abandon the free enterprise system altogether, but what these policies together sought to introduce was a system very different from the one operating under the colonial regime. Except for the brief interregnum of World War II, the colonial government had seldom imposed overt restriction on the freedom to conceive, organize, and implement business plans, and the business actors were free to manage their show on the basis of their understanding of the world around them. In contrast, it would now be the government that would determine what they would produce, how much they would produce, where they would produce, and at what price they would sell.

State participation in business was another new element in the business environment of independent India. A few departmentally run commercial undertakings like the railways and postal services and ordnance factories engaged in defence production were all that the colonial state could boast of in the name of business undertakings under its direct control and management, whereas the entire scheme of industrial rejuvenation under the new dispensation visualized the public sector dominating the commanding heights of the economy. Incidentally, 'public sector' and 'private sector' were new entrants into economic vocabulary. As business in pre-Independence India was synonymous with private enterprise, there had been no need then for the binary classification.

The obvious constraints for the free enterprise system, inherent in these policy pronouncements, did not cause much concern in the Indian business world. For one thing, they were expected and, as mentioned earlier, were in tune with the general sentiments of the country. More importantly, no one including the worst pessimists, had any doubt that the new government's emphasis on industrial transformation within the shortest possible time (which had been at the lowest end of the priorities of the colonial regime) would unquestionably open up a whole new vista for the private sector. Moreover, certain aspects of these policies were a source of comfort to the Indian business world. Protection to industries requiring heavy capital outlay, for instance, was in keeping with a long-standing demand of the industrial leaders, and emphasis on import substitution promised to bolster the competitive ability of the Indian producer to exploit the vast domestic market. No wonder then that apart from voicing, for the sake of form, some feeble ritualistic reservations about the licensing provision, the private corporate sector had little to find fault with the overall development strategy of the government, at least during the First Five-Year Plan period.

TOWARDS A SOCIALIST RHETORIC

Sections of the private sector, however, started developing some misgivings about this strategy towards the close of the First Five-Year Plan, as the ruling Congress Party began to adopt a somewhat more radical tone in its economic programme. The stage was set by the Prime Minister himself who, fresh from a trip to the People's Republic of China, declared in a public statement in December 1954 that the picture of India that he had in mind was definitely a 'socialistic' one. The Congress Party and the Indian Parliament formally endorsed this stand and suitable changes were made in the object clauses of the Second Five-Year Plan, still at the drafting stage, to declare that India would henceforward move towards a 'socialist pattern of society'—substituting a more emphatic expression for the feeble sounding 'socialistic'! In keeping with the changed stance of the government, a new Industrial Policy Resolution was issued in 1956, and the ruling party went a step further when it declared in its manifesto for the general elections of 1957, that its ultimate goal was to establish a 'socialist society' in India—sounding still more radical. The nationalization of Imperial Bank of India (which now became State Bank of India) and of the life insurance business around the same time in 1955 must have added to the insecurity of the private sector.

The fact of the matter is that the new policy enunciations, in real terms, changed little except the rhetoric. The Industrial Policy Resolution of 1956 was essentially a mere reiteration of the earlier document except that the number of industries reserved for the exclusive exploitation of the state or where the state would progressively expand its presence was now substantially larger. The new policy also did away with the ten-year guarantee against nationalization of the existing industries contained in the old document. Lest this cause undue apprehension among private sector industrialists, Prime Minister Nehru declared in the Indian Parliament almost on the morrow of the new enunciations:

I have no shadow of doubt that if we say 'lop off the private sector', we cannot replace it. We haven't got the resources to replace it, and the result would be that our productive apparatus will suffer. And why should we do it, I do not understand. We have our industries; there is a vast sector. Let the state go on building up its plants and industries as far as its resources permit. Why should we fritter away our energy in pushing out somebody who is doing it in the private sector? There is no reason except that the private sector might build up monopoly, might be building up economic power to come in the way of our growth.... Prevent that, control that, plan for that; but where there is such a vast field to cover, it is foolish to take charge of the whole field when you are totally incapable of using that huge area yourself. Therefore, you must not only permit the private sector but, I say, encourage it in its own field.

The Prime Minister would continue to offer such assurances to the private sector throughout his tenure.

The government's pragmatic approach to private enterprise was also reflected in the new company law enacted in 1956. It gave a new lease of life to the managing agency system despite the fact that the system had been under heavy attack for years from various quarters because of the wide powers it gave to the managing agents—powers that were not always used fairly and scrupulously. Whatever its role in the nation's industrialization, it had become synonymous with family management and did not have many supporters, beyond the business circles, in free India. Its abrupt abolition, however, would have caused a great deal of disruption in the managerial set-up of the private sector enterprises. The government, therefore, decided to retain the managing agency structure until 1 April 1970, and introduced only cosmetic changes in the powers and privileges of managing agents. No managing agency could now have more than ten companies under its direct care, but there was no limit placed on the number of firms for which it could act as secretary and treasurer. Interestingly, in terms of actual powers, a secretary and treasurer's role was no different from that of a managing agent. For all practical purposes, thus, the existing business groups were left with their business empires intact. And even this harmless document did not come into force until 1 April 1960. Significantly, in deciding upon the phased abolition of the managing agency system, business opinion was fully taken into account by the government and Parliament.

It can easily be seen from the foregoing discussion that the new policy enunciations did not offer much of an immediate threat to the private enterprise, socialist rhetoric notwithstanding. This was so because the private sector was left undisturbed in the areas in which it had been operating or in which it was likely to expand. Barring a few distinguished exceptions like TISCO, most private sector companies were engaged in consumer goods industries, which the state was unlikely to enter under the new dispensation, and the industries that were sought to be promoted under the state's auspices demanded resources of such magnitude, both financial and technological, that the private enterprise would have found them too risky. The emphasis in the Second Five-Year Plan, it may be recalled, was on the development of capital-intensive industries such as machine tools, heavy electricals, iron and steel, heavy engineering, and petroleum and natural gas.

In this context, the emergence of government-sponsored credit facilities must have been a source of great comfort to the private sector as they were meant to help the private enterprise with large funds for industrial projects on a long-term basis, that the Indian banking system, as it stood then, was ill-equipped to advance. The first in this genre was Industrial Finance Corporation of India (IFCI) set up soon after the announcement of the Industrial Policy of 1948. Then followed in quick succession a number of institutions with similar objectives. The most important of these were National Small Industries Corporation (NSIC), Industrial Credit and Investment Corporation of India (ICICI), Industrial Development Bank of India (IDBI), and Industrial Refinance Corporation of India (IRCI). Apart from these national-level institutions were the financial corporations set up by practically every state government to meet the credit needs of medium- and small-scale industries under its jurisdiction. The Nehru government also successfully resisted pressure from the left parties backed by a powerful section in the ruling Congress to bring the nation's banking system under the ownership of the state.

UNANTICIPATED DISTORTIONS

It should be clear from the foregoing discussion that seen in a proper perspective there was little in the policy pronouncements that can be dubbed as anti-private enterprise per se. In fact there was much in them that opened up new opportunities for the private sector. Given the socio-economic realities in the country and the public sentiment favouring a radical economic stance, it is indeed doubtful whether another government, more inclined to the free enterprise system, could have come with an essentially different programme. In fact, the new policy parameters did not cause much problem in the beginning. As the years passed, however, many unanticipated distortions set in, overshadowing their intended purpose and positive features. This was primarily because of faulty implementation.

The licensing policy is perhaps the most notable of these. As has been pointed out earlier, the main purpose of the policy was to make sure that industrial expansion proceeded along the lines determined by the Planning Commission and the targets set by it. The responsibility to clear applications for licences was vested in an inter-ministerial Licencing Committee set up for this purpose. The Committee, however, acted on the basis of recommendations made by a plethora of committees or agencies functioning at parallel as well as hierarchical levels. This inevitably caused delay and frustration. Moreover, the Licensing Committee never developed or published explicit criteria for assessing the applications and operated in an ad hoc manner. In many cases, an application for expanding existing capacity was rejected on the grounds that sufficient capacity had already been allowed to another investor, without going into the merits of alternative applications. Whenever expansion of capacity involved more than one stage, sanction was normally given for the first stage without any assurance that the licence for subsequent stages would follow as a matter of course and without undue delay. One of the objectives, as mentioned earlier, was to prevent the rise of monopolies. But the licensing system was heavily weighted in favour of large houses, because being better informed and organized they could jump the queue and thus pre-empt others. In fact, some business houses submitted multiple applications with a view to cornering a substantial part of the targeted capacity, and thus to develop a dominant position for themselves in a particular industry, or simply to foreclose the capacity without any intention to utilize the licences secured.

Other control measures too were rendered ineffective, even counterproductive, because of procedural inefficiencies. The avowed purpose of the import policy, as pointed out earlier, was to ensure the optimum utilization of the scarce foreign exchange for importing goods and services that were required for the success of the import substitution strategy or were absolutely essential for the social good of the republic. Such goods and services could be imported against permits issued by the government after examining the applications at various administrative levels by a multitude of departments and agencies with reference to a labyrinth of rules and regulations. This complicated apparatus could have presumably worked had there been a set of principles and criteria to guide the decision makers. But as in the case of the licensing policy, these were grievously lacking with the result that ad hocism ruled the roost at the cost of efficiency. The same can be said of the measures to control prices and distribution of essential commodities such as steel, cement, motor cars, and a large number of other products that were in short supply in the country.

All this is amply borne out by the findings of a number of expert groups appointed by the government to examine the working of the various control measures. Apart from defeating the very purpose they were intended to accomplish, the procedural deficiencies in implementing the control measures created needless bottlenecks, caused avoidable delays, and generated widespread frustration and indignation among the applicants. However, perhaps the most pernicious, though unintended, byproduct of the system of controls was widespread corruption in bureaucracy. For, in the absence of clarity in criteria and guidelines, government officials at almost every level had a field day obliging the applicants, both deserving and undeserving, in exchange for illegal gratifications. Though it is not possible to document such misdeeds, committee after committee has pointed to this monstrous side effect of the control system that has been eating into the vitals of the nation's body politic ever since. The popular sobriquet 'License-Permit Raj', with its pejorative connotation, for the post-colonial regime was born out of these numerous failings of implementation that brought the entire system into disrepute.

Why were these failings allowed to occur? How did the decision makers fail to realize that too much control in an economy characterized by shortages was bound to breed corruption? It can be argued that this could have been due to sheer inexperience. While the political wing of the new regime responsible for determining the broad directions had no experience of governance, the administrative or bureaucratic wing whose task was actually to carry out the policies and programmes had never been involved in implementing a development strategy in the real sense. The colonial regime had basically remained a sort of night watchman government, concerned mainly with law and order.

Regardless of who was responsible for creating or nurturing them, the control measures did distort in many ways the development strategy of the post-colonial regime. And yet despite all the constraints that this strategy created for the private enterprise, no discerning observer could miss the fact that private capital now had a much wider and more promising horizon for investment and profit. Continued political stability within a democratic framework—something that few countries emerging from colonial domination at that time could boast of—and growing signs of the Indian populace craving for material comfort—the revolution of rising expectations—added to the overall optimism.

Indian business after Independence had to chart its course against these conflicting trends in the business environment.

1. Drawn in AD 1858 by the Amreli (in Baroda State) branch of the firm of Haribhaktis, this *muddati* (date specific) *hundi* entitles the payee (who is probably identified on the reverse) to receive Rs 14 from the main office of the firm in Baroda on a particular day. The hundi is written in old Gujarati.

Source: Haribhakti Collection, Department of History, M.S. University of Baroda.

2. Dwarkanath Tagore

Source: A Claude Campbell,
Glimpses of Bengal (New Delhi,
2003, reprint), vol. 2, p. 211.

3. Ranchhodlal Chhotalal

Source: Govt. of Bombay,
*Representative Men of the
Bombay Presidency*
(Bombay, 1890), p. 161.

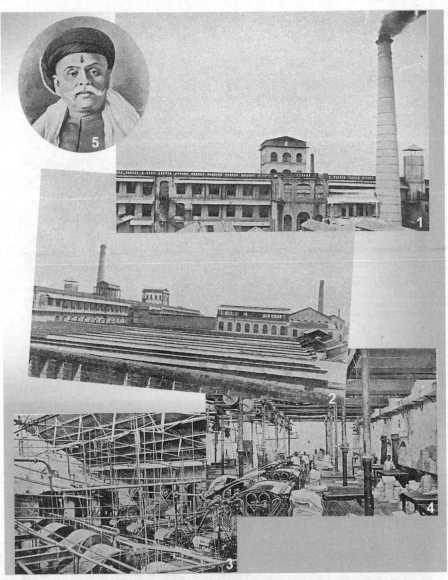

4. Gujarat Ginning and Manufacturing Company Ltd, Ahmedabad and its founder Mansukhbhai Bhagubhal (top) in 1915. Mansukhbhai was the first member of the mercantile class to branch out into modern industry in Ahmedabad.

Source: S. Playne (comp.), *The Bombay Presidency etc.* (London, 1917), p. 93.

5. Bombay Dyeing and Manufacturing Company, founded by Wadia's successors, *c.*1915.

Source: S. Playne (comp.), *The Bombay Presidency etc.* (London, 1917), p. 291.

6. Taj Mahal Hotel, Bombay, the oldest surviving enterprise of the Tatas.

Source: F.R. Harris, *J.N. Tata* (Bombay, 1959), p. 95.

7. Elgin Mills, Kanpur, *c*.1915.
From the top:
  i. General view
 ii. Tents made for the army
iii. Carding room
iv. Spinning room

Source: S. Playne (comp.), *The Bombay Presidency etc.* (London, 1917), p. 445.

8. Parry's Corner, Madras, *c.*1860.

Source: Hilton Brown, *Parrys of Madras* (Madras: privately printed, 1958), p. 116.

9. Alembic Chemical Works, *c.*1915.

From the top:

 i. Chemical laboratory

ii. Front view of the works

Source: S. Playne (comp.), *The Bombay Presidency etc.* (London: 1917), p. 77.

10. Laxmanrao Kirloskar with
    wife Radhabai and eldest
    son Shantanu, c.1904.

Source: *Yantrikachi Yatra* in Marathi
(Kirloskarwadi, 1958), p. 16.

11. J.N. Tata (white beard) with his brother-in-law, R.D. Tata, and sons, Ratanji
and Dorabji (clockwise) sometime in the 1890s.

Source: F.R. Harris, *J.N. Tata* (Bombay, 1958), p. 111.

12. Ford Automobiles (India) Ltd, Bombay, *c*.1915.
From the top:
  i. Assembled chassis to be tested
 ii. Ford de Luke Car
iii. Showrooms
Ford Motor Company (USA) was the first motor company to open a sales agency in India.

Source: S. Playne (comp.), *The Bombay Presidency etc.* (London, 1917), p. 182.

13. Tatanagar, a light armoured vehicle built by TISCO. The Indian army used it on the North African front during World War II and found it very dependable.

Source: *Tata Steel Diamond Jubilee* (Jamshedpur, 1967), p. 138.

14. Aditya V. Birla

Source: Minhaz Merchant, *Aditya Vikram Birla* (New Delhi, 1997), p. 168.

15. Volkart Brothers, Bombay, *c*.1915.

From the top:

   i. Interior of an oil mill

  ii. Ginning factory, Nagpur

 iii. Cotton press, Nagpur

 iv. Hide godown, Karachi

Source: S. Playne (comp.), *The Bombay Presidency etc.* (London, 1917), p. 367.

16. Various views of Sassoon Spinning and Weaving Company Ltd, Bombay, c.1915.

Source: S. Playne (comp.), *The Bombay Presidency etc.* (London, 1917), p. 325.

17. Dhirubhai Ambani
Source: A Reliance
company release.

18. Grand Hotel, Calcutta, *c.*1920.
Source: A Macmillan (comp.), *Seaports of India and Ceylon* (London, 1928), p. 125.

19. Ready-for-sale Maruti cars in the company yard.

Source: From a Maruti Udyog Ltd promotional handout.

20. Reliance Petrochemicals Ltd: Oil refinery at Jamnagar, Gujarat under construction. When completed, this will be the largest oil refinery in the world.

Source: Reliance Industries Ltd.

21. Corporate Block, Infosys Technologies Ltd.

Source: Infosys Technologies Ltd, Bangalore.

22. MC Room, Infosys Technologies Ltd.

Source: Infosys Technologies Ltd, Bangalore.

23. Airtel customer centre showroom, New Delhi.
Source: Hindustan Times.

24. Shopper's stop, Ansal Plaza, New Delhi.
Source: Hindustan Times.

25. Laboratory, Dr. Reddy's Laboratories Ltd, Hyderabad.
Source: Dr. Reddy's Laboratories Ltd.

26. Corporate Building, Dr. Reddy's Laboratories Ltd, Hyderabad.
Source: Dr. Reddy's Laboratories Ltd.

CHAPTER 12

BUSINESS IN THE NEHRU ERA

THE LEFT-OF-THE CENTRE DEVELOPMENT STRATEGY EVOLVED DURING THE initial years of the Nehru government enjoyed widespread support in the country in his lifetime. The Indian masses in general endorsed it through the results of successive general elections held between 1952 and 1962 and, barring stray elements on the extreme right and left, few in the intelligentsia found fault with its basic approach. The Nehru model did not evoke much explicit opposition from organized business either, with the exception of some ritualistic noises from the trade associations.

Obviously, the Indian business interests were more inclined to exploiting the opportunities that freedom had brought in its wake than wasting their energy on combating the restrictions imposed on their operations. A small section of them did extend lukewarm support to the Swatantra Party formed by the venerable C. Rajagopalachari, the first Indian Governor General of free India, but it soon withered away without anybody noticing it despite the enormous respect its founder commanded in the country. Throughout the colonial period, the leaders of Indian commerce and industry had lamented an essentially non-interventionist economic policy the government of the day pursued. How could they seriously complain against the Nehru model that on the whole struck a judicious balance between freedom for enterprise and an interventionist state?

DEFINING THE NEHRU ERA

This balance remained virtually undisturbed for about five years following Nehru's death on 27 May 1964. These five years can easily go down as the most difficult period in the economic history of India. A bloody war with the People's Republic of China in 1962 had already left the economy in a shambles when Nehru died; another war with Pakistan soon after Nehru's death made the situation worse. As if this was not enough, in many parts of the country the monsoon failed for three years in succession. The foreign exchange position, never too happy after the First Five-Year Plan period, became dangerously precarious because of the worsening performance in exports. Accumulating budgetary deficits, rising inflation, spiralling prices, expanding money supply, and mounting unemployment consequently formed a vicious circle to aggravate the distress. So grim was the economic scenario around the mid-1960s that even the breakthrough in wheat production, popularly known as the Green Revolution, offered no more than a mere glimmer of hope. The Green Revolution marked the end of food deficit, tormenting the country since much before Independence, but it was not enough to provide the requisite momentum to an ailing economy. Radical rhetoric under these conditions struck a responsive chord. Communists and socialists of all hues and leftist elements in the ruling Congress Party itself—the so-called Young Turks who had been kept under check by the titanic personality of Nehru—turned more shrill in their demand to further tighten the noose around the private enterprise.

Nehru's immediate successor, Lal Bahadur Shastri, had much too brief a tenure—barely twenty months—to leave any imprint on the strategy to grapple with the crisis. It was Indira Gandhi, Shastri's successor and Nehru's daughter, who had to face the music. During the first two years of her tenure, her government sought solution to the mounting economic problems in the Nehruvian model but could not arrest the downward trend in the economy. No wonder that her party received a severe drubbing in the general elections of 1967, reducing an already insecure Prime Minister into a political cripple.

A powerful section of the Congress Party now began to conspire to remove her from power. To ward off the impending danger to her position, she decided to bring all major Indian commercial banks under state control through an ordinance on 19 July 1969. The demand for bank nationalization, which Nehru had resisted throughout his tenure, had become the battlecry of all the leftists in the country after his death. By acceding to their demand, the Prime Minister hoped to win their support against the conspiring old guard in her party.

Much can be said in favour of bank nationalization as an economic measure, as also much against it. But the fact of the matter is that Mrs Gandhi used it as a purely political measure to consolidate her power. As a political weapon, the decision vindicated itself in full, as it had an electrifying effect on the party and nation, elevating Mrs Gandhi, until then an insecure head of a government riven with dissension, to be the tallest figure on the nation's political firmament. The measure, however, was a major departure from, if not a total negation of, the Nehruvian framework. Throughout his lifetime, he had kept on reiterating his opposition to nationalization as a strategy and, barring a few exceptions, his government refrained from resorting to this expedient. As for Mrs Gandhi, having profited from the impact of one radical measure on her political fortunes, she had to initiate many others to retain her radical credentials. Viewed in this fashion, the bank nationalization marked the end of the Nehru era. Significantly, most of the unanticipated distortions in the development strategy of the Nehru government, discussed in the last chapter, started setting in only after his daughter had emerged as the undisputed leader of the country.

Undeniably, the socialist rhetoric that reverberated through the corridors of power after 1969 claimed sanction in the policy pronouncements of the Nehru government. But during his time, the private enterprise system did not suffer from undue insecurity and, in fact, registered good progress. Practically all the old established Indian houses registered impressive gains and many new groups emerged during the Nehru era.

PROGRESS OF THE OLD HOUSES

Let us first look at the performance of the old established houses—the houses that defined the contours of the private corporate world on the eve of India's Independence. How did they fare in the Nehru era?

The starting point obviously has to be the house of Tatas who had all along retained their numero uno position in the private sector of the Indian business world. Tata Iron and Steel Company (TISCO), their flagship and the largest company in the country on the eve of Independence, needed urgent attention because it had emerged from the war with its production capacity greatly impaired. Even though the house had maintained a discrete distance from the freedom movement and the Congress Party, TISCO was too important an undertaking for the nation to be allowed to languish as would have happened if the new government had not advanced a sum of Rs 10 crore. This helped the company initiate a programme of modernization and expansion that eventually culminated in doubling the capacity from 1 million tonnes to 2 million tonnes by 1958. The Tatas encountered little problem in securing the necessary permits and licences from the government and a huge credit from International Bank for Reconstruction and Development—the largest industrial loan so far granted by World Bank and the largest loan ever granted for any purpose in Asia. Steel had been reserved for the public sector under the new industrial policy, but the Government of India did everything possible to facilitate TISCO's expansion.

Around the same time Tata Locomotive and Engineering Company reorganized itself and became Tata Engineering and Locomotive Company (TELCO). As the manufacturers of locomotives for Indian Railways, the old company had only one customer. In its new incarnation it would make trucks and other commercial vehicles for which there was growing demand not only in India but in other developing countries as well. TELCO was not entitled to a licence for making commercial vehicles as, under the guidelines laid down by the Tariff Commission in 1953, only existing automobile makers, barring exceptional cases, could be considered for the purpose. But this hurdle was crossed without much difficulty. TELCO entered into collaboration with Daimler-Benz AG of Germany, a world leader in the automobile industry. The giant automobile maker was willing to collaborate with the Tatas to produce passenger cars also, but the government did not permit this. Despite this setback, TELCO developed into a formidable concern. Starting with the manufacture of merely 3000 vehicles in 1954–5, it doubled its production of vehicles in just three years.

The Tatas' other major ventures experienced little difficulties in adjusting to the post-Independence scenario. Tata Chemicals, struggling for survival in the face of competition from multinationals on one hand and technological deficiencies on the other, finally attained a measure of stability by the end of the 1960s. However, the company was denied permission to diversify into fertilizers because of a feeling in government circles, according to J.R.D. Tata, that the Tatas were already too big. In the meantime, the management of the Tatas' hydraulic power companies had reverted to the house in 1951 after the expiry of the contract with the American syndicate. Power generation was reserved for the public sector, but the Tatas were left undisturbed, although the government refused to permit further expansion of capacity. This, however, was a minor setback in comparison with what happened to the aviation companies of the house.

Under the Industrial Policy Statement of 1948, air transport had been included among industries that were reserved for the public sector. There was nothing, however, to indicate any threat to the existing private sector companies at that time, nine in all including Tata Airlines, operating within India. The Tatas' planning for launching an international carrier was already at an advanced stage when the new policy was announced. However, instead of blocking the Tatas plan, the government agreed to J.R.D.'s suggestion to launch the company in the joint sector. Thus was born Air India International in 1948 in which the government had 49 per cent stake and the Tatas 20 per cent, while the remaining 31 per cent was left for public participation. Within barely five years, however, the government decided, in spite of stiff opposition from the Tatas, to nationalize air transport. Instead of several aviation firms in the private sector, there would now be only two companies, both in the public sector: Indian Airlines to operate domestically and Air India to operate internationally. To recognize the role J.R.D. Tata had played in promoting air transport in India, he was made chairman of Air India and a member of the Indian Airlines board. Two years later, the Tatas also lost a part of their insurance business to the government consequent upon the nationalization of life insurance. Their New India Assurance Company, however, continued to handle general insurance, which would not be nationalized until much later.

New acquisitions and floatations, however, more than compensated for these losses. The acquisitions included Forbes, Forbes, Campbell & Co. and a minority interest in Macneill and Barry, one of the oldest and largest British houses in Calcutta, controlling a number of collieries, jute companies, and tea. Volkart Brothers, a Swiss trading firm operating in Bombay since 1851, was taken over to form Voltas Limited in 1954 which would specialize in large-scale air-conditioning and supply of machinery for agriculture as well as industry. A large investment firm, controlled by David Sassoon, who had practically withdrawn from India long ago, was another acquisition of the early 1950s. The new floatations during the period were few and far between and were relatively modest ventures. Two of these, however, would later grow into significant enterprises. They were Tata Finlay, launched in 1963 in partnership with James Finlay as a sterling firm to produce tea, and Tata Consultancy Services (TCS) set up in 1968.

The 1950s and the 1960s, however, were more a period of adjustment for the house of Tatas than of new initiatives. Between 1958, when TISCO completed its expansion, and 1969, when TELCO's collaboration agreement with Dailmer-Benz ended, the only big industrial project the house proposed to launch was fertilizer production by Tata Chemicals in 1967 which, as mentioned earlier, the government turned down. TELCO's car project was also turned down by the government, and there was no sanction in sight for the applications to expand the capacities of Associated Cement Companies (ACC), or of the group's power companies and TELCO. Modernization of the ageing TISCO plant was also held up for the same reason. Price control on steel and cement only added to the constraints. And yet the Tatas not only retained their number one position in the Indian business world but also grew both in size and range of operations. The number of companies controlled by the house had risen to more than 150 by 1969 as against only 102 in 1951, and the total assets from a little less than Rs 163 crore to more than Rs 505 crore during the same period. At an average of just about 2 per cent annually, the growth rate of the Tatas was admittedly somewhat slower than that of some other houses during the Nehru era. But this was partly due to the fact that most of their product lines, being subject to price and distribution control, would have greatly constricted the business manoeuvrability of the management, and thus adversely affected the generation of capital.

The Birlas were one of those groups that registered a more impressive growth during the Nehru era than the Tatas. This, however, was the continuation of a trend that had started during the war when the house had relentlessly pursued the twin strategies of acquisition and flotation. The birth of their first major post-war venture, Gwalior Rayon, coincided with the coming of Independence. Among the first producers of rayon fabric in India, the company developed, after some teething troubles, into one of the most successful undertakings of that time. In the process, Grasim Industries (as Gwalior Rayon would later be known) transformed the sleepy, deserted, and wild Nagda in Madhya Pradesh, where its factory was set up, into a busy industrial township pulsating with life and activity.

However, despite all the links G.D. Birla had built with Gandhi and many other leaders of the Congress before Independence, his proposal to launch a steel mill was turned down by the new government. But the group's initiative for producing aluminium resulted in the birth of Hindustan Aluminium Company (HINDALCO) at Renukoot in Uttar Pradesh. Launched in collaboration with Kaiser Corporation of the United States in 1958, it would grow into the largest company in its field within a few years. Another important floatation of the post-Independence period was Digvijay Woollen Mills registered in 1948. A large number of investment and trading companies were also added during the first decade of freedom, and the Birlas also invested heavily in cement to become the second largest producer in the field, next only to ACC. Also, some of the Birla firms, though conceived earlier, became operational after Independence. The most important of these were Textile Machinery Corporation (TEXMACO), and Hindustan Motors.

Acquisitions too were pursued with relentless vigour. The Century Spinning and Weaving Mills was the first in this category. It was an old cotton company, originally founded by the famous Wadia family in 1898 in Bombay, that in 1951 had passed under the control of Chunilal Mehta, a nephew of Walchand Hirachand. Other acquisitions of the period included Sirpur Paper, Sirsilk, Hyderabad Asbestos, Bally Jute, Rameshwar Jute, Soorah Jute, and Air Conditioning Corporation in the eastern region and Digvijay Cotton in Saurashtra. Some of these companies were earlier under the control of British expatriate firms. A few of the newly acquired or promoted companies were in areas in which the Birlas had already registered a noticeable presence, but many others heralded the entry of the house into fields hitherto unexplored by them, such as banking, insurance, coal, tea, starch, engineering, and passenger cars.

As a result of the twin strategy of promotion and acquisition, the group had by 1969 expanded far beyond where they were in 1947. Within a space of twenty-two years, they had added at least thirty major companies; on the eve of Independence they had had only thirteen. They also had a much more variegated product portfolio now. The number of companies in their empire would have been still larger had they utilized all the licences they had acquired from the government. Many business groups in post-colonial India acquired licences without any intention of actually using them. Their main purpose was to pre-empt others from entering the field and thus thwart competition. The Birlas seem to have been far ahead of others in this respect.

The group's resources and expansionist ambitions, however, far outstripped the opportunities the India of the 1960s with its highly regulated economy could offer. The Birlas, therefore, began to explore investment possibilities outside India in other developing countries. A textile mill in Ethiopia, set up as a joint venture with the government of that country in the late 1950s, was the first venture of this kind. Then followed three companies in Nigeria to produce engineering goods, paper, and asbestos, and a paper mill in Kenya. These early initiatives seem to have inspired Aditya Vikram Birla, reportedly G.D. Birla's favourite grandson (son of G.D.'s youngest son Basant Kumar) to adopt overseas expansion as an integral element of his overall strategy to get around the constricting business climate in India. He had taken over the command of a few domestic enterprises in the group after returning with an engineering degree from the prestigious Massachusetts Institute of Technology

(MIT) in 1964. His first overseas venture was Indo-Thai Synthetics set up in 1969 at Bangkok, to be followed by a host of others.

Among other houses that were at the centrestage of Indian business at the time of Independence and continued to remain prominent even later were the Thapars, Kirloskars, Mafatlals, Lalbhais, Walchands (or Doshis), and Shri Rams. Some of them improved their relative positions, while others were overtaken by new entrants. The Thapars, the Mafatlals, and the Kirloskars were in the first category.

A major factor in the ascent of the Thapars was the acquisition of Greaves Cotton, one of the oldest and most prominent British houses in Bombay tracing its origin back to 1859, and its affiliate, Crompton Greaves. Primarily trading in engineering products, the acquired firms had just started manufacturing oil engines and electrical equipment at the time of the transfer of management. The acquisition, thus, led the Thapars into a wide range of manufacturing activities, often in collaboration with world leaders in their respective fields. Another acquisition that gave new direction to the group's operations was that of Ballarpur Paper and Straw Board Mills Limited, originally floated by a Sikh family with the support of the government of Madhya Pradesh. With its merger with Shri Gopal Paper Mills, already under the Thapars' control, this would become Ballarpur Industries Limited. In the meantime, a few sugar mills and several coal mines had been added to the group. New floatations seem to have been avoided during this period as a matter of policy. For a general insurance company was the only notable promotion by the group in the 1950s.

As a natural consequence of the acquisitions and new floatations, the Thapars had already become a fairly diversified group, with more than fifty companies under their umbrella, by the time their founder died in 1962. Even though his four sons, all grown up and well educated, decided to split the same year, it caused no disruption in management, as each one of them already had a particular industry group under his care. The progress of the group, therefore, remained unhampered, and at the end of the Nehru era it was counted among the four largest houses in the country—a significant achievement for a group that was still counted among the backbenchers in Indian business in 1947.

The Mafatlals, led by Navinchand, the founder's sole surviving son, were essentially a textile group at the time of India's Independence. Having made handsome profits during the war, they had substantial surplus to invest in new businesses. The desire of the Sassoons to withdraw from India altogether provided them an opportunity to acquire Sassoon Spinning and Weaving Company and Union Mills that were among the few companies still under the control of the expatriate house. Two years later, they acquired another textile concern at Dewas in Madhya Pradesh. These acquisitions placed the group in the front rank of textile producers in the country. The acquistion of Indian Dyestuffs Industries, set up by one Anandlal Sheth at Kalyan near Bombay in 1954, took them into an allied line in 1957. From dyestuffs to chemicals and then to petrochemicals was only a short distance and these were the fields the Mafatlals entered after stabilizing the operations of the dyestuffs company. The result was the emergence of National Organic Chemical Industries (NOCIL) and Polyolefins Industries Ltd (PIL) in the early 1960s with American and German collaboration respectively. The manufacturing facilities of these companies together represented the largest chemical complex of its kind in the country.

Though concentrating mainly on acquisition, the Mafatlals also promoted National Machinery Manufacturers Ltd soon after Independence to produce spindles and looms for the textile industry. Reputed international firms including Platt Brothers—the famous British suppliers of textile machinery to Indian cotton producers before Independence—collaborated in this venture. Tariff protection coupled with efficiency of management helped the company carve out a large market for its products within just a few years of its birth. The Mafatlals also promoted a few other concerns of modest size during this period, but it was acquistion and not new floatation that resulted in the phenomenal growth of the house during the Nehru era. This was reflected in their rise to third position in the Indian business world by 1969. As long as cotton textiles was the mainstay of their business, they hovered between ranks 8 and 12.

The Kirloskars during the Nehru era were led by S.L. Kirloskar, the eldest son of the founder, as Laxmanrao had practically retired from active management in 1945. Neither his retirement nor death eleven years later affected the unity of the group, as each one of Laxmanrao's sons had already been placed in charge of a specific group of industries. This reduced the possibility of conflict in the group to the minimum. Functioning under a unified command, therefore, the house pursued a coordinated strategy. This involved seeking new markets for the products of their existing companies and launching new companies to enter new markets. The strategy pursued by Kirloskar Oil Engines is a case in point. To cope with declining demand for its products, the company resorted to exports and eventually captured the market in fourteen different countries. At the same time it added new models of engines, based on its own R&D efforts.

As Kirloskar Oil stabilized its operations, two major concerns were floated. These were Kirloskar Pneumatic set up in 1958 to manufacture compressors for air-conditioners, and Kirloskar Cummins Limited in 1962, the latter being a joint venture with a famous American firm, to produce internal combustion engines. After initial teething problems Kirloskar Cummins developed into one of the most profitable concerns in the private sector. Kirloskar Electricals charted a similar course.

Among the factors that helped the Kirloskars to improve their performance was the choice of product lines. Most of the goods they produced were such that the expanding economy of India could easily absorb, even though the demand situation sometimes became precarious. The Lalbhais were not so fortunate. Their product portfolio was dominated by cotton textiles. Fortunately for them, in the Nehru era the industry was still far from the crisis that would grip it later. Being among the best managed in the industry, the Lalbhais' mills continued to maintain their profitable course. However, their starch factory, because of slackening demand, only somehow kept its head above water. Their chemical operations, centred around Atul Products Limited, too went through teething problems but eventually emerged as a most important producer of several batches of sophisticated dyes and pharmaceutical products. As in the case of the Kirloskars, the group remained united but various members of the family had responsibility for specific concerns.

The Walchand group too remained united during this period, but no more enjoyed the high profile image of the pre-Independence days. This was because the two remaining symbols of the founder's aggressive entrepreneurship (after the acquisition of Hindustan Aircraft by the government during the war) were lost to the group soon after Independence. Irreconcilable differences with Morarjee's widow Sumati and her son Shantakumar caused Walchand to sell off his entire holdings in Scindia Shipping in 1950 to them, and his Air Services of India was nationalized by the government in 1953—the year Walchand died. More down to earth and less aggressive, his successors continued to manage the remaining enterprises—Premier Automobiles, Premier Construction, and Ravalgaon Industries—with quiet determination, exploiting profitable opportunities both in India and abroad. But the group's focus was now mainly on consolidation; it showed little enthusiasm for expansion in the post-Independence era. The strategy paid rich dividends as reflected in the growth of its physical assets—from merely Rs 18 crore in 1951 to Rs 81 crore by 1969. The contribution of its construction company to this development was particularly significant. The Shri Rams also primarily concentrated on consolidating their diverse businesses but their gains were not as impressive. The death of Lala Shri Ram in 1963 could have been one of the factors that arrested their growth, although they did add a couple of companies during the 1960s.

The Shapoorjis, Khataus, and Seshasayees were among the other older houses that prospered only marginally or even declined after Independence. The Shapoorjis had come into the limelight with the acquisition of F.E. Dinshaw's interests in Associated Cement Companies just before the outbreak of World War II. Soon after the war, they acquired a 42 per cent minority interest in Bombay Dyeing, India's largest single exporter of cotton textiles then, and took over control of a reputable British managing agency firm, W.H. Brady. The house, however, remained practically aloof from the actual management of these concerns and continued to concentrate on its construction business. The Seshasayees' decline was due to the loss of a number of government companies for which they were managing agents up to 1960. Consequent upon a change in the Companies Act, no concern in which government had substantial interest was allowed to be under a managing agent. Most of their companies, including their flagship Fertilizers and Chemicals Travancore Ltd. (FACT) belonged to this category. Other companies under their management were modest ventures in which they had slender financial participation. With the loss of the government-controlled companies, the Seshasayees faded out of the Indian industrial scene by the end of the 1960s. The Khataus declined because of their overdependence on a single product.

No business house, however, suffered as steep a fall in its position in the Indian business world as the house of Dalmia-Sahu Jain did. The upward progress of the house continued unabated for more than a decade after Independence. During this period, the group acquired a number of companies which were previously under British control including Bennett, Coleman & Co. (the publishers of the *Times of India*) and the Govan group of companies. Several others, such as Punjab National Bank and three large jute mills of Andrew Yule came under the Dalmias umbrella through stock manipulation. Their Rohtas Industries, in the meantime, diversified into sugar, paper, vanaspati, chemicals, spun pipe, etc. Trading and speculation continued simultaneously. As a result of these expansions, effected between 1947 and

1951, the group developed into one of the four largest business houses in the country.

The fortunes of the house, however, declined as fast as they had risen. The process started with the quiet break-up of the combine in 1952—the first major business split in independent India—with Ram Krishna Dalmia and his son-in-law Shreyans Prasad Jain dividing the assets. The split did not immediately affect the fortunes of the group and remained a closely guarded secret for a number of years. What really hurt the group was the involvement of the founder in several cases of tax evasion. Many shady business practices were brought to light in 1962 by a special commission appointed by the Government of India. Dalmia was convicted and imprisoned. This caused an irreparable damage to the reputation of the group from which it never recovered. No other business group in India had such a meteoric rise or such an abrupt and disgraceful fall. The two factions that emerged from the split, the Dalmias and the Jains, continued to remain in business but neither ever reached anywhere close to the position they had unitedly held almost up to the end of 1950s.

Among the major business groups that met their doom after freedom were two prominent diversified business groups of pre-Independence days. One of these was the mighty Calcuta-based Martin Burn. It remained the third largest group in the country with interest in iron and steel, engineering, power, construction, light railways, and refractories well until the end of the 1960s. Decline set in because the management headed by Sir Biren Mookerjee could not cope with the continuing labour troubles that vitiated the business environment in West Bengal beyond measure during the mid-1960s. The situation became so serious that it became necessary for the Government of India to acquire the companies under the Martin Burn management in 1967. Thus passed into history one of the oldest and most distinguished industrial families Bengal ever produced.

The other was the house of Indra Singh that had developed during the two World Wars and undergone substantial expansion during the first decade after Independence. Though counted among the largest twenty groups in the country during the 1950s, it disappeared from the scene during the next decade, though the exact circumstances of its exit are not known. Another business house that had a brief period of glory had come into being soon after Independence thanks to the enterprising zeal of V. Ramakrishna of the Indian Civil Service. Belonging to the Kamma caste of Andhra Pradesh, he prematurely retired from service to launch an industrial concern in 1948. He soon expanded his interest in sugar, cement, and engineering during the 1950s. The division of his assets among his children after his retirement from business resulted in the house losing its prominence in the Indian business world by the mid-1960s.

THE NEW ENTRANTS

Cases of total eclipse, however, were few and far between. In the meantime, a multitude of new groups emerged. Some of these, though still backbenchers in the pre-Independence days, had already achieved a measure of success before 1947. This included the Bajajs, the Mahindras, the Godrejs, the Singhanias, and the Bangurs. Trading was the mainstay of the Bajajs before Independence though they had a small sugar mill under their control. During the post-freedom era, the group under the leadership of the founder's two sons, Kamal Nayan and Ramkrishna, and grandson Rahul diversified into electrical appliances and two-wheelers and three-wheelers, in collaboration with reputed producers of these goods in developed industrial countries. The group carved out an enviable position in the production of scooters for which they captured a sizeable market both in India and abroad. Though technically a part of the Bajaj group, Mukund Iron and Steel Company developed almost independently of it under the direction of Viren Shah, the son of Jeewanlal Motichand who had joined hands with Jamanlal to acquire this concern from its original founder in 1937. Engaged in producing steel and alloy castings, high carbon wire rods, cranes, and equipment for steel plants and chemical industry, the company captured a substantial export market for its products.

The Mahindras' upward growth started in 1947 when they secured a franchise for distribution of jeep vehicles in India from Willys Overland Company of the United States. They later undertook the assembly and phased manufacturing of jeeps, in which field they became market leader within a decade. The house also acquired a well-known British trading firm, Turner Hoare, in 1948 with minority participation by the Tatas. Manufacturing became the Mahindras' principal activity as they gained strength, producing, in collaboration with well-known international firms, goods that few in India produced such as elevators, tractors, alloy steel, and hydraulic equipment. Although most of their products had a ready market in India, some, particularly jeeps, were in demand in other countries as well. The group had its own share of troubles, but on the whole it achieved tremendous growth within a relatively short period, primarily because of imaginative mangement by well-educated and technically qualified leaders. Not only the founders but also their successors, Keshub and Harish, who guided the destiny of the firm during a major part of its still very short history, had their education in some of the best institutions in the world. Significantly, the Mahindras' control over their companies was primarily due to the faith the financial institutions and foreign collaborators, who together held a substantial chunk of the equity, had in their managerial capabilities.

The Bangur house too emerged as a major player in Indian business only after Independence. Although the Bangurs had made a fortune through trading before the outbreak of World War II, their industrial presence was inconspicuous when the war ended. Acquiring a number of jute mills from the European managing agencies after the war, the Bangurs had already grown sufficiently big by 1951 to be counted among the twenty largest groups in the country. Acquisitions of companies, then under the British control, continued unabated during the 1950s: Kettelwell Bullen, an old British agency house in 1954, and a little later Bengal Coal and Midnapore Zamindary from Andrew Yule, and Bengal Paper from Balmer Lawrie. Though the house teamed up with G.D. Somany, another Marwari family, to float a few small concerns during this period, acquisition remained its preferred route to growth. So fast did the Bangurs expand that within a short period of a decade after Independence, the number of companies under their control had gone up to more than one hundred with an aggregate share capital of about Rs 20 crore.

Preceding the Bajaj, Mahindra, and Bangur groups by several decades, the Godrejs still had modest-sized operations making security equipment, refined oils, and toilet soaps in 1947. It was only after World War II that they began to move into more complex fields such as typewriters and office furniture. Launching a refrigerator production unit in the 1960s was a pioneering initiative, as Allwyn of Hyderabad was the only other company in the field. Strangely enough, the Godrej group did not float new companies; it preferred to consolidate its gains and expand under the umbrella of the two companies formed before 1920: Godrej Boyce & Co. and Godrej Soaps. Both these companies remained closely held. And yet the house of Godrej, that had an insignificant local presence in 1947, became an all India group within just two decades, and also expanded abroad—mainly in Malaysia and Singapore. Much of the credit for this remarkable record goes to the second generation of leaders—founder Ardeshir Burjorji Godrej's sons, particularly Ardeshir and Pirojsha, and grandsons Sohrabji, Burjorji, and Naoroji (Naval).

The Singhanias too, previously confined mainly to Kanpur, developed into an all-India group only after Independence when they took control of Muir Mills in Kanpur from the British owners, Raymond Woollen Mill in Bombay from the Sassoons, and Ganges Manufacturing from Macneill and Barry in Calcutta. These acquisitions helped them diversify into chemicals, synthetics, manmade fibre, sugar, paper, tyres, cement, aluminium, and insurance. With factories in Uttar Pradesh, Rajasthan, Maharashtra, Orissa, and Bengal, they acquired a national character by the end of the Nehru era.

Unlike the five groups discussed above, who had already developed some industrial interests when Independence came, at least twenty new industrial groups—counting only those whose businesses had national dimensions—developed almost from the scratch during the Nehru era. Some of these had a trading background while many were new entrants in the world of business. The most important in the first category were the Goenkas, Kalyanis, Khaitans, and Ruias, and the three houses based in Goa—the Chowgules, Salagaonkars, and Dempos. Those who started from the scratch but carved out niches for themselves in the world of Indian business included Dhirubhai Ambani of Reliance fame, Mammen Mappillai of MRF Tyres, Brij Mohan Lall Munjal of Hero, S. Anantharamakrishnan of the Amalgamations Group, Ramanbhai Patel of Cadila, Uttambhai Mehta of Torrent, Raunaq Singh of Apollo Tyres, Hari P. Nanda of Escorts, Bhai Mohan Singh of Ranbaxy, and Mohan Singh Oberoi of the Oberoi group of hotels. Brief accounts of their antecedents and growth should provide an understanding of the changing character of Indian business during this period.

Among the groups mentioned in the first category, the Goenkas had the most spectacular rise. A family of Rajasthani traders, the Goenkas' fortunes began to rise when they moved to Calcutta around the turn of the nineteenth century. Operating as banians to some prominent British agency houses, and general traders and moneylenders, they gradually became one of the most influential Marwari families in Calcutta, next only to the Birlas whose might Badridas (later Sir), the head of the Goenka clan, openly challenged soon after World War I. Unlike the Birlas, however, the Goenkas primarily remained traders until Independence, working as banians for Duncan Brothers, Octavius Steel, Ralli Brothers, and Kettelwell and Bullen, which were counted among the most important European agency houses of their time.

By the time India became free, Badridas had practically retired from active leadership and the next generation—his sons and his brother Hariram's sons—had already assumed command. The family's industrial career started under their leadership with Keshav Prasad, Badridas's elder son, playing the most critical role in the affairs of the house. Transition from trade to industry was marked by the acquisition of Octavius Steel, controlling a sugar mill, a colliery, and four power supply companies. Having decided to pull out of India soon after Independence, this British managing agency firm sold off its interests to its erstwhile banian. The process of acquiring Duncan Brothers, the other firm for which the Goenkas had acted as banian, started soon after the Octavius Steel acquisition and was completed in gradual stages by 1963. Duncan Brothers had several tea gardens and a jute mill under their control. As the tea business was badly hit by a continuing slump during the 1950s, Duncan Brothers turned to their banian for funds, who were glad to oblige their erstwhile patrons, until the former decided to transfer control of their companies to the Goenkas. This happened in 1963. In the meantime, Keshav Prasad and his brother Lukhi Prasad had split from their cousins, the sons of Hariram, with the Octavius Steel companies going to the share of the Hariram faction and the Duncan Brothers' companies remaining with Keshav Prasad and his brother.

While the Hariram faction showed little interest in expansion, it became a passion with the Badridas branch. Although new companies were occasionally floated, acquisition was the most preferred strategy adopted by Keshav Prasad and his brother. During a short period of three years between 1966 and 1969, no less than three major concerns were acquired, including Coorla Mills and Asian Cables in Bombay, the latter founded by a cotton trader in 1959 with foreign collaboration to produce electric cables. The group also acquired a minority interest in an expatriate group, Balmer Lawrie. With these acquisitions, Keshav Prasad and his brother not only made a successful transition to industry, but also acquired a foothold in Bombay—the busiest business centre in the country.

The Khaitans were another Marwari family that rose to great prominence after Independence through acquiring British-controlled businesses. Unlike the Goenkas, however, the family had done little to distinguish itself in business, nor was it particularly wealthy at the time of Independence. Brij Mohan, the creator of the Khaitan business empire, started out as the supplier of fertilizers and plywood packaging crates to the tea plantations of Assam during the

1950s. In this process he became particularly close to Richard Magor, a partner in Williamson Magor, a tea plantation company operating in Assam since 1869. The firm was at one time counted among the three largest tea planters in India, but by the late 1950s it had been left with only eighteen gardens, and these too did not seem quite safe from the greedy designs of corporate raiders. Under these conditions, the partners offered to Brij Mohan a one-third interest in their firm. Because of his holdings in the firm and the absence of the British partners from India, Khaitan now became managing director of Williamson Magor. A few months later, he bought out the shares of a British shipping company in the firm, amounting to one-third of its equity. This gave him control of Williamson Magor and he became its chairman. The British partners, unable to deal with the growing restrictions on the functioning of private enterprise and continuing labour trouble, were happy to surrender the management to him. This was the beginning of a process of acquisitions of tea gardens that would eventually end up in Brij Mohan becoming the biggest individual tea planter in the world.

The Goenkas and the Khaitans were not the only Marwaris who made their debuts in industry with the acquisition of expatriate houses after Independence. Most other Calcutta-based Marwari trading families did likewise. It was a much easier way to register one's presence on the Indian industrial horizon than to float and organize new undertakings. And profits earned during the war came in handy for this purpose. The Ruias based in Madras took a more challenging route to growth. Nand Kishore Ruia had been trading in imported trucks and exporting groundnut oil and cotton from Bombay and Madras before Independence. Madras, however, had become the effective headquarters of his business by the mid-1950s. This is where the Essar group (from the pronunciation of the first letters in the names of his two sons Shashi and Ravi) was born in the late 1960s. Though the company's operations were limited at this stage, the Ruias had already laid the foundation of a business with unlimited potential. Incidentally, the three Goa-based houses—the Chowgules, Salgaonkars, and Dempos—who got integrated with the mainstream of Indian business after the liberation of this Portuguese colony in 1962, also built their fortunes through shipping and iron ore export. All these three were controlled by Maharashtrian Brahman families. The Kalyani group too was founded by a Maharashtrian Brahman—Neelkanth A. Kalyani. His father was a trader in turmeric and groundnut. Encouraged by Y.B. Chavan, the-then Chief Minister of Maharashtra, and S.L. Kirloskar both of whom had been very close friends of his father, Neelkanth set up Bharat Forge with the financial support of Industrial Credit and Investment Corporation of India (ICICI) in 1964.

Very different from the persons whose entrepreneurial initiatives and exploits have already been discussed was Dhirubhai Hirachand Ambani, who would soon dwarf all other post-Independence entrants in the world of Indian business. The son of a village schoolteacher in western Gujarat, he started his career as a gas filler at a petrol station in Aden. The start to his business career came in 1958 with the setting up of a trading firm, Reliance Commercial Corporation, in Bombay which concentrated on exporting cashewnuts, pepper, nylon, rayon, and such other profitable commodities. The contacts he had built during his eight-year-long stay in Aden and the money he had earned from his various salaried jobs in the British colony stood him in good stead in this respect. He then started dealing in imported nylon which sold at a high premium in India as nobody in the country produced it. The government in the meantime launched a scheme permitting the import of nylon against the export of rayon that India produced. Taking advantage of the scheme, Ambani made substantial profits which helped him launch his own manufacturing operations. Reliance Textiles, was a modest undertaking which went entirely unnoticed when it was set up in Ahmedabad in 1966, but proved later to be the nucleus of a huge business empire.

While Ambani started his industrial career with a traditional line, many others made their industrial debuts with more sophisticated industries. K.M. Mammen Mappillai and Raunaq Singh, for instance, proved their mettle in producing automobiles tyres. Originally from Kerala, Mappillai brought his family back into business (his father had lost all his businesses way back in 1939) by setting up a rubber balloon factory in Madras soon after Independence. Tyre manufacturing started only in 1961 in collaboration with Mansfield Tyre and Rubber Company of the United States. Raunaq Singh, a refugee from Pakistan, started off as a trader of spices and steel pipes in 1947, but later took to producing steel pipes himself, with the bulk of the funds provided by Punjab National Bank. He moved into tyre manufacturing much later with the setting up of Apollo Tyres and Premier Tyres.

A number of new entrants into business concentrated on drug manufacturing. Prominent among these were Bhai Mohan Singh of Ranbaxy, Ramanbhai Patel of Cadila, and his fellow Gujarati Uttambhai Mehta of Torrent. Like Raunaq Singh, Bhai Mohan Singh was also a refugee from Pakistan, though in a much better financial position. He and his son Parvinder started off with a financing business in the course of which they advanced funds to Ranbaxy, a Delhi-based distributor of pharmaceutical products and sole franchisee of an Italian drug manufacturer, Lepetit. They acquired the firm when it became bankrupt in 1954 and started manufacturing drugs themselves. As the profits soared, the company went public, and its shares were sold at a high premium. The group later diversified into health-care by setting up MAX India, and also floated Montari Industries. Cadila was the joint creation of Indravadan Modi, the chief chemist in a company, and Ramanbhai Patel, a pharmacy teacher in a college at Ahmedabad, who decided in 1951 to put their expertise to better use. Torrent owed its origin to the founder's own health problem. Uttambhai Mehta, a medical representative, had to quit his job with Sandoz (India) because of physical illness. Using the small amount of money he had received as severance pay, he launched the company, producing drugs for the kind of ailments from which he himself suffered. By early 1969, Torrent had already grown into a substantial concern.

The emphasis on steel and steel-based industries in India's Five-Year Plans attracted a number of new entrepreneurs to these fields including Kulwant Rai, Om Prakash Jindal, and Mohan Lal Mittal. Rai, belonging to Haryana, traded in steel pipes in Calcutta for some time before setting up a steel rolling mill with Japanese technology in Madras in 1956, the first enterprise of this kind in south India. As the business developed, he diversified into semi-conductors in collaboration with an American company. The joint venture, Usha Rectifier, was later named Usha India. Jindal, another Haryanvi, also started off as a trader in Calcutta but returned to his native state where he set up Jindal India to make steel buckets in 1957. He later integrated backward to make steel strip in 1970 which eventually took the group into stainless steel. Mittal's first business was an oil mill that he set up in Kanpur, leaving his family in Karachi, just before the partition. A flood in 1949 swept away his factory and forced him to take to trading in scrap metal. Hindustan Shipyard was one of the sources from which he bought the scrap. This eventually led to the setting up of a rolling mill, Andhra Steel Corporation, in 1956 which would later develop into the Ispat group.

Five major groups—SPIC-MAC, Escorts, TVS, Hero, and Amalgamation—originated with the entrepreneurs perceiving an opportunity in the need to produce power-driven vehicles within easy reach of the relatively less affluent sections of society. M.A. Chidambaram who later developed the SPIC-MAC group, was the first to take a meaningful initiative in this respect. Belonging to a family of indigenous bankers, he started his industrial career with the manufacture of scooters in 1957 under the brand name of 'Lambretta' in collaboration with an Italian company. This was a pioneering initiative as his Bombay-based company, Automobile Products of India, was the first to produce scooters in the country. However, with the entry of new manufacturers in the field, including Bajaj, Lambretta could not writhstand the competition. Chidambaram, therefore, moved out of this line altogether and took to producing fertilizers in 1969 for which purpose he set up a plant at Tuticorin, a backward area in Tamil Nadu. This led the group into chemicals and petroproducts under the leadership of Chidambaram's son, A.C. Muthiah.

Escorts was the creation of Hari Prasad Nanda. Originally set up as Escort Agents Limited in 1944, the firm held the franchise for distributing electrical appliances produced by Westinghouse, the well-known American corporation, in Punjab. The division of the subcontinent and of Punjab put paid to all Nanda's dreams and forced him to move to Delhi with his entire family but without any money. Using a bank loan, he first launched into a transport business, but later acquired a franchise from an American firm famous for producing agricultural implements. Trading in second-hand cars, acquired from the British officials departing after the end of colonial rule, was a side business. The cars, bought relatively cheaply, were renovated and sold with substantial profit. As its financial position improved, the firm took to manufacturing motorcycles, tractors, and earth-moving equipment with Polish, American, and Japanese collaboration. Its progress was so rapid that within less than three decades, Escorts emerged as one of the most prominent manufacturing concerns in the country.

Like Escorts, two of the major corporate houses in the south started off as transport operators. T.V. Sundaram Iyengar, the founder of TVS and Sons, was an automobile dealer before Independence. After Independence, he launched a road transport service and then moved into manufacturing of automobile parts and power-driven bicycles. The other, the Amalgamation group of companies, emerged from the Indianization of Simpsons, an expatriate firm operating a transport service in Madras. S. Anantharamakrishnan, who had been inducted into the Simpsons board in 1938, acquired the controlling interest in the group, gave it its present name, and led it into industry, manufacturing tractors, diesel engines, farm implements, machine tools, automobile parts, and other such items. Both these groups are controlled by Tamil Brahmans.

Hero's is a rags-to-riches story. Its founder Brij Mohan Lall Munjal was a refugee from Pakistan who set up a cycle repairing shop in Ludhiana to begin with but later moved into manufacturing bicycle parts, and eventually bicycle itself in 1956. Until then, all bicycle-manufacturing units were located in metropolitan centres and none of them was particularly noted for quality. Munjal challenged their monopoly. Munjal was not the first to launch cycle production in Ludhiana. Two other companies, Atlas and Avon, founded by refugees like him, had already started production. Offering quality products at reasonable prices based on large volumes and tight cost control, these companies eventually drove the products of enterprises set up by large business houses, including the Birlas' Hind Cycles, out of the market. By 1969 the Hero group emerged the most successful of them.

The entry of an Indian, with no business experience, into liquour manufacturing was a somewhat surprising development. For this had been the exclusive preserve of expatriates so far and the influence of Gandhi, a champion of prohibition, was still substantial during the early years of freedom. But Vittal Mallya, the son of an army doctor and trained as a scientist, defied these discouraging factors. He had started his career as a stockbroker in Calcutta. Watching the operations of the stock markets from close quarters, he started acquiring shares of United Breweries, a British brewery firm based in Bangalore with McDowell and Company as its flagship enterprise. The process eventually culminated in Mallya acquiring a controlling interest in United Breweries soon after Independence. New breweries were added to United Braweries during the 1960s.

A prominent house emerged in the hospitality industry with the rise of the Oberoi group of hotels. Its founder Mohan Singh Oberoi was a clerk in Clark's Hotel at Simla in 1933 when a plague epidemic in Calcutta gave him an opportunity to be the owner of a hotel himself. The Grand Hotel in the city, one of the most prominent hospitality outfits in the entire country, was virtually deserted because of the epidemic. Mohan Singh took the premises on lease, and ran it so efficiently that within a few years he was able to buy it up. Oberoi earned huge profits during World War II which enabled him to acquire control of the British-owned Associated Hotels combine, operating the largest chain of hotels in India at that time, soon after the war. The real expansion of the group, however, took place after Independence through a twin strategy of acquiring existing hotels and building new ones—not only in India but also abroad.

The foregoing is only a small sample of the new businesses that emerged during the period under review. But it is sufficient to indicate that the new policy regime, despite restrictions placed on the working of the free enterprise system, also opened up new opportunities for native entrepreneurs. The fact that, barring a few exceptions, practically all the major houses that dominated Indian business before Independence underwent substantial expansion and consolidation, suggests the same thing. The Nehru government is very often criticized for introducing an economic system that was inherently obstructive of the private sector. But the brief review here of the performance of Indian private sector proves just the opposite.

THE PUBLIC SECTOR

Nehru is also criticized for giving undue importance to the public sector at the cost of the private sector in his development strategy. The facts, however, suggest otherwise. Out of the total number of sixty-seven public sector undertakings set up during his lifetime, only about fifty were engaged in what may be considered business activities in the real sense. Others were mainly concerned with providing consultancy services in various fields, developing physical infrastructure like roads and bridges, and organizing warehousing facilities or helping agriculture with better seeds and other inputs. Only fifteen of these fifty companies were large organizations requiring heavy outlay such as Bharat Heavy Electricals Ltd, Oil and Natural Gas Commission, Indian Oil Corporation, Air India and Indian Airlines, Hindustan Machine Tools, four steel plants, and a few oil refineries and chemical companies. The goods and services that most of these companies produced were urgently needed to create a multiplier effect on the development efforts. The private sector, constituted as it was at that time, was ill-equipped to undertake the task with alacrity, given the cost and complexity involved. It should also be borne in mind that the geopolitical situation in and around the country at that time made it incumbent on the government to keep certain strategic sectors under its control. It is possible that some of the public sector undertakings were set up primarily because of the overenthusiasm of the bureaucracy to prove its commitment to the ideology of the new government, as I.G. Patel, a knowledgeable insider has suggested. On the whole, however, the public sector during Nehru's times remained essentially within the bounds of the balance between the private enterprise and state intervention that was at the heart of his development strategy.

Much of the hue and cry against the public sector was due to the fact that most of the state undertakings had a much longer gestation period than expected or planned. None of them started showing profits when they should have, and even when they turned the corner, only a few registered profits on a sustained basis and at a reasonable rate. Lack of experience in enterprise management on the part of the government was primarily responsible for this state of affairs. The colonial administration had left behind a reasonably efficient bureaucracy but it was hardly equipped to manage industrial enterprises. In the absence of an alternative, the post-Independence government had to depend on the same administrative infrastructure to run the public sector undertakings that ran the general administration. In fact, heads of public undertakings and general administration were drawn from a common pool, and persons occupying top posts in the two streams moved back and forth. As positions in the general administration were more eagerly sought after, perhaps because they carried more power and prestige, public sector appointments were looked upon merely as transit points or even as punishment postings.

Realizing that this was hardly conducive to efficient management, towards the close of the Nehru era the government decided to develop a special managerial cadre for public-sector undertakings. This, along with some other measures, eventually helped some of the major public sector companies turn around, vindicating to an extent the philosophy behind the concept. But before they could sufficiently wash off the stigma of non-performance, other factors intervened, as shall be discussed in the next chapter, to bring undeserved disrepute to the concept itself.

EXPATRIATES AND MULTINATIONALS

While the public sector was still struggling to live up to the expectations towards the end of the Nehru era, the private sector was displacing the British expatriates who had been in an unassailable position in India almost until the onset of Independence. A large number of expatriates began to feel shaky as the end of the British rule drew closer and decided to sell off their enterprises. In fact, a few of the major Indian groups like the Goenkas made their debut in industry with the acquisition of expatriate firms, and some entered new product lines through the same route. Even a few brave spirits among the expatriates who decided to stay on felt compelled to reconsider their decision as the years passed. Andrew Yule and Bird are examples of such firms. Of these, the former began to divest itself of its companies in bits and pieces soon after Independence, either selling them off to Indian houses such as the Dalmias, Bangurs, and Goenkas or diluting its interest. By the mid-1960s, Andrew Yule was left with only a few companies under its control. Even these the house could not effectively manage, largely because of the continuing labour unrest in West Bengal during this period, and they were taken over by the Union government in 1967. Thus disappeared from the Indian business one of the largest and oldest European groups. Martin Burn too, as mentioned before, was taken over by the government because the management could not cope with the difficult labour situation in West Bengal. Many other sick units belonging to expatriate houses were taken over by the government during the latter half of the 1960s and early years of the 1970s.

Bird fared slightly better and lost only a few companies to Indian houses after Independence. The foreign investors in the firm continued to disinvest to individual Indians and institutions during the 1950s, but these disinvestments seem to have been guided by normal business consideration; they did not necessarily indicate gradual steps towards ultimate withdrawal from India. In fact, Bird was still the third largest group in the Indian corporate sector at the end of the 1950s. But the management could not have viewed without misgiving the rising restrictions on the functioning of the private sector and the deteriorating labour situation in Bengal where most of its companies were located. Whatever the case, a custom enquiry in the affairs of the company in 1964, resulting in substantial penalties, broke the old camel's back and the Benthall family which held the controlling interest decided to withdraw from the scene altogether. The method chosen for disinvestment was unique in the Indian context. Instead of selling out to others in the corporate sector, the management decided to let the employees and executives acquire the controlling stocks of the foreign owners mainly through their pensions and savings funds. This was perhaps the first and only occasion in the history of Indian business when the employees of a large enterprise became its virtual owners through an imaginative and innovative strategy—quietly and painlessly executed. It is another matter that this arrangement did not last very long and the company was eventually taken over by the government in 1976.

Many other Calcutta-based expatriate firms resorted to a variety of ways to meet the situation. Some like Shaw Wallace, Mackinon Mackenzie, and James Warren, that had remained partnership firms ever since their inception, were converted into public limited or private limited companies, opening themselves to financial participation by Indians. A few like Macneill and Barry, James Finlay, and Gillanders Arbuthnot sold off large equity stakes to reputed Indian houses or individuals, while people like Lord Inchcape decided to disband their Indian enterprises, and several expatriate groups, as already discussed, were acquired by Indian houses. The net result of these various processes of disinvestment was that by the end of the 1980s, expatriate enterprise in eastern India became virtually a thing of the past. Assam Company was the only prominent undertaking that did not fall into Indian hands until 1991, when it was taken over by the Mehta group, founded by Nanji Kalidas Mehta in the early 1930s with a textile mill at Porbander in Gujarat. A Marwari group headed by K.K. Jajodia later acquired the controlling interest in this company from the Mehtas who now operate abroad and have a rather inconspicuous presence in India.

Like their counterparts in the east, the major expatriate groups in the south also tried to hold on to their Indian empires for some time but eventually gave up. Both Parry and Binny went through expansion and reorganization during the 1950s and 1960s. Both ceased to be sterling firms under the British law soon after Independence, and were registered as joint stock companies in India—Parry in 1948 and Binny in 1963. This change in their status provided an opportunity to Indian investors, including financial institutions, to acquire their shares as the foreign interests continued to dilute their holdings. Parry in the process gradually came under the control of public financial institutions by the end of the 1960s and was eventually taken over by the Murugappa group in the mid-1970s. The Inchcape group, however, held on to its controlling interest in Binny until the end of the 1970s. But with textiles being the mainstay of the Binny business, the firm continued to make losses as the industry was overtaken by an unending crisis. To add to Binny's problems, a disastrous flood in Madras in 1978 caused considerable damage to its factories. The company could not withstand the cumulative assaults. The government eventually took over its management in 1980.

While the older expatriate firms gradually disappeared from the scene after Independence, a young expatriate enterprise ran against the current. This was Larsen & Toubro (L&T), founded by two Danish engineers, Henning Holck-Larsen and Soren Kristian Toubro shortly before the war. Both of them had worked as the representatives of a reputed firm of their country in India for a number of years before hitting upon a business proposition of their own. Shortly before the outbreak of World War II, they decided to quit their jobs to form a partnership—Larsen & Toubro—to import and supply capital goods to Indian industry. The outbreak of World War II, however, conspired against all their plans, forcing their firm to maintain a shaky existence, doing odd jobs.

Their most ambitious venture launched during the war was a public limited company, Hilda Limited, registered in June 1943. The sole business of Hilda

Limited was to operate a floating workshop for ship repairing off the Bombay coast on board R.V. Hilde, an Italian vessel the British navy had captured. As the government compensated the company at a fixed rate over the actual cost incurred, the operations involved virtually no risk and proved quite lucrative while the hostilities lasted. With the end of the war, however, the very *raison d'etre* of Hilda's existence disappeared, consigning it to the status of a mere paper company. It was wound up and amalgamated with a new company, Larsen & Toubro Private Limited, in 1946 to resume the business of importing and supplying capital goods to Indian companies, demand for which multiplied with the coming of Independence. Despite its manufacturing pretensions, Larsen & Toubro essentially remained a trading concern for more than a decade after Independence. However, it had to launch a vigorous manufacturing programme in 1958 mainly because the Government of India, concerned about a dwindling foreign-exchange position, cancelled the bulk of its import licences. This proved a blessing in disguise, for progress on the manufacturing front was swift thereafter, with the result that within just a decade, L&T emerged as one of the most reputed and largest engineering enterprises in the nation's private sector.

With the loss of political patronage, a major source of their strength before Independence, the expatriates felt rather insecure in the new India but the subsidiaries controlled by foreign multinationals continued to expand their presence. At least six large undertakings of British origin alone were set up during the Nehru era. They by and large operated in fields in which they faced relatively less competition from indigenous interests. As Indians were increasingly expanding into new fields, responding to the emphasis on import substitution, in the government policies, the multinationals seem to have exercised a great deal of caution in setting up new subsidiaries. The parent firms continued to exercise very tight control over the financial structures of these subsidiaries, but were keen to identify their Indian operations with India. They Indianized their management gradually and at least two of them changed their names to signify a closer link with the main theatre of their business. Unilever (India) was the first to do so when it became Hindustan Lever Limited (HLL) in 1956. The company was also the first to appoint an Indian, Prakash L. Tandon, as the chairman of its board in 1964. The Imperial Tobacco Company followed suit with the appointment of Ajit N. Haksar to succeed C.A. Bone as chairman in 1969. A year later the company replaced the obnoxious 'Imperial' in its name with 'India'.

Both HLL and India Tobacco Company (ITC) registered substantial growth after Independence. They entered new fields and set up their own subsidiaries. HLL developed an enviable reputation in fields such as soap, toiletries, detergents, and animal feed; with with the acquisition of Lipton Tea Company, it emerged as a major player in this field also. Its subsidiaries set up during this period included Indexport, Lever Associated Trust, Levindia Trust, and Hindustan Trust Limited. Its manufacturing programmes were fed not only by the production process developed by its parent firm but also through a vigorous programme of research and development—not a common feature of the Indian business scene at that time. As for ITC, it remained essentially a cigarette manufacturing concern until the end of the 1960s.

Most of the other multinational subsidiaries also registered good progress. The subsidiaries set up by petroleum multinationals, however, deserve special mention. At the time of Independence, India was almost wholly dependent on imports for petroleum products. The government of free India would have liked to develop the oil resources under the exclusive control of the state—the industrial policy statements unambiguously reserved the field for the public sector—but for the fact that it was almost impossible to undertake this gigantic task, given the resources of the government at that time. Three major international producers of oil—Burmah Shell, Standard Vacuum, and Caltex—were invited to set up refineries on terms extremely favourable to them. Controlling every aspect of the operation, from exploration of crude to the marketing of petroleum products, the Indian subsidiaries of these vertically integrated giants reaped enormous profits for more than a decade. The entry of the erstwhile Soviet Union into the world oil market in the late 1950s and its offer of crude to India in the middle of the 1960s on very reasonable terms enabled the government to establish state-owned oil refineries in India under the overall supervision of Indian Oil Corporation—a public sector undertaking incorporated in 1964. This, however, made little dent on the fortunes of the foreign firms during the period under review. Things would change drastically for them only a few years later.

At the end of the Nehru era, no major constituent of Indian business, except the expatriates, had any reason to complain.

CHAPTER 13

THE LICENCE–PERMIT RAJ

TO THE GENERAL MASSES, THE 1969 BANK NATIONALIZATION MUST HAVE appeared to be in tune with the left-of-the centre programme of economic transformation evolved by the Nehru government. This was obvious from the rousing reception the decision spontaneously received from the nation. It was perhaps taken for granted that Indira Gandhi would not deviate from the basic prescriptions of her father for nation building. But the measure, was in fact, a cruel blow to the Nehruvian balance between state intervention and freedom of enterprise. And many of her other radical measures to tighten the noose around private enterprise went far to the left of the Nehruvian model.

These included the establishment of Monopolies and Restrictive Trade Practices (MRTP) Commission, vested with the statutory authority to check the rise of monopoly positions in the private sector. Business groups whose assets were Rs 200 crore or more could not now undertake any substantial expansion without scrutiny and clearance from MRTP Commission. A year later, a new licencing policy was announced which barred large houses from a number of key sectors. Further modifications effected in 1973 added new and sharper teeth to the licencing requirements. That some of these policy measures emerged from the recommendations of committees appointed before Mrs Gandhi assumed power (for example MRTP Commission and Industrial Licencing Act of 1970) does not absolve her government from the responsibility of enacting them. Her regime also witnessed indiscriminate expansion of the public sector, nationalization of the coal industry, and mounting restrictions on foreign capital investment. Even more serious was an impression that the Indira Gandhi government was against private enterprise—an impression that Nehru never allowed to gain strength about his government. Nehru had built a great deal of national consensus behind his left-of-the-centre strategy for development. His daughter caused serious rupture to that consensus, if not completely destroyed it—perhaps unwittingly.

As if this was not enough to vitiate the business climate, another war with Pakistan in 1971 added to inflationary pressure. The mounting economic crisis for the common people, coming in the wake of rising prices of essential goods, injected a new life in the opposition offensive—disorganized and ineffective until the mid-1970s. Unable to meet their united challenge, a confused Prime Minister declared internal Emergency—a measure provided for in the nation's Constitution to meet extreme situations posing a serious threat to the republic—and for all practical purposes suspended the democratic processes. Between 20 June 1975, when Emergency was declared, and March 1977 when Mrs Gandhi's Congress Party lost the general election to the Janata Party (formed on the eve of the elections by the entire Opposition minus the Left parties) all governmental activities were directed to one single objective: the survival of the beleaguered Prime Minister. The Janata Party government, however, remained more preoccupied with infighting than governance and had to make room for Mrs Gandhi and her party within a little more than two years when she emerged triumphant in a mid-term poll held in January 1980. The entire decade of the 1970s, thus, was by far the most tumultuous period in the life of the young nation.

This is the kind of milieu that normally breeds inefficiency, misgovernance, sycophancy, and corruption, and India during those fateful years was no different. Practically every aspect of the development strategy perfected during Nehru's times was, as a result, overstretched, distorted, and even mutilated to accommodate the interests of those who were in a position to ingratiate themselves to the powers that be and their hangers-on. In fact, all those unanticipated distortions of the Nehru strategy, which have been discussed in an earlier chapter, began to surface and eat into the vitals of the body politic only during the 1970s. Since the distortions basically sprang from the control regime originally introduced by the government of Indira Gandhi's own party, headed by her own father, the entire Nehru–Gandhi administration is very often dubbed as the licence–permit raj. The sobriquet, however, appropriately belongs to Indira Gandhi's tenure alone. For it is unfair to hold Nehru accountable for the subsequent disfigurement of the basic policy structure created by his government.

The economic consequences of this disfigurement were disastrous for the nation. Except for agricultural production, all other indicators reflected consistently negative trends. Particularly hard hit was industrial production which grew at a snail's pace during the 1970s. Prices of practically everything continued to rise resulting in runaway inflation, and the rising budgetary deficit further aggravated the situation. Matters went so much out of control that even the draconian powers the government had assumed during the Emergency proved incapable of arresting the downhill trend, and the Janata interlude was too short-lived—and perhaps too rudderless—to repair the damage. For the most part of the 1970s thus private business had to contend with an exceedingly uncertain environment. In her second coming as Prime Minister there were some feeble indications of Mrs Gandhi adopting a more business-friendly posture, as will be seen in the next chapter, but she had yet to move into a definite direction in this respect when she fell to the assassin's bullets on 31 October 1984. The licence-permit raj was thus still quite entrenched until the middle of the 1980s. The performance of the private sector during this period has to be understood against this backdrop.

THE LEADING GROUPS

Let us first look at the older established groups, almost all of which had grown bigger and more prosperous by the end of the Nehru era. The largest of them all, the Tatas, had fully adjusted to the post-war situation as well as to the constraints and opportunities inherent in the post-colonial regime. They were still waiting for the government clearances of their proposals to expand the capacities of ACC and of the group's power companies and TELCO. Also, there was no sanction in sight for the plan to modernize TISCO's ageing plant. A number of other business proposals had either been turned down or had evoked no action. The government intransigence slowed down the Tatas' progress, and by 1976–7 they had to concede, for the first time, their first rank in the Indian business to the Birlas, their traditional rivals.

Surprisingly, the government sanctions for expansion the Tatas had been waiting for came only after Indira Gandhi was voted out of power. J.R.D.'s personal relations with the Prime Minister had always been very cordial and he had even supported the internal Emergency. His equation with the Janata Party leaders was never so close. In fact, one of the first acts of the new government headed by Morarji Desai was to remove J.R.D. from the chairmanship of Air India which he had held ever since the company was born. George Fernandes, Industry Minister in the new government, with his socialist professions was no friend of big business. He, at one stage, even contemplated nationalizing TISCO, a move that had to be given up because of vociferous protest from all quarters including Tata Workers' Union. And yet it was he who awarded the much awaited sanctions to the Tatas' applications for expanding their major undertakings. According to Fernandes, the earlier government had withheld the sanctions because, as a top Tata executive confided to him, 'the Tatas were not in the business of buying favours with money even if it meant a setback to their interests'.

With these sanctions, the Tatas moved forward with utmost vigour. With the financial help from World Bank, a new thermal power plant was added to the electric companies to generate 500 megawatts more power. The progress of the Tata system brought to it many turnkey projects in Africa and West Asia which were successfully completed. The TELCO expansion resulted in the setting up a brand new factory at Poona which more than doubled the existing capacity. A part of the money for the TELCO expansion was raised from subscriptions from non-resident Indians on a repatriable basis, although Reserve Bank's schemes for inducing the non-resident Indians to invest money in India on a repatriable basis had not yet been introduced.

As a result of all these initiatives, the Tatas once again regained their number one position in the Indian corporate world by the beginning of the 1980s. Around the same time, the first phase of the modernization programme of TISCO was completed under the dynamic leadership of Russi Mody who became the chairman of the company in 1984—a position that J.R.D. himself had held till then—and Tata Chemicals finally launched its fertilizer plants. As the national environment turned a little more stable and the ferocity of the licence-permit raj showed signs of waning by the beginning of the 1980s, the Tatas' suppressed energy for new initiatives received a boost and they set up as many as fourteen new companies during the 1980s. The house also acquired in 1983 the shares of James Finlay & Co. in Tata Finlay, their joint tea venture with the British firm, which now became Tata Tea.

The Birlas too concentrated on nursing what they already had instead of launching new ventures during this period. They were much less constrained than the Tatas in this respect, as they already had a number of licences. If they refrained from utilizing them, it was perhaps because they found the environment in the country during the 1970s too volatile for prudent investment. Their propensity for business expansion found expression in setting up overseas ventures—a course which Aditya Birla had already embarked upon with the launching of Indo-Thai Synthetics in 1969. Between 1970 and 1981, almost a dozen companies were set up in Indonesia, Malaysia, Thailand, and the Phillipines. Winning the support of the governments in these countries and raising finances for their ventures through stock markets, Aditya's initiatives resulted in substantial expansion in the Birlas' overseas empire during the 1970s. The Birlas' enterprises emerged as leaders in the manufacture of viscose staple fibre, palm oil, and carbon black in these countries which badly needed these products in their bid for speedy industrialization. The success of these ventures encouraged the Birlas to add about half a dozen more companies overseas during the 1980s.

With signs of improvement in the business environment by the beginning of the 1980s, the Birlas would probably have turned their attention to inland expansion also but for the problems they had to face as a result of the death of Ghanshyam Das Birla on 11 June 1983. Although the Birla companies, both in India and abroad, functioned in the name of the group, various members of the large Birla clan were handling the affairs of the companies under their charge almost independently, subject to the general guidance of the patriarch. Most of the old business families were falling apart due to reasons that shall be discussed later. If the Birlas still maintained a semblance of unity, it was because of the unifying force of the founder's personality. Soon after the patriarch's death, the forces of disintegration that had been kept in check asserted themselves, and the process of adjusting to the new situation took several years. Six independent groups of the Birlas eventually emerged by the end of the decade out of what had remained a unified house until the middle of the 1980s. Going through the painful, and often acrimonious, process of division, the Birlas were hardly in a position to expand their empire.

The division of the group was based on a blueprint prepared by G.D. Birla in his lifetime. The lion's share went to the Basant Kumar–Aditya Birla combine which claimed most of the prized companies in the group, accounting for almost half the total assets of the entire house. The division was essentially informed by a practice common among the Marwaris whereby the businesses created and developed by a member normally go to his share in the event of a family split. Notwithstanding the family spilt, the Aditya Birla group retained its number two position in the Indian business world, next only to the Tatas.

Though the Tatas and the Birlas did not expand very much during the 1970s, they also did not contract by losing any of their existing companies consequent upon growing governmental intervention in the economy. The

Thapars were not so lucky, losing all their collieries as a result of the nationalization of the coal industry in 1973. This, however, made only a minor dent on the prosperity of the house as it was left undisturbed in its coal distribution operations. Also, its Ballarpur Industries made impressive progress. The company took to manufacturing glass containers in 1975 and acquired or set up a number of factories in various parts of the country. The group also acquired substantial interest in a glass container unit in Malaysia, and set up two paper plants in Indonesia, collaborated with textile and paper producers in Thailand, and mounted trading operations and completed several turnkey projects in West Asia. Although the Thapars' bid to acquire some Indian ventures, including Scindia Shipping, failed, they succeeded in pushing up their total sales to more than Rs 900 crore by 1984 through careful management of their existing resources.

The Kirloskars followed a similar strategy. Keeping abreast of changes in demand, they placed new products on the market without setting up any major new companies. The fact that most of their products were important for agricultural operations was an added advantage for them. At the same time, the group looked outside for investment opportunities. Kirloskar Electricals was particularly active in this respect and set up a few joint ventures in Malaysia and Kenya to manufacture diesel engines and electric motors and pumps.

Significantly, the only major company the Kirloskars founded during the 1970s remained a source of trouble. This was Kirloskar Tractors, set up in 1970 that had a bumpy ride until it was merged with Kirloskar Pneumatic in 1982. The same year Kirloskar Computer Systems was set up as a consulting unit. A rather modest venture, it would help the house utilize the excess capacity of a large computer system that the Kirloskars had installed essentially for the in-house use.

Most of the other prominent groups defining the contours of Indian business at the end of the Nehru era too followed the path of least resistance during the uncertain years of the 1970s and early 1980s—restricting themselves to areas of activities in which they had already proved their mettle instead of launching new initiatives. The Walchands, for instance, concentrated on civil engineering projects in India and West Asia and earned huge profits in the process. Their Premier Construction as a result emerged as the ninth largest enterprise in this field by the beginning of the 1980s. Ravalgaon Farm also prospered but Premier Automobile, the makers of the most popular of the three brands of passenger cars produced in India, had to contend with a continuing series of labour troubles that did not end until the beginning of the 1980s. The mainstay of the Mahindras operations remained the production and distribution of jeeps, elevators, tractors, and alloy steel, and the Godrejs continued with their proven lines—security equipment and office furniture— or the lines they had entered during the Nehru era—refrigerators and electric typewriters. Acquisition remained the principal route to growth for the Goenkas and the Khaitans—the route through which they had come into prominence—and the Bangurs remained more concerned with consolidating the diverse businesses they had brought under their control during the 1950s. Likewise, the Bajajs, reaping huge profits through their scooter operations had no time to think of any major diversification.

Apart from the general environmental factors that affected the pace of progress of most business groups in the country during the 1970s, many had to weather family splits that added to their woes. Among the most important business families (besides the Birlas) that split during the period were the Mafatlals, Shri Rams, Singhanias, Bangurs, and Goenkas. The Mafatlals split in 1979 into three factions, each led by one of the three grandsons of the founder, and thus lost the number three position in the Indian corporate world that they had attained by the end of the Nehru era. The Shri Ram group was divided in 1984 amongst Lala Shri Ram's three sons—Murlidhar, Bharat Ram, and Charat Ram. Before the spilt, the group had expanded into rayon tyre chord, chemical engineering, PVC cables, and fertilizers. With the entry of the Lala's grandsons into the management, the group found it difficult to pull together. None of the three factions could sustain the pace of progress maintained during the two decades following the founder's death in 1963. The Singhania division in 1979 amongst the three sons of Kamlapat, representing the third generation, slowed down considerably the onward march of the house that had attained an all India position only after Independence. The Bangurs too lost their front ranking as a result of division between two factions.

The Goenka split in 1979 was somewhat special in the sense that it marked the second break-up of the house within two decades. As we saw in the last chapter, following the first split, the Duncan group led by Keshav Prasad had continued with its policy of aggressive acquisition, placing his group at the forefront of the private corporate sector in the country by the end of the Nehru era. Continuing with their acquistion strategy, Keshav Prasad and his brother took over another major concern in 1973 when Indira Gandhi was at the zenith of her power. This was a group of enterprises under the control of a Calcutta-based Jewish family, B.N. Elias. Unable to cope with the labour troubles in Calcutta during the mid-1960s, the Eliases decided to retire to Britain, and therefore sold off their Indian interests comprising a jute mill, a tobacco company, and Murphy India, a radio-manufacturing firm.

The 1979 split—this time between Keshav Prasad's three sons: Rama Prasad, Jagdish Prasad, and Gauri Prasad who had already joined the management of the group as their father was gradually weaning himself away from active leadership—was the result of the expansion and resultant prosperity. By the time of the second split in the family, the Goenkas' presence in Bombay had become as strong as in Calcutta, thanks to a spate of acquisitions in the western metropolis.

Out of the three new branches of the family, Rama Prasad (R.P.G.) and Gauri Prasad (G.P.G.) continued with the policy of aggressive acquisition. R.P.G., who started off with a clutch of companies with the combined sales of Rs 75 crore, increased his group's sales to Rs 800 crore within a short period of six years mainly through acquiring some of the most important companies in the private sector. These included: Wiltech India set up in 1982, a joint venture of the Karnataka government and Asian Cables, to manufacture razor blades; Deccan Fibre Glass which was passing through difficult times; Ceat Tyres of India, originally set up as a joint venture between Ceat of Turin, Italy, and the Tatas in 1958; and Kamani Engineering Corporation, a pioneer in the field of power transmission towers, founded in 1945 by Ramji M. Kamani whose fighting grandchildren proved incapable of managing their precious inheritance.

The G.P.G. group (also known as Duncan Group as most of the companies belonging to the erstwhile Duncan Brothers fell into Gauri Prasad's share) followed a similar route to expansion so that it had as many as nine companies, having sales of more than Rs 370 crore, under its control by 1984. At the time of the family division in 1979, it had only three companies with combined sales of around Rs 72 crore. The group's success was largely due to the policy of producing new, sophisticated brands of tea and cigarettes, and promoting their sales through aggressive marketing. In contrast to the groups headed by his two brothers, the Jagdish Prasad (J.P.G.) group made only modest progress during this period and remained confined mainly to cotton textiles and jute.

The exploits of all business houses in India during the 1970s and 1980s are dwarfed into insignificance in comparison with those of Dhirubhai Ambani, who was still an unknown figure in India when the Nehru era ended. His Reliance Textiles, the only enterprise under his control, was still too small to attract much notice even in Ahmedabad where it was located. Starting from this slender base, he reached the top of the ladder with startling speed, using methods that few in India had ever used with so much finesse and such success. His rise, without question, is the single most momentous development in the business history of free India.

The process started in 1971 when the government launched a special scheme to boost foreign exchange reserves. One could, under this scheme, import polyester filament yarn against the export of art silk that Ambani's mill produced. This gave him an opportunity to produce high-quality goods from the imported yarn, and by exporting these goods, he could import still more yarn. As his mill could not use the whole, a part of the imported yarn was sold to other producers of synthetic fabrics at high premium. So successful did this operation turn out to be that the Reliance sales jumped more than one hundred times by 1977.

The manufacturing facilities now needed expansion, and expansion needed money. Ambani, therefore, went public. However, instead of asking the investors to buy shares of his company, he issued convertible debentures of Rs 7 crore. From the investor's point of view, it was a much safer system as it guaranteed returns in the form of interest while holding out the prospects of capital appreciation in the future through the conversion of debentures into shares. For someone who was still a little known figure in the Indian industry, this was a much better method of attracting investors. The convertible debenture method to raise industrial finance was not unknown in India, but few had used it before, and none on the scale on which Ambani did. Following his success, this heretofore neglected instrument became immensely popular with the Indian industrial class; for the Ambanis, raising funds through the stock market became the preferred method. To retain the investors' confidence, they offered consistently high dividends and occasionally bonus shares. It is not surprising, therefore, that the Reliance shares were eagerly sought after, which pushed up their value to dizzy heights. At one time in the late 1980s, the value of shares of the Ambani company had appreciated to an incredible 450 per cent. None in the entire industrial history of India had ever used the stock markets with so much success to raise industrial finance. Ambani's experiment, in fact, has been the single most important factor in energizing the Indian stock market.

The post-1977 history of the Reliance group was one of unhampered growth. While the Ahmedabad facilities were vastly expanded, another factory, equipped with state-of-the art machinery was set up in Bombay in 1981 to produce polyester filament yarn in collaboration with DuPont of the United States. The Reliance Industries would not have to import this crucial input for its own production any more; the company in fact would supply polyester filament yarn to other Indian producers of synthetic fabrics as well. Four years later, the house entered into another related field—petrochemicals. An amount of Rs 270 crore—the largest ever in the Indian corporate history—was raised through a non-convertible debenture issue. By this time Ambani's reputation for giving more than fair returns to the investors was so firmly established that the enthusiasm for the issue caused a stampede-like situation in the capital market. The Ambani firm now had the distinction of having a much larger number of shareholders than any other company in the country, and the house of Ambanis emerged as the third largest group, next only to the Tatas and the Birlas, in India. Never before had an Indian business house, starting virtually from the dust, risen so high within such a short time.

Suprisingly, the Ambani saga unfolded itself during the heyday of the license-permit raj. It is widely believed that the Ambanis' success was to a large extent due to Dhirubhai's ability to manipulate, using fair and foul means alike, the government machinery to his advantage. The scheme to offset the import of polyester filament yarn against the export of art silk, of which Ambani's mill was the largest producer in India, is believed to have been launched at his persuasion. And a steep rise in the import duty on polyester filament yarn in the mid-1980s, forcing domestic users of the product to turn to Dhirubhai's company, was widely attributed to his uncanny influence in the corridors of political power. It is very difficult to be certain about the veracity or otherwise of these charges, but no one can accuse Dhirubhai and his associates of failing to appreciate the opportunities inherent in the environment during the license-permit raj, and to exploit them to the maximum possible extent.

Ambani's feat appears even more impressive considering that his launching pad was the textile industry for which the 1970s and the 1980s proved to be the most stressful period in its long history. For this state of affairs, most of the mill owners had themselves to blame to a large extent, for they had failed to modernize their plants and machinery during the years of prosperity. The government policy, forcing the mills to supply yarn to the powerloom sector at fixed rates and include what was called 'Janata cloth'—material of lower or medium quality generally used by the relatively poorer sections of the population—in their product portfolio added to their problems. In the face of all these adversities practically all business groups involved exclusively or primarily with the industry suffered immeasurably.

Barring only a few distinguished exceptions, most of the mills in Ahmedabad including the Sarabhais proud possession, Calico, and the companies under the control of the prestigious Mangaldas group either closed their doors or were taken over by the government-controlled National Textile Corporation. In the process the Manchester of India, boasting as many as seventy-two mills at one time, was left with only a handful of functioning companies in the private sector by 1984. These included Arvind Mills of the Lalbhais who found it difficult to expand or even retain some of their other ventures or diversify into new fields. Bombay too suffered a similar fate. Apart from the general crisis that hit the cotton mills everywhere in the country, the Bombay industry had also to contend with a year-long labour strike under the leadership of a firebrand trade unionist, Datta Samant. The industry never recovered from this blow and, with the exception of a few concerns like Bombay Dyeing under the management of the Wadia family headed by Nusli Wadia, and the Singhanias' Raymond Mills, most older companies were consigned to history. A major reason for the survival of the mills like Arvind, Bombay Dyeing, and Raymond was their focus on producing high-quality goods meant for exports.

YOUNGER GROUPS

While none of the other younger groups of enterprises that had appeared on the Indian business horizon during the Nehru era came anywhere close to Ambani's achievements, most of them consolidated their positions fairly well by the end of the 1980s. Of these, the progress of the Hero, Ispat, TVS, Murugappa, and Oberoi groups deserves special mention. Brij Mohan Lall's Hero group emerged as the largest cycle producer in the world, deserving a place in the *Guinness Book of Records* in 1991. In the meantime, ploughing back its profits supplemented by institutional finance, it diversified into the production of mopeds and motorcycles. Honda Motors of Japan, the world leader in the field, collaborated with Hero in the motorcycle venture and its product 'Hero Honda' emerged as a most successful brand in the Indian two-wheeler market. Mohan Lal Mittal's Ispat group achieved prominence through pursuing a strategy of acquiring sick steel mills in other countries and reviving them. It thus emerged as the owner of steel mills in Egypt, the Carribean, Indonesia, and Mexico by the end of the 1980s. Using the same strategy with greater finesse and aggressiveness, his son Lakshmi Nivas, as a non-resident Indian, would later emerge as the largest producer of steel in the world.

TVS, like the Hero group, also moved into producing motorcycles. It also began producing auto-ancillaries in which field it would later establish a great reputation. The Murugappa group, under the leadership of the founder's son, A.M.M. Arunachalam, moved beyond steel furniture and coated abrasive, with which it had made its debut in the industrial field, and took to producing steel strips and steel tubes in the 1970s in collaboration with Tube Investments, a British firm. This was followed by further diversification when the house entered a few other industrial lines such as fertilizers, chemicals, petrochemicals, paper, cement, agro-products, and confectionary. The acquisition of Parry in the mid-1970s marked the entry of the house into the big league of Indian business.

As for the Oberoi group, so fast was its expansion during the 1970s, that it had five-star hotels not only in most of the major cities and tourist centres in the country but also in Egypt, Saudi Arabia, and Australia. Accent on promoting tourism in government policy was a major factor in the growth of the Oberoi operations. A few other players (such as India Tobacco Company, as we will see later) too entered the field during the 1970s, and Indian Hotels Company running the prestigious Taj group of hotels, also expanded its operations. But the Oberois had gained sufficient strength by the mid-1980s to be able to withstand the stiffest of competition.

A few entrepreneurs who were still feeling their way at the end of the Nehru era also stabilized their positions during the period under review. Prominent among these were the promoters of enterprises in the electronic industry which was still at a nascent stage during the Nehru era. These included T.P.G. Nambiar, to whom belonged the credit of developing BPL into an all-India group, and Nandlal Dhoot, the builder of the Videocon group. Nambiar was born in a business family. His father's company based in Kerala specialized in designing products like carrier communications systems (for the state electricity boards) and electro-audiograph machines. The family shifted to Bangalore in 1971 because of labour troubles in their home state and began to produce television sets in collaboration with Sanyo of Japan in the early 1980s. Other consumer durables like washing machines were added later.

The BPL group would face a crisis of existence by the mid-1990s. In contrast, the Dhoot group never looked back. The group originated in 1955 with the establishment of a sugar mill by Nandlal Dhoot, a Marwari sugar and cotton grower based in Aurangabad. He, however, lost his mill to the cooperatives that almost entirely took over sugar manufacturing in Maharashtra by the mid-1960s. He then took up the production of light dimmers and electronic gadgets. These, however, were small operations. In the early 1980s, he took a bank loan and launched an ambitious programme of producing colour television in collaboration with Toshiba Corporation of Japan. Pioneers of colour television in India, the Dhoots would later diversify into a whole range of electronic products and spread into many countries of the world.

LULL IN ENTERPRISE CREATION

Whether the companies or groups whose progress has been traced in the foregoing pages would have done better if the business climate had been more favourable during the period under review is debatable. But the fact that much fewer new enterprises were launched during the 1970s and 1980s suggests that regressive environment did have an adverse impact on business confidence. In contrast with the Nehru era when not less than twenty enterprise groups appeared on the scene and gained in strength over the years, new enterprises founded during the heydays of the licence-permit raj that carved out a national niche for themselves within a reasonable time frame, can be counted on the finger tips. These were: the Nirma group of Karsanbhai Patel, Shahra group of Mahadev Prasad Shahra, Nagarjuna of K.V.K. Raju, Llyods Steel of Raj Narain Gupta, and Biocon of Kiran Mazumdar (Mazumdar-Shaw after marriage). Even when the situation slightly eased during the 1980s, only one group of some significance, Lohia of Mohanlal Lohia, came into being.

Nirma started rather accidentally. Karsanbhai Patel, born in a farming family, was working as a salaried employee in Ahmedabad when he set up Nirma Chemical Works in 1969 with a view to earning some side income. It was a small workshop, producing washing detergent. Although it was not easy to procure the necessary inputs, the distribution of which was rigorously regulated, Karsanbhai somehow managed his show, producing through manual manufacturing process and distributing the products on bicycle from door to door. As the product gained acceptance because of its good quality and low price, Karsanbhai gradually expanded and modernized his operations. By the end of the 1970s, the detergent and also washing soap produced by him had gained so much public acceptance that the mighty Hindustan Lever, the major detergent maker in the country at the time, had to take notice of the unknown competitor. Nirma, in the process, emerged as a national concern and Karsanbhai an entrepreneur of rare quality.

The Shahras had had a long family history of trading in agro-products before moving into industry with the establishment of General Foods in 1973, specializing in the soyabean-based products. They also set up a research and development (R&D) unit to produce seeds of better quality, that developed into Ruchi Soya Industries. With their base at Indore in Madhya Pradesh, the family later diversified into steel strips and alloys.

K.V.K. Raju, with a Chemical Engineering degree from the United States, started his career with an American petroleum company in India, but later joined Union Carbide. After a long stint of seventeen years with this firm, at the age of 48, he decided to be his own employer. Looking for an industry with potential for expansion and involving relatively less risk of obsolescence and cost escalation, he zeroed in on the production of cold-rolled steel strips. This is how Nagarjuna Steel came into existence in 1974. Fertilizers and chemicals were added to the group's product line a few years later, as the company stabilized itself.

Lloyds Steel of Raj Narain Gupta came into existence just about a year after Raju's Nagarjuna Steel. Gupta's interest in making steel products resulted from his long experience of trading in such products. This was a highly lucrative business during the licence-permit raj as the dealers could manipulate in numerous ways the control measures that regulated the production and distribution of steel products. Having made their money by selling steel, the Guptas eventually decided to become producers of steel pipes. This is how Lloyds Steel was born which in the next two decades would develop into a sizeable group, though the family never took leave of trading altogether.

Like Gupta, Mohan Lal Lohia also came from a trading background. Belonging to Rajasthan, his family had been involved in trading operations in Singapore, Burma, and Japan, but later set up a textile mill in Indonesia. Mohan Lal spent a number of years with the family businesses abroad before returning to India in 1986. The government had decided to reduce import duties on raw material for the textile industry just a year earlier. Responding to this concession, he launched his Indo Rama Synthetics in 1988 to produce polyester intermediates, which soon developed into a respectable concern.

Kiran Mazumdar was very different from these five entrepreneurs in every respect. The daughter of a brewmaster, she was barely twenty-five years old, when she launched her Biocon India Limited soon after securing a Master's degree in brewing technology from Melbourne University in Australia. Formed to produce food and non-food industrial enzymes required by a vast group of industries ranging from food and beverages to textiles and pharmaceuticals, the company was registered in 1978. Mazumdar had barely Rs 1 lakh as her start-up capital, but her real assets were her technical expertise and her Irish partner, Biocon Biochemicals Limited. The progress was necessarily slow in the beginning, but the company started exporting enzymes to Europe and the United States—the first Indian company to do so—within a year after its birth, and its sales touched Rs 10 crore by 1987 making Biocon an undisputed market leader.

There were, of course, a few others whose names can be added to the list: Vijay and Bharat Shah of Palanpur, Gujarat, who laid the foundation of a stupendous business in diamond trading; Ramesh Chauhan of Parle Exports, whose firm operating since the early 1950s emerged as a prominent soft drink producer, thanks to the expulsion of Coca Cola and Pepsi from India by the Janata Party government in 1977; and Satish Kaura's Samtel producing television colour tubes. But history on the whole would not remember the 1970s and 1980s as an era of new enterprise creation.

The post-Nehru era also witnessed the rise of the Hinduja Brothers— Gopichand and Srichand—and Manohar (Manu) Chhabria, both Sindhis. The foundation of the business fortunes of both these families had been laid by the previous generation through extensive trading operations in Iran and the adjoining regions in the early years of the twentieth century. Their Indian presence is simply an extension of their international operations which they conduct from their headquarters abroad—the Hindujas from London and the Chhabrias from Dubai—and thus neither is an Indian group in the strict sense of the term. In fact, the Hindujas' involvement in Indian business well until the mid-1980s was primarily limited to their having a minority interest in Ashok Leyland, the well-known manufacturers of trucks and buses. The Chhabrias too had a rather insignificant presence in India until 1987 when they acquired Shaw Wallace, an expatriate firm that had emerged as a major producer of liquor after Independence. Until then they had operated from Dubai where their firm, Jumbo Electronics, set up by Manohar (Manu) Rajaram Chhabria had its headquarters. The Chhabrias later acquired Ceat Tyres (which was eventually sold to the Goenkas) and Dunlop India Limited from their British owners. Manohar's differences with his brother and conflict with the Goenkas created considerable problems for his Indian operations, and yet he diversified into a number of new lines such as chemicals, engineering electrical machinery, leather products, detergents, and personal care products, and expanded his liquor operation by setting up Maharashtra Breweries and Skol Breweries. However, following Manu's death in 2002 the entire business edifice erected by him seems to be facing risk of collapse.

The ventures and businesses discussed here undoubtedly represent impressive examples of entrepreneurship. But surveying the entire business canvas of the 1970s and 1980s, it is difficult to avoid the conclusion that the gains registered by the Indian business during this period were far below the potential.

STRUCTURAL–STRATEGIC POSTURES

The period was also marked by the lack of any significant development in the realm of structure and strategy. In fact, this observation applies to the entire post-Independence period, including the Nehru era. Family control over the private sector remained undiminished, despite the formal abolition of the managing agency system with effect from 1 April 1970 and the socialist rhetoric of the new rulers to curb family power. But the new structure did strengthen the tendency towards greater autonomy on the part of individuals placed in charge of various units in a group even if they belonged to the family, as was generally the case, with which the group was identified.

Also, the post-Independence leaders of Indian industry were by and large much better educated and professionally qualified in comparison with their counterparts of the earlier times. Most of those who took over the reins of management in the older houses after Independence had, unlike their predecessors, the benefit of higher education or technical training relevant for managing the enterprises under their charge. The same is true of most of the founders of the new enterprises. The decision-making processes in the Indian industry as a result became much more informed than in the past when business leaders depended more on intuition and gut feeling than on a knowledge-based understanding of the situation. Professionalization in the sense of separation of management from control was still a far cry, but a more professional approach to conducting business was definitely taking shape during the period under review.

The emergence of a new breed of business leaders should have encouraged technological experimentation and innovation. But this did not happen. For, with the luxury of a vast domestic market largely protected against external competition, they paid less than necessary attention to the quality of their products as well as research and development. Instead of attempting to develop new technological processes on their own, they by and large preferred the softer option of collaboration with reputed producers in the developed world for launching into new directions. The end of colonialism thus seemed to have had little impact on the technological inertness that had been the bane of the Indian industry before freedom.

Changes in the financial structure of the private sector were much more significant as the family in most cases ceased to be the principal source of business finance during the period. The nature of industrial undertakings, in the context of the nation's goals and aspirations, was such as to render their financing beyond the resources of the wealthiest of families. Practically all private groups, therefore, increasingly turned to government-controlled financial institutions and the stock market for necessary funds to realize their business dreams. As a consequence, in most cases, it was financial institutions that in effect had the controlling interest in the companies identified with certain families. Although the financial institutions in most cases refrained from interfering in routine management, they were in a position to tilt the balance for or against the family. Swraj Paul, a British businessman of Indian origin, would have devoured both Escorts and Delhi Cloth Mills but for the support of the financial institutions. He had acquired substantial interest through stock market operations by the mid-1970s to challenge the control of the Nanda and Shri Ram families over these enterprises, but the financial institutions firmly stood by the families and thus frustrated the designs of this high-profile corporate raider. Financial institutions also saved Larsen & Toubro from the covetous gaze of the Ambanis in 1990.

An indirect outcome of the family ceasing to be a major source of industrial finance was the rise of splits in business families. The process received additional reinforcement from the growing pressure on the joint family system in general in the wake of the growing urbanization and westernization of the Indian society. The tendency towards greater autonomy on the part of individuals placed in charge of various units in a group, as a consequence of the abolition of the managing agency system, could also have played some role in this development. It is no accident that the number of family splits rose substantially after 1970. In the next two decades at least twenty business families splintered— some amicably while others clumsily and bitterly. And these, as already discussed, included such illustrious names as the Birlas, Modis, Bangurs, Singhanias, Mafatlas, and Shrirams—in fact, most of the older houses that defined the contours of the private corporate sector at the time of Independence. Most of the splits took place after the third generations had come to the helm, by which time family ties normally tend to weaken. In contrast, relatively younger groups retained their unity. Most of the houses based in the south too defied the general trend perhaps because family ties in the south have traditionally been much stronger.

Despite the growing tendency towards business splits and myriad restrictions on the functioning of the private sector, the Indian business class registered substantial expansion after Independence. Not only did the number of persons opting for business as a profession increasingly go up, the new entrants into the profession came from a more varied background than was the case at the time of Independence. Caste and conventional social divisions were already losing much of their hold on occupational choices even before Independence. In free India, the process gained momentum, as prospects of economic gain and self-fulfilment became the principal determinants of the choice of career. All socio-cultural barriers against entry into business seem to have collapsed as attractive business opportunities unfolded themselves.

Decline of Foreign Firms

While the Indian private sector continued to expand under the post-Nehru regime, though at a slower pace than earlier, expatriates and multinationals came under much greater strain. Expatriates had already started disbanding their operations during the Nehru era. The process accelerated in the later period as Indira Gandhi's growing radicalism added to their insecurity. Her policies also affected the fortunes of the multinationals, which had been treated rather leniently by the Nehru government. The Indira regime looked upon them with suspicion. The Foreign Exchange Regulation Act (FERA), passed in 1973, was one of several measures her government took to regulate their Indian affairs. Requiring the multinationals to dilute their holdings in their Indian subsidiaries to 40 per cent, FERA was intended to restrict the inflow of foreign capital into the country. Mrs Gandhi around this time very often referred to the foreign conspiracy against India.

Among those companies on whose fortunes FERA had the most dramatic effect were the subsidiaries of the petroleum multinationals—Burmah Shell, Standard Vacuum, and Caltex. These subsidiaries had already been pushed into a defensive position, thanks to the progress of indigenous efforts to discover new sources of oil in the country and develop refining operations since the birth of Indian Oil Corporation in 1964. FERA further added to the insecurity of the oil subsidiaries. They, therefore, gladly accepted the government's decision to nationalize their Indian operations. With the completion of the nationalization process between 1974 and 1976 emerged Hindustan Petroleum and Bharat Pertroleum, incorporating the erstwhile Indian subsidiaries of the three oil multinationals.

FERA did not affect companies like Hindustan Lever and Indian Tobacco Company (ITC) which had already reduced foreign holdings in their ownership structure and also Indianized their management. They were therefore no more affected than many indigenous companies. ITC, in fact, substantially expanded its operations during the period under review. It was still essentially a tobacco manufacturer until the end of the 1960s. Realizing the danger inherent in depending on a single product line, and that too at a time when there was a strong anti-smoking movement around the world, the management decided to diversify into the hospitality industry, marine products, paper, and export trading. A beginning was made with the launching of exports of marine products in 1971, followed by the setting up of a chain of luxury hotels in various parts of the country and exports of carpets, handlooms, and handicraft items. Bhadrachalam Paper Boards, set up in a backward area of Andhra Pradesh, was perhaps the most ambitious project the company launched in the priority sector. A few years later, it moved into cement by acquiring an existing concern that had accumulated huge losses.

The diversifications undertaken by ITC after 1976 completely transformed the character of the company to emerge as a multiproduct firm. Its simplistic managerial set-up, therefore, yielded place to a divisionalized structure, leaving each division with considerable freedom to handle the product line under its charge. Perhaps no other structure would have suited a company engaged in producing goods or in businesses almost wholly unrelated to one another.

PUBLIC SECTOR: INDISCRIMINATE EXPANSION

More than the slower growth of the private sector or the plight of the expatriate and multinational companies, what distinguishes the Indira regime from the Nehru era was a huge increase in public sector undertakings. This is clear from the simple fact that as many as 131 new enterprises were added to the public sector within a space of fourteen years from 1970 to 1984, whereas only 67 companies in this category had come into being during the seventeen-year-long reign of Nehru. Also, whereas the emphasis before 1969 was by and large on the key sectors, in the later period public sector enterprises (PSE) intruded into consumer-oriented sectors as well, such as drugs, hotels, and food-processing industry with the objective of ensuring easier availability of vital articles of mass consumption. Enterprises to operate in national and international trade, consultancy and contract services, and inland and overseas communications also came up under state ownership.

Further expansion of the area of operation of the PSEs occurred when the state stepped in to take over a large number of private enterprises, mostly cotton mills, which had become sick and would have closed down, rendering a large number of persons unemployed. A few expatriate firms, producing goods and services considered important for the economic health of the country, also came under government control as they found it difficult to cope with the post-Independence regime of regulation. These included some of the dominant concerns of the pre-Independence days. In addition, the central government controlled all major banks, financial institutions, and insurance companies. And then there were enterprises set up by different state governments or those in the joint sector in which the government, central or state, and private business houses were equal partners. In the process, the public sector emerged by the mid-1980s as a vast conglomerate of heterogeneous industries—a veritable leviathan dominating almost every major branch of the nation's business.

Given the state of the economy at the time of Independence and the reluctance or inability of the private sector to risk investment in fields that did not promise quick returns, or in geographically less developed regions where setting up industrial units was relatively more difficult, the idea of the public sector as a catalyst of change had a lot to commend it. However, it is doubtful that the early leaders of the republic whose political-economic philosophy provided the basic framework for the birth and development of the public sector, as contained in the Industrial Policy Statements of 1948 and 1956, ever visualized that their ideas would lead to the emergence of such a gigantic, overarching umbrella. What they perhaps had in mind was an economic system in which the public sector would function as a facilitator rather than competitor of the private enterprise.

The compulsions of electoral politics during the late 1960s and later, however, seem to have been responsible for indiscriminate multiplication of state-owned or state-controlled enterprises, which to a poor, backward nation suspicious of the free enterprise system, appeared to be a panacea for all its economic miseries. Poverty and hostility to profit motive often go hand in hand.

The PSEs mostly continued to make losses year after year; and practically all the sick units taken over by the government continued to be sick. It is not surprising, therefore, that the profits before interest and taxes as the percentage of capital employed in the public sector remained on an average very low—between 10 and 15 per cent—during all these years. The worst performers were public sector manufacturing enterprises; they yielded only between 3 and 5 per cent returns on investment from 1976–7 to 1986–7 as compared to 17–23 per cent in the private sector manufacturing. Few of the profit-making units were operating in a competitive environment; the bulk of the profits, 70 to 75 per cent, came from companies operating in sectors in which the public sector enjoyed a near monopoly position.

There were sector-specific, even enterprise-specific, reasons for the less than satisfactory performance of the public undertakings, which it is not possible to discuss here. Mismanagement was a basic factor. Reforms initiated in public-sector management during the closing years of the Nehru era were not seriously pursued in later years. Lack of requisite autonomy and constant interference by the ministries in vital areas of pricing, expansion, modernization, diversification, and appointments to the top positions continued to plague the working of the government undertakings. A former head of a public-sector undertaking observed as late as 1986: 'The Government Ministries adopt a superior attitude of an owner and try to run the enterprises coming under their administration. While creating a myth of autonomy all decisions pertaining to the state enterprises, even of operational nature, are made in the corridors of the Government Secretariat.' On many occasions and in many cases, crucial vacancies remained unfilled because the Appointments Committee of the Cabinet could not act on time, while many units were saddled with excess manpower, thanks to political interference. In short, even though the PSEs were business organizations in form and content, most of them were run in a totally unbusiness-like manner. And given the management structures of these units, it was not easy to hold anybody accountable for their woes.

Because of these disabilities, a large majority of PSEs achieved limited success as business ventures and most of them failed to yield satisfactory returns. Only a few earned consistently good profits. These included Bharat Heavy Electricals Limited, Indian Oil Corporation, Hindustan Petroleum Corporation, Bharat Petroleum Corporation, Oil and Natural Gas Commission, State Trading

Corporation, Minerals and Metals Trading Corporation, and National Thermal Power Corporation. The profit-making PSEs by and large belonged to the core sectors, and most of them had been set up during the Nehru era. It is the companies launched or acquired by the government after 1970, under the compulsion of political expediency, that were largely responsible for the accumulating losses of the public sector. Perhaps the public sector would have not earned so much disrepute—in fact it might have vindicated the faith of the early leaders of the republic in the concept of public sector—if the post-Nehru regime had not deviated from the original idea of keeping the state confined to the key sectors. Not the concept itself but the indiscriminate application of it seems to have been the real villain of the piece.

Whatever the reasons for most of the public-sector companies failing to deliver the goods, it would be unfair to evaluate them purely in terms of monetary returns on investments. While it would be difficult to justify the state entry into such areas as consumer goods, hotels, drugs, and fertilizers, most of the enterprises in the capital-intensive category, particularly those set up during the first two decades of Independence, opened up new areas of investment that held little attraction for the private sector at that time. Enterprises in backward or relatively less developed regions reduced the existing regional imbalances in industrial development. The PSEs also created employment opportunities for the sections of population that the private sector had largely neglected, that is persons belonging to the disadvantaged strata of society. While judging the PSEs, we cannot ignore the social good or the complementarity effect they generated, even if as an economic activity most of them failed. However, these indirect benefits that the PSEs brought to the nation remained unnoticed because of their failure as business enterprises.

The case of Maruti Udyog Limited may illustrate what a public-sector project, if properly executed, can achieve. Originally conceived in the mid-1970s as a private sector concern by Sanjay Gandhi, the irrepressible younger son of Prime Minister Indira Gandhi, the company planned to make small cars within easy reach of the middle class but made absolutely no progress until 1980, when the Government of India decided to acquire it. Strictly speaking, it was not a public sector company as only half the share capital was provided by the Government of India. The other half was subscribed by Suzuki Motor Company, a Japanese firm which agreed to supply the technology. It was thus a joint venture functioning under the joint management of the collaborating parties. The manufacturing facilities were set up near Gurgaon in Haryana—a relatively less developed area near Delhi. The Japanese partner not only provided the technology but also inspired the adoption of some of the Japanese managerial practices. The very first model produced by the company became immensely popular with Indian users.

Maruti 800 was not a very inexpensive car, but in comparison to the price that the Indian consumer then paid for indigenously produced automobiles that were, far inferior in quality—'tinboxes' in the words of C. Subramaniam, once a cabinet minister—it was without question a very good bargain. It was not surprising, therefore, that the model registered instant success and within no time became something of a status symbol among middle class consumers. Not only the quality of the vehicle but also the easily accessible after-sales service facilities arranged by the company made the Maruti venture hugely successful. As the wide acceptability of its first product boosted the coffers and confidence of the management, the company placed new models in the market, targeting relatively more affluent segments of consumers.

The value of the Maruti experiment, however, did not end here. It forced the other car producers in India to improve the quality of their products. For more than forty long years, Hindustan Motors and Premier Automobiles, the only producers of passenger cars in the country (the Madras-based Standard Motors, another automobile manufacturer, had stopped production by the mid-1970s) continued to produce the same models, without so much as exploring the possibility of bringing about even marginal improvement. With a near-monopoly position—and there always remained a wide gap between demand and supply—the manufacturers felt no pressure from the consumers to improve quality. The coming of the Maruti, however, forced both these companies to bring about whatever improvement was possible within the range of technology available to them. It is commonly believed that private enterprise, if allowed to compete with public sector firms on equal terms, can inspire salutary changes in the working of the latter. But here was a case of a pubic sector firm waking up the private sector to its responsibility to consumers.

Another experiment also suggested that productive enterprises could be successfully launched and efficiently managed under systems other than the private sector. This was Amul Dairy, founded at Anand in Gujarat on the initiative of Kaira District Cooperative Milk Producers' Union Limited (KDCMPUL). Kaira in Bombay Presidency (later in Gujarat state) produced a large quantity of milk, which had enabled a Parsee entrepreneur, Pestonji Edulji Polson, to run a flourishing business in dairy products—butter, cheese, casein, ghee, etc.—since 1915. His operations provided the only outlet for the huge quantity of milk produced by the farmers. Naturally, therefore, Polson exploited them in many ways. KDCMPUL came into being in 1946 as a response to this state of affairs on the initiative of Tribhuvandas K. Patel, a freedom fighter, who received valuable support from political stalwarts like Sardar Vallabhbhai Patel and Morarji Desai. During the first ten years of its history, however, the milk producers cooperative did little more than collect milk from the farmers and supply it to dairies in Bombay and Gujarat, including Polson's Model Dairy. This was by no means a mean achievement, as the milk contractors or middlemen who paid only a pittance to the farmer for his product, were eliminated in the process. Having stabilized its position, KDCMPUL launched its manufacturing operations at Anand, and within just a few years drove Polson's enterprise out of business. Led by an engineer, Verghese Kurien, Amul (acronym from Anand Milkproducers' Union Limited) Dairy started with the production of pasteurized milk and butter and then went on adding new items—cheese, ghee, milk powder, baby food, cattlefeed, refined cooking oil, etc.—to its product portfolio. Combining an imaginative product-development programme, backed by relevant research and development and aggressive marketing, Amul emerged by the mid-1980s, a highly diversified, multiproduct enterprise in the country, placing in the process the sleepy town of Anand on the dairy map of the world. The success of a number of sugar cooperatives in Maharashtra state, like Amul, also exploded the myth that enterprise management was a monopoly of the private sector.

Maruti Udyog, Amul Dairy, and the sugar cooperatives, however, were among the exceptions. The management of most of the public sector, and even cooperative sector, enterprises left much to be desired. Private sector companies were not always well-managed; many of them too had to close down or maintain a precarious existence. But private sector failings did not create as much rancour and public outcry as the continuing crisis in the public sector. The common citizen, impressed by the socialist rhetoric, expected the public sector to achieve what private enterprise had failed to do. Failure to deliver the goods by public sector undertakings, therefore, was bound to cause much greater frustration. Moreover, depending on the national exchequer for finances and, therefore, accountable to the legislatures, public sector undertakings were much more exposed to public scrutiny than private concerns. In the beginning, a few economists and right-wing politicians were the only ones who questioned the wisdom of locking up colossal public funds in enterprises that for years yielded little or no returns. With the passage of time, however, the disillusionment with the public sector became much more widespread. The supporters of the public sector ideology in the meantime dwindled in number and declined in influence, as the generation of the political class, for which the left-of-the-centre ideology was an article of faith, disappeared from the scene, and social hostility towards private enterprise, prevailing at the time of Independence, became less and less acute in the face of the gathering disaffection against the public sector.

This, among other things, was a clear signal that the ideology that had guided the economic destiny of the nation since Independence and propped up, perhaps unwittingly, the licence-permit raj was fast losing its *élan* by the middle of the 1980s.

CHAPTER 14

AFTERMATH OF
LIBERALIZATION*

POLITICAL PARTIES ARE GENERALLY SLOW TO ABANDON OR SUBSTANTIALLY modify their socio-economic programmes. This at any rate was true of the Indian National Congress—the party that almost uninterruptedly controlled the central as well as most of the state governments for the first forty years after Independence and thus fashioned the economic-industrial policies of the young republic. While the Congress brand of socialism was losing its lustre, the government controlled by the party continued to tighten the noose around the private sector particularly after Indira Gandhi came to the helm of affairs in 1969. The Janata Party, a motley crowd of politicians that ruled the country between April 1977 and January 1980, remained too busy sorting out its own internal contradictions to leave a meaningful impact on the policies and programmes of the union government. There is some ground to suggest that after she returned to power in the general elections of 1980, Mrs Gandhi began to feel the need to expand operative freedom for the private sector. For, as eminent economist Jagdish Bhagwati recalled a few years ago, 'tentative moves towards delicensing had been planned towards the end of [her] term before her assassination, in the wake of a series of official examinations of licensing regimes'. But it is hard to believe that Mrs Gandhi's government would have gone far along the road, even had she lived. 'This scenario', as Bhagwati rightly suggests, 'seems wholly out of character with her past thought processes'. The licence–permit raj, after all, blossomed fully under her regime.

---

*This chapter was written in November 2005.

INITIATING THE CHANGE

The real push to the forces of change came with the assumption of office by Rajiv Gandhi as the Prime Minister of the country in October 1984 after the assassination of his mother. Young, energetic, and with a clean public image uncontaminated by ideological shibboleths, he placed great emphasis on technological progress to enable India to enter the twenty-first century well equipped to face international competition. He visualized an India that would be a major global player instead of a cloistered economy behind the walls of protection. This could be achieved, he visualized, only by liberalizing the economy—by liquidating the licence-permit raj. Though he too on occasions sang ritualistic paeans to socialism, this was no more than mere political strategy to retain the goodwill of the old guards in the party, who still clung to the old dream. There was little doubt that for him liberalization of the economy was the key to realizing his vision.

The first two budgets of his government bore ample proof of this. Taxes and tariffs were lowered; as many as twenty-five industries were taken off the list requiring licences, restrictions on product diversification were relaxed for, with the broadbanding of capacities, it was now possible to diversify into related products, and asset size qualification for MRTP scrutiny was restored to the 1969 level so that the number of industrial groups requiring clearance from MRTP Commission for capacity expansion was reduced to half, and the number of companies to nearly 15 per cent of the earlier total. Some other changes included dereservation of a few areas reserved for the small-scale sector and opening of telecommunication equipment manufacturing to private enterprise. The telecommunication scene was virtually transformed with the establishment of the Centre for Development of Telematics (C-DOT), an autonomous agency of the Government of India, under the leadership of Sam Pitroda who brought in young software professionals to provide the necessary boost to information technology (IT). Although little was done explicitly to encourage foreign investment, there was a perceptible change of attitude in this respect after 1985 as a result of Rajiv Gandhi's drive for advanced technology. His government also initiated the move to open up the civil aviation sector to private operators, although the so-called 'open sky policy' could not be finalized before he was voted out of power in 1989. These measures in themselves did not amount to much, but a long-term fiscal policy announced in 1986 was a clear indication of the new government's seriousness of purpose to continue with its programmes for change.

Unfortunately, Rajiv Gandhi's vision got entangled in unanticipated political controversies and dissensions in his government, prematurely halting the process of reform in the later years of his tenure. But the initiatives his government had taken greatly buttressed the sentiment for change not only among intellectuals and economists but also among the general population. Significantly, no political party, except the Communists, was explicitly opposed to economic reforms, if we go by their manifestos issued for the parliamentary elections of 1991. Thus the ground for the acceptability of reforms was well prepared when P.V. Narasimha Rao formed the new government in June 1991. Supplementing the mounting national sentiment against the restrictive economic regime was a severe foreign exchange crisis, because of which the country was on the verge of defaulting on payments to its external creditors. All this left the new government with no option but to resume the liberalization drive in right earnest no sooner than it assumed the reins of administration.

The very first budget that Rao's able Finance Minister, Manmohan Singh, presented barely weeks after the formation of the new government was a proof in point, while his next budget presented in February 1992 was a landmark document in the history of independent India. These two documents together with a new industrial policy announced in July 1991 shook the foundations of the licence-permit raj and ushered in a brave new world for the private enterprise. The system of industrial licencing was completely done away with except in eighteen industries; the MRTP Act was abolished, eliminating the need for pre-entry clearances imposed on large groups under the old regime; the list of industries reserved exclusively for the public sector was drastically reduced, leaving only such manufacturing areas in the list as were related to defence, strategic concerns, and petroleum; the 40 per cent limit for foreign investment in Indian companies was raised to 51 per cent with the proviso that proposals for higher percentage, even up to 100 per cent, would be considered on a case-by-case basis; the automobile sector was opened to foreign manufacturers; and import and excise duties were drastically cut on a large number of products. With one stroke, as it were, Singh caused a veritable upheaval in the Indian economy and eliminated many of the shackles that had held back the creative energy of the Indian private sector. Strangely enough, this was the man who had earlier been accused of pro-left tendencies by a respected British journal! Reserve Bank of India followed up by making the rupee convertible on current account so that market forces would henceforward determine the value of the Indian currency vis-à-vis the major currencies of the world.

The Rao government introduced some other reforms during its tenure. The most important among these were allowing private participation in power generation, giving a statutory status to Securities and Exchange Board of India (SEBI), determining the price of new issues based on market forces, and permitting private sector participation in the road sector. These changes, with the exception of the last mentioned, were introduced during the first two years of the Rao regime. By 1994 the pace of reform unfortunately slowed down under pressure from vested political interests. This prevented Manmohan Singh from attending to some other items on his agenda that included full convertibility of the rupee, overhaul of tax structure, and reining in the subsidy regime. He had, nevertheless, set in motion a process that proved irreversible.

Rao's government failed to win another mandate in the parliamentary elections of May 1996, largely because of its mishandling of the Hindu–Muslim imbroglio centred around the Babri Mosque–Ram Janmabhumi temple at Ayodhya in Uttar Pradesh and other failings on the political front. But even the governments that followed at the centre (there were three between 1996 and the general elections of 2004) continued with the tempo of change, despite having different political persuasions. The appointment of a Disinvestment Commission in August 1996 to decide the public sector enterprises to be privatized, massive cuts in income tax and tariff rates in 1998, the disinvestment or strategic sale of government holdings to the tune of Rs 44,882 crore in government-owned companies by March 2004, and opening up of the insurance business to private enterprise in 2000, amply bear this out. Admittedly, the post-Rao governments could not provide the same kind of dynamism to the agenda for reform largely because of their own internal contradictions. But none tried to put the clock back. The Rao–Singh initiative thus not only achieved a much-needed breakthrough in what had become a static economic scenario, but also helped evolve a national consensus in favour of change. The left parties were the only political formation that still continued to voice reservation, although many people believed that the approach of their own government in West Bengal to matters relating to economy and business was closer to the reform agenda than to the official party line.

The abolition of stifling restrictions and introduction of salutary changes in what may be termed as 'confiscatory' taxation policies unleashed the creative energies of the Indian private sector that had been kept under tight control during the licence-permit raj. All impediments to expansion, experimentation, and even innovation suddenly vanished as if by the waving of a magical wand. Business confidence, never too high during the licence-permit raj, became all pervasive. The will to partake of the emerging opportunities, not only in the country but also in other parts of the world, received a great spurt. Global competition became the buzz word in the Indian business circles. Old established business houses entered new lines of business that had earlier been out of bounds for them and a host of new entrepreneurs came to the fore to mount undertakings in areas they would not have earlier thought of. Banks and financial institutions came out with generous schemes to support business initiatives, and venture capitalists, almost an unknown tribe in the age of restrictions, emerged on the scene with vigour. Foreign investment, looked upon with suspicion if not downright hostility under the old regime, was now eagerly sought after, and for the multinational enterprises India with its 300 million strong middle class emerged as too attractive a market to be ignored. A small but influential group of industrialists, the so called Bombay Club led by Ratan Tata, would have liked the government to create what they called a 'level playing field', a euphemism for differential treatment to Indian-controlled enterprises vis-à-vis the Indian operations of multinationals. But few followed their lead. The consumer, who had earlier been at the shortest end of the priorities of the producer, was the greatest beneficiary of these developments. For as the competition for providing goods and services increased, he became a force to reckon with in the total scheme of things.

Admittedly, these steps taken to dismantle the licence-permit raj severally or individually did not amount to a revolution—much more needs to be done to deserve that description—but no other word can signify the change more appropriately. It is neither possible nor even necessary for the purpose of this volume to recount and analyse the impact of this 'mini revolution' on the Indian private sector. The developments at any rate are still too close to our own times to admit of a proper historical assessment. The best we can do is to point to the major business trends that have come to the surface in the wake of liberalization.

IMPACT ON PRIVATE ENTERPRISE—INDUSTRY AND TRADE

The most visible effect has been on the general industrial scene. New industries not existing before liberalization have come to the fore and existing industries have become more productive and competitive. These can be classified, though at the cost of some arbitrariness and overlapping, in the following four categories.

The first category includes industries now producing goods and services that had virtually no domestic demand earlier. Of these, information technology and allied industries have demonstrated the most spectacular rise. The birth of this industry can be traced back to as early as 1968 when Tata Consultancy Services (TCS) was set up at the initiative of J.R.D. Tata. The first software company in the country, it somehow kept its head above water until Rajiv Gandhi's technology-friendly team opened up new opportunities for enterprises like TCS. Demand for the services offered by the company, both in India and abroad, multiplied by leaps and bounds as liberalization gained momentum, and TCS's turnover touched almost the Rs 5000 crore mark by 2002. There has been no turning back since.

Most of the software companies formed during the 1970s and 1980s experienced similar spectacular growth. Infosys Technologies, Bangalore, offers the best illustration. Led by N.R. Narayana Murthy, its founders had neither the money to mount a business enterprise nor the experience to run it. Belonging to a south Indian Brahman family and the son of a schoolteacher, the leader of the group, an electrical engineer by training, had started his career as a systems analyst at the Indian Institute of Management, Ahmedabad (IIM-A)—a pretty low position in the Institute's academic hierarchy. His co-promoters, all young software professionals, also came from families with modest resources. To launch their company, they borrowed small amounts from various sources, including their wives. Their real struggle, however, started after the company was launched in 1982 when the licence–permit raj still held sway. Financial limitations apart, it was not easy to import necessary equipment because of a high tariff wall and many other constraints. Things began to improve only with the opening of the economy. The ever-growing demand for software services in the developed world catapulted Infosys to frontline position in the Indian business world. With its shares being traded at prices several times their face value, the market value of the company that had started with barely Rs 5000 touched dizzy heights by the turn of the century. In March 1999, Infosys Technologies became the first Indian company to be listed on an American stock exchange.

The rising fortunes of the IT industry attracted many others already engaged in some other lines. One of these was Azim Hasham Premji. His Wipro Corporation, like TCS, was a small concern when its present head assumed its leadership in 1966 after the death of his father M.H. Hasham Premji. At that time the family was in the business of processing vegetable oil. This appeared to be too restricted a field to young Azim who diversified first into medical systems and later computer hardware when IBM closed its Indian operations in 1977. What, however, gave a real boost to his business was his entry into software development in the early 1990s. Providing software services to several top companies in the world, some of which were in the Fortune 500 list, Wipro became a household name by the turn of the century with its net worth amounting to several billion rupees, and Azim Premji the richest Indian, according to Forbes rating. Like Wipro, technocrat Shiv Nadar's Hindustan Computers Ltd. (HCL), struggling with computer hardware manufacturing since its inception in the mid-1970s, developed into a respectable enterprise only after a liberalized economy provided it the necessary space to diversify into software services. These success stories encouraged others to launch IT-related enterprises. One of these was B. Ramalinga Raju who moved away from the family business of cotton spinning and construction to set up Satyam Computers in 1992 and propel it on to the global stage through a high-capacity satellite link.

These examples are illustrative of how liberalization transformed the atmosphere for software companies. This is eloquently reflected in the turnover of the Indian software industry that jumped from a mere Rs 430 crore in 1991 to Rs 28,350 crore by 2001. The progress of the software industry has resulted in the rise of another industry, Business Process Outsourcing (BPO), in the last few years. In fact, little was heard of it in India until 1999. BPO is basically a cost-cutting device involving transfer of mundane white-collar jobs—such as preparing routine reports, processing voluminous financial data, and compiling statutory reports for governments—by large companies to specialized firms, thus obviating the need for maintaining in-house staff for the purpose. India's BPO industry started with large foreign companies opening their own captive organizations in the country for this purpose. This inspired the rise of call centres owned and managed by Indians which could offer the required services at much cheaper rates because of the lower labour cost. The ability to handle the English language along with computer technology has given a great deal of competitive advantage to India vis-à-vis many other countries with lower labour costs. The result has been the mushrooming of BPO centres in India. So successful have the Indian call centres been that the developed West has started feeling the pinch of the outflow of jobs that in ordinary course of things would have been handled by their own nationals. As for India, IT or IT-related industries have been the fastest growing sector with almost 90 per cent of the sales coming from abroad.

The second category consists of industries that had large domestic demand for their product but could not develop before liberalization because of supply-side constraints. The automobile industry is the best example. Well until the beginning of the 1990s the Indian consumer had to put up with a long waiting period for acquiring a car and commercial vehicles and had to remain content with shoddy products (with the exception of Maruti), for nothing better was available. With the facility for making foreign direct investment (FDI) available to them after liberalization, multinational automobile manufacturers entered the Indian market in a big way. Almost all the major international auto firms have set up their manufacturing facilities in India. These companies have brought with them the manufacturing and technical skills as also the management systems required for making quality products. The result is that Maruti 800, which was seen as the ultimate status symbol for an average middle class Indian well up to the end of the 1980s, has now been reduced to the position of a basic model!

Significantly, foreign models or models based on borrowed technology are not the only quality vehicles available in India. For Indica, designed and produced by Tata Motors (TELCO renamed), is successfully competing with the products of multinational companies both in India and abroad. Just a few years ago it would have been inconceivable for an Indian company to produce a passenger car based on designs and technical know-how developed indigenously. The entry of the multinationals and the rise of the Indian automobile industry have also given fillip to the auto components industry. For, the automobile industry could not have developed without the development of a supplier industry. Spurred by companies like Bharat Forge and Sundaram Clayton, the Indian auto ancillary industry has by now become globally competitive at least for low-value components.

Apart from the auto industry, the opening of the Indian market has attracted multinationals to some other sectors as well. Their Indian operations, carried on alone or jointly with Indian companies, are now producing a variety of goods for which Indians earlier visiting the developed countries would flock to the stores: Kelloggs cereals, McDonald's fast food, Arrow shirts, Levis jeans, Gillette toiletries, Rexona deodorants, beauty care products, wines, spirits, and a host of other articles. These are now available, made or processed in India itself, under licence from the parent company. It is difficult to think of any prominent multinational—whether American, European, British, Japanese, or Korean—that has not yet entered the Indian manufacturing industry either through setting up its own independent operation or through collaboration and franchise arrangements. Multinationals have also entered the service industry in a big way, alone wherever possible and jointly with Indian firms wherever necessary. A good example is the insurance sector. Even though the FDI participation in this line cannot exceed 26 per cent, a number of foreign concerns have joined hands with well-known Indian business groups to promote at least twelve insurance companies in the last few years. These young concerns have not only broken the monopoly of the government-controlled Life Insurance Corporation of India, but also brought about a much needed modernization of this sector to the immense relief of harried consumers.

How attractive a market India has become for the foreign investors is clear from the fact that whereas the total FDI investment in India in 1991 stood at merely US $ 234 million, the average yearly investment between 1998 and 2003 has been around US $ 2.5 billion. Foreign institutional investors (FII) have played a critical role in this development. Their principal route to participation in the Indian business has been through buying equity shares in the Indian companies. The cumulative FII investment since the equity market was opened up in 1992 until the end of 2003 was US $ 21 billion. The rate of growth can be measured by the fact that within a single year from 2002, FII investment increased by almost ten times—from US $ 739 million to US $ 7.59 billion. There are at present over 620 FIIs registered in India for participating in the equity market. Dwelling upon the value of the Indian market for foreign investors, an American TV commentator recently observed: 'For American CEOs [Chief Executive Officers] trying to grow their companies, the issue is whether they embrace globalization. If they do, they must have a presence in India.'

Significantly, the emerging climate for business in India has also inspired some Indians who have made a name for themselves in business abroad, to seek investment opportunities in their home country. These include the Hinduja Brothers occupying a prominent place in the British business and Lakshmi N. Mittal, the largest steel producer in the world, also based in the UK. Before liberalization they had limited presence in India, and showed little inclination to expand it.

The vigour of the multinational invasion and growing FDI have caused some alarm among assorted groups of politicians, intellectuals, and economists. But the Indian middle class, fed up with shoddy, unattractive, and inefficient products and services offered by the Indian firms for more than four decades after Independence, is happy with these developments, unmindful of the political and economic costs to the nation—real or imaginary. For the entry of the foreign firms and the resultant competition have led to the much-needed improvement in the products and services of indigenous firms as well.

Apart from the auto industry and others discussed in the foregoing pages, telecommunications is another example of industries in the second category. Despite its large population, India still had a small telephone network until as late as 1990. The government-controlled Posts and Telegraph Department could not meet the enormous demand for phone connections in urban centres simply because the state-owned Indian Telephone Industries (ITI) could not produce instruments in sufficient number. A long waiting list was the inevitable consequence. With the opening of the telecommunications sector for private participation, a number of manufacturers, including established business groups such as the Tatas, Godrej, and BPL, took to producing telephones. Short supply of instruments thus became a thing of the past. By the end of the 1990s, in most Indian cities one could get telephone connections almost for the asking. In more recent years, the telephone network has expanded to the villages as well. No pre-liberalization observer could have foreseen this development.

The telecommunications revolution is also reflected in the spectacular growth of cellular phone services. No sooner was the telecom sector open for public participation, than a number of established business houses branched out into mobile phone services. The beginning was made by the Aditya Birla group; others such as Reliance, Tatas, and Essar followed soon. Collaboration with foreign operators in the field greatly aided this development. The foreign companies were prevented from establishing telecom services on their own because the government did not permit more than 49 per cent foreign investment in this sector.

While the big houses were competing for their share of the cake, a young Punjabi was slowly but surely emerging on the centre stage of Indian business through this line of business. This was Sunil Bharti Mittal. A graduate of the Harvard Business School, this Ludhiana-based entrepreneur was still confined to small businesses such as producing bicycle parts and telephone equipment until 1993 when the telecom sector was opened for private participation. Making a cautious beginning with a cellular service for Delhi under the brand name of Airtel, the first in the nation's capital city, he soon consolidated his position in this field by expanding his operations to Himachal Pradesh, Madhya Pradesh, Andhra Pradesh, Karnataka, Tamil Nadu, and Gujarat. In the process his company, Bharti Enterprises, acquired J.T. Mobiles in Andhra Pradesh and Sky Cell in Chennai to emerge as the largest cellular operator in the country by the end of the century. Within a brief span of five years after entering the telecom line, Bharti Enterprises increased its turnover from Rs 30 crore to Rs 500 crore—almost seventeen times—and it is still steadily increasing. As a result of enormous expansion of the cellular phone services, a facility that was limited to the rich alone until just a few years back has become a common convenience at grassroots level.

Industries that could not realize their full potential before liberalization owing to the stranglehold of the public sector constitute our third category. Civil aviation is a case in point. With monopolistic control on air transport in the country the state-owned Indian Airlines had become an apology of a flying organization by the end of the 1980s because of callous inefficiency and mismanagement. The announcement of the open air policy in 1990 followed by the repeal of the Air Transport Act (that had reserved air transport for the public sector) in 1994 opened up a new business opportunity for private enterprise. Beginning with 1993, a host of private carriers, most of them promoted by well-established business houses, sprang up within no time. All of them except two exited the scene as fast as they had emerged because of mismanagement and conflict among the promoters. The exceptions were Jet Airways and Sahara Airlines. The promoters in both cases were upstart businessmen and both started their operations in 1993. Jet Airways was founded by a group of non-resident Indians led by Naresh Goyal with 40 per cent participation of two West Asian airlines, while Sahara was an initiative of the Sahara group of companies headed by Subroto Roy about whom little had been heard before 1990.

We still know precious little about Roy's family background and the strategies that helped him carve out a distinct niche for himself in the Indian business world within a very short time. Air transport occupies a rather modest part of his total operation that includes IT-related businesses such as e-commerce, e-learning, and video conferencing, and life insurance, housing finance, urban housing, media, and entertainment. He launched his business, shortly before the onset of liberalization, with parabanking—collecting small deposits, sometimes as small as Re 1 a day or Rs 5 a month, and offering unusually high rates of interest on them—which still remains an important lifeline of his operations. Rising from a small town in the backward eastern Uttar Pradesh to become one of the most powerful business figures in north India, Subroto Roy is an entirely post-liberalization phenomenon.

Jet and Sahara, both went from strength to strength during the 1990s—Jet much more so than Sahara—and both are now flying on international routes. In the meantime more private airlines have come on the scene, offering a variety of fare structures and, in the process, expanding the base of the air travelling class. The quality of services offered by the private airlines has forced Indian Airlines to wake up to its responsibilities to its passengers. The efficiency now visible in the operations of the state-owned company is wholly due to the competition offered by the private airlines. And now with their flexible fare structure, these new airlines are likely to put pressure on Indian Railways also to improve its services.

Electronic media is another example of the industries that have made great strides in recent years because of the receding shadow of the public sector. During the pre-liberalization days, television mogul Rupert Murdoch's Star TV, beaming special programmes for Indian viewers from Hong Kong, was the only private channel to break the monotony of the government-controlled Doordarshan's offerings. A quiet entrepreneurial initiative of an unknown Indian gave to the country its first satellite channel. Coming from a family of small traders and with modest education, Subhash Chandra had shown some feeble signs of entrepreneurial ability and also made some money through a couple of innovative but small ventures when the electronic media was thrown open for private participation. Joining hands with Star TV, he first launched Zee TV, a Hindi news and entertainment channel, to gauge the market. As the channel became immensely popular with the Hindi-speaking viewers, both in India and abroad, he bought out Star TV's holdings in the enterprise to bring Zee TV under his sole control and launched several subsidiary channels, each specializing in specific kind of programmes. His example was emulated later by many others including Prannoy Roy, the promoter of New Delhi Television, but the fact that Subhash Chandra was the first to enter the line, challenging the might of Murdoch, makes his case somewhat special.

Our fourth category consists of industries that had large, though latent, domestic demand for their products and services but remained grossly underdeveloped during the age of control because of difficulties in assembling requisite technology, equipment, and infrastructure. Health care is perhaps the best example; it remained in a pitiable state all through the licence–permit raj because state and urban governments and a few charitable institutions, apart from private practitioners, were the only providers of these services. Barring a few distinguished exceptions, the Indian corporate system remained aloof from the field. When Dr Prathap Reddy pioneered the idea of corporate hospitals with the launching of the Apollo Group of Hospitals in 1983, few in the Indian business world followed his lead. The result was that secondary and tertiary health-care facilities, by and large unavailable in the country, were out of reach for ordinary citizens. Post-liberalization, a number of hospitals with state-of-the-art facilities have come up at the initiative and under the management of private enterprise. These have proved to be a boon to Indians in the middle income groups. Patients from the United Kingdom and some other developed countries are also trickling in to these facilities because the cost these patients have to incur for treatment in India is a fraction of what they would pay for similar services at home. If this trend continues, the kind of medical infrastructure that is developing in the country may give a great boost to what is generally called health tourism.

Liberalization has impacted not only industries but also the trade sector. The most visible impact is on retailing which never realized its full potential in the past. As big companies never showed any interest in this branch— shops owned by some companies to sell their own products is not what is meant by retailing here—it remained synonymous with small operators until very recently. A fast-developing educated middle class in urban India coupled with growing contact with the West and a modern lifestyle has changed this and a number of new enterprises operating a chain of retail stores and supermarkets have come up in recent years. Kishore Biyani showed the way by launching Pantaloon Retail (India) in 1992; a host of others followed such as Lifestyle, Shoppers's Stop, and Piramyd. Some of the established houses, including the Tatas, have also moved into retailing in a big way. Because of their initiative, big shopping malls and departmental stores on western lines have now started dotting the streets of major urban centers in the country. The success of these early ventures has attracted many more large players to the field such as Reliance, Wipro, Hero, K.K. Modi, and Godrej who are planning to set up stores or shopping malls in various cities. No one would have imagined just a few years ago that retailing, always a poor relation in Indian business, would emerge as such a promising area of investment for corporate India. A number of global retailing giants like Wal-mart, Tesco, and Correfour are ready to expand into the vast Indian market the moment the government clears FDI in this sector.

All this is indicative of growing dynamism in Indian business. This is also reflected in another area, acquisition and merger (A&M) activity, which is usually considered to be a necessary concomitant of a dynamic business environment. The statistics are revealing. Whereas the five years antedating 1991 witnessed a total of only 160 attempts of A&M, of which 120 were successful, the figure for just 1999–2000 was 205. The industry areas that account for the largest number of cases include telecommunications, chemicals, and the financial sector. The most celebrated examples of acquisitions, though not of merger, have been the taking over of Videsh Sanchar Nigam Limited (VSNL) by the Tatas, and of Indian Petrochemical Corporation Limited (IPCL), Baroda, by the Reliance group. The Tatas acquired VSNL, a public sector company providing transnational telephony that was divested in 1996. The IPCL too was a public sector company that came into the Reliance fold in 2002 through the process of disinvestment.

While the Tatas' acquisition consolidated their position in the telecommunications sector, the taking over of IPCL by Reliance seems to have been in continuation of a plan on the part of the group to diversify into petroleum and allied sectors. For, soon after the liberalization process was under way, the group had started developing a petrochemicals complex at Hazira near Surat and an oil refinery at Jamnagar. It later moved into some other areas such as electric power generation and supply, industrial finance, and oil and natural gas exploration. The aggressiveness with which the Reliance group pursued its goal of expansion through acquisition and diversification is reflected in the fact that by the end of the century it beat the Tatas to the number one position in Indian business—fulfilling a cherished dream of its founder, Dhirubhai Ambani.

Some other important acquisitions in recent years pertain to areas other than those listed above. These include Hindustan Lever's acquisition of Tata Oil Mills and Brooke Bond Tea Company, Aditya Birla's group taking over Larsen & Toubro's cement operation, the acquisition of Ahmedabad Electricity Company by Torrent—primarily a pharmaceutical company—brewery firm Shaw Wallace exiting from Manu Chhabria's fold into Vijay Mallya's United Breweries, and the B.M. Khaitan group acquiring Williamson Tea Assam Ltd from the Magor family of Britain. While Mallya has now emerged as the second largest producer of alcoholic drinks in the world, the Williamson acquisition has made Khaitan's McLeod Russel India Ltd (MRIL) the world's largest integrated tea company. Ajay Piramal built up a whole new line of business through acquisitions and mergers. He had, after completing his education, joined the textile mill that the Piramal family controlled. He, however, branched out into the pharmaceutical industry in 1988 by acquiring an old company. This marked the beginning of a series of acquisitions and mergers that made his enterprise, Nicholas Piramal, the fourth largest pharmaceutical company in the country by the turn of the century.

All said and done, however, there have been more acquisitions than mergers, and most of the acquisitions have resulted from mutually agreed arrangements. Hostile takeovers have been few and far between. This is partly due to legal safeguards created by the Government of India which has always disfavoured hostile takeover. As for the mergers, most of these have been intra-group in nature effected with a view to restructuring the existing businesses for better performance. The recent merger of three companies belonging to the Aditya Birla group into a single enterprise, Aditya Birla Nuvo, is a case in point. On the basis of the available examples it is hard to indicate the direction in which Indian business will move in this respect, but in all likelihood consolidation through merger will gain momentum. It may be recalled in this context that in the post-Civil War America, merger and acquisition went hand-in-hand with an unusually accelerated pace of development of business that put that country on the road to becoming the most industrialized society in the world. The recent European experience suggests the same thing.

THE FINANCIAL SECTOR

Like the industrial sector, commercial banking too has undergone significant changes. Before liberalization, public financial institutions, created soon after Independence to support large industrial projects, and nationalized banks dominated the banking sector in the country with a sprinkling of a small number of branches of a few foreign banks. The public sector banks and financial institutions may have been well-equipped to meet the demands of banking services in the age of economic restrictions, but they were hardly capable of coping up with the needs of the more dynamic times that liberalization brought in. The emergence of new banks with a modern outlook in consonance with the temper of the times was a natural consequence. As it was far easier now for private parties to float new banking firms, as many as eight institutions in this genre emerged within barely eight years of Reserve Bank of India (RBI) issuing new guidelines for setting up new private sector banks in 1993. Of these HDFC Bank, in the setting up of which the Housing Development Finance Corporation played a critical role, and ICICI Bank, an offshoot of Industrial Credit and Investment Corporation of India (which would later merge with the Bank) were the most important. Emulating these examples, Industrial Development Bank of India (IDBI), another financial institution set up in the early years of the republic, also floated a commercial bank of its own. Fresh opportunities in the field also attracted private players of which Kotak Mahindra Bank, promoted recently by Uday Kotak of an old trading family in association with Mahindra & Mahindra, is a good example. That the new private banks accounted for 6 per cent of the total assets and 10 per cent of the total profits of the banking industry by the turn of the century (2001) tells us something about the position they have carved out for themselves.

The new private banks, when they appeared on the Indian business horizon, were very different from their public sector counterparts in terms of the range of services offered and customer care. Their most distinguishing feature, however, has been the use of computer technology to cut transaction costs and the introduction of modern-day services such as the automated teller machine (ATM) and credit card. The origin of such services can be traced to a pilot project known as 'Suvidha' launched by the Indian subsidiary of the multinational Citibank at Bangalore under which customers were encouraged to conduct transactions by telephone, over the net, or through ATM. How far Citibank's experiment inspired the new private banks to introduce these devices is difficult to ascertain. But the fact is that they, particularly HDFC Bank and ICICI Bank, have managed to leverage technology to centralize the backends, reduce the number of employees, cut transaction costs, and add to their services. Such has been the impact of the new banks on the Indian business scene that even the nationalized banks have been forced or inspired to emulate their younger counterparts to leverage technology to modernize their operations. Significantly, banks now provide not only working capital loans to industry but also 'consumer loans', which they seldom did before liberalization. Consequently, the housing industry and consumer-durables industry have gained because the consumer can get loans at low cost.

All this indicates that the Indian banking sector has entered a more competitive phase than at any time before in its history, making it almost imperative for the weaklings to merge with more solvent entities. Significantly, the banking industry has witnessed eleven cases of mergers since 1993, when RBI made it obligatory for Indian commercial banks, both in public and private sectors, to have a minimum of Rs 100 crore as the capital base. These developments suggest that the Indian banking sector is going to gather enough strength to become a more effective engine of business growth than has been the case so far.

The venture capitalist is another engine of business growth that has emerged after liberalization. Venture capitalists usually provide the start-up capital through equity participation to operationalize a promising business idea but have neither the inclination nor perhaps the ability to run the venture. They proactively scout for competent individuals, preferably with some evidence of proven ability and experience in the field, to launch and run the company as a joint enterprise. This route to entrepreneurial initiative, very much established in the West, did not exist in India at all until the mid-1990s. The beginning in this respect was made by the entry of some of the world's leading venture capital players such as Warburg Pincus and the Carlyle group. But not more than Rs 90 crore of venture capital had been invested in India until as late as 1997. By the end of the century, however, the figure had jumped to Rs 4800 crore with more than fifty venture capital firms operating in the field. Most of them are American and European. But a few Indian institutions of this kind have also emerged as a sort of multiplier effect. The most important of them all is ICICI Venture Funds Management Company, which has emerged as the second largest venture capital firm in the country, Warburg Pincus being the first.

The areas in which the venture capitalists have been active so far are IT or IT-related businesses, but other fields may also attract them in the future. For venture capital investments have been consistently rising and India is likely to absorb close to Rs 50,000 crore before long, according to an authoritative estimate. The figure is still a drop in the ocean but it is a potent pointer to the shape of things to come.

These developments in the Indian financial sector, though important, are almost dwarfed into insignificance in comparison with what has happened to the stock markets. Some crude statistics will bear this out. While the number of companies listed on the Bombay Stock Exchange (BSE), then the most important capital market in the country, in March 1992 was just 2601, it had jumped to 5937 by December 2000 despite the establishment of the National Stock Exchange (NSE) in 1992 to which some of the companies, that would have otherwise turned to the BSE, were diverted. In 1991–2, the highest level to which the sensitivity index (sensex) of stock values reached was 4285; by the end of 2005 it had crossed the 9000 mark. And the end of the upward spiral was nowhere in sight. Another indicator is that whereas the sensex showed merely 2 per cent average appreciation between Independence and the mid-

1980s, the average annual increase between March 1992 and November 2005 has been more than 14.5 per cent. Although the Indian stock markets had started gaining momentum since the mid-1970s, thanks largely to Dhirubhai Ambani's successful experiment of using this medium to raise finance for his ventures, it was only after the relaxation of controls that they began to be seen as an important source of business finance.

The process began in May 1992 with the abolition of the Capital Issue Control Act of 1947. A few months later, foreign institutional investors (FIIs) were permitted to invest in the Indian securities market. The birth of the NSE in November 1992 was a milestone in strengthening the institutional base. The significance of this development is clear from the fact that within less than three years after its birth the NSE overtook the BSE as the largest stock exchange in terms of the volume of trading.

The revitalization of the stock market has not been an unmixed evil. Persons like Harshad Mehta who manipulated the system to cause a major scam in May 1992, and Ketan Parekh who was responsible for repeating Mehta's mischief in March 2001, are cases in point. Despite the statutory powers granted to Securities and Exchange Board of India (SEBI) as early as January 1992 to regulate the stock markets, the agency has not been very effective in its mission, and unscrupulous individuals still somehow find ways to beat the system. This drawback notwithstanding, the rise of stock markets as a major source of business finance must be considered a significant development in liberalized India.

ENTREPRENEURS AND ENTREPRENEURSHIP

The new climate for enterprise, emerging in the wake of liberalization has shown, to quote Shitin Desai the managing director of DSP Merrill Lynch, an American venture capital firm operating in India, that 'there are huge local and global opportunities in India'. It is natural under these conditions for new enterprise creators to emerge. The exploits of some of these have already been referred to in the section on industry and trade in this chapter. A few more names may be added to the list. Significantly, a large majority of the businesses launched by new entrepreneurs belong to the knowledge-based category, and most of them have taken the venture capital route.

One of the most successful of such businesses has been Dr Anji Reddy's, Dr Reddy's Laboratories, a health care and pharmaceutical company at Hyderabad. With a degree in Medical Chemistry from a prestigious American

University, he started his career with Indian Drugs and Pharmaceutical Corporation (IDPL), a public sector enterprise, but later set up his own company to produce drugs based on his own formulations. The products of his company found a market in the United States too where he had to face a court case on the charge of patent violation which he won. With his confidence boosted, he turned global and set up a production base in China's special trading zone near Shanghai, his being the first Indian enterprise to do so. Although Anji Reddy had launched his venture a few years before the onset of liberalization, the real consolidation of his operations occurred only during the 1990s when his Laboratories transformed from a small bulk drug manufacturer into a fully integrated drug research company. By listing his firm on New York Stock Exchange in 2001, he has also measured up to global benchmarks of performance and evaluation. Like Dr Reddy's Laboratories, Habil Khorakiwala's biotechnology and pharmaceutical company Wockhardt, though formed as early as the 1960s, came to life only after liberalization. Almost unheard of before 1990, it now boasts of an annual turnover of more than Rs 1280 crore.

Ashok Soota is another example of a salaried man turned entrepreneur, thanks to the new business climate. Working as vice president in the IT giant Wipro, he decided to become his own employer, and to that end set up Mindtree Consulting in Bangalore in association with a colleague, Subroto Bagchi, and with the help of a venture capital firm that provided the start-up capital. Srini Rajan, the country head of Texas Instruments, and Suresh Rajpal, the CEO of a joint venture promoted by Hindustan Computer Ltd (HCL) and Hewlett-Packard (HP), did likewise, setting up their IT firms—Ittiam Systems and Trigyu Technologies respectively. Both are now respected names in their fields of operation. Many more examples of this kind can be cited.

While knowledge-based enterprises have been the most distinguishing feature of the post-liberalization entrepreneurship, traditional businesses too have thrown up new entrepreneurs with visible impact on the national scene. Ahmedabad-based Gautam Adani is perhaps the best example. Born in a trading family of modest means, he started his business career as an importer of plastics, but later switched over to exports in 1989 when the Government of India announced a policy of granting 100 per cent tax exemption for export items. Thus was born Adani Exports Limited (AEL). The progress was swift, and by 2004 the company was trading in almost sixty commodities spread over fifty countries with a turnover of US $ 1.6 billion. The Adanis in the meantime also diversified into vegetable oils, natural gas distribution, retailing, and the BPO business. But what has given the group a distinctive identity is their involvement in port development following the Gujarat government's decision, announced in 1995, to invite private sector participation for updating facilities at the port sites on the Gujarat coast. Responding to this policy the Adanis joined the state government to launch Gujarat Adani Port Limited (GAPL) in 1998 for the development of Mundra port. The infrastructure that has been developed at this port by the company is rated amongst the best in the country. It is a measure of the Adanis' entrepreneurial quality that within the short period of a decade and a half their group has acquired a national status and developed into a Rs 11,000 crore empire.

The post-liberalization period has also witnessed an upsurge of entrepreneurship among women. Although a few women did play critical managerial roles in family-owned enterprises—such as Sumati Morarjee and Anu Agha who assumed leadership of their family concerns, Scindia Steam Navigation Company and Thermax Limited respectively, after the death of their husbands—and some small-scale undertakings came up at the initiative of women, few women, except perhaps Kiran Mazumdar with her Biocon, were visible on the contours of Indian business before the liberalization process set in. Things began to change as the business climate improved. As per the reports of Federation of Indian Chambers of Commerce and Industry's (FICCI's) ladies organization, there was a 100 per cent growth in its ranks between 1996 and 2001. Federation of Women Entrepreneurs has estimated the increase in the number of women entrepreneurs in the country during this period to be in the order of 35 per cent. Although their entrepreneurial exploits in all cases may not be directly attributable to the opportunities created by liberalization, the new environment has had something to do with the inspiration behind their initiatives. Some of the noteworthy names among the women who have emerged on the business scene in the post-liberalization era are Ishita Swarup and Tina Sapra who set up a flourishing call centre in Delhi; Revathi Kasturi who launched Tarang Software in 2000 jointly with her brother at Bangalore; Shahnaz Hussain whose herbal empire is now estimated to be worth Rs 300 crore; Suhag Khemlani who has chosen skyscraper cleaning for her business; and Ekta Kapoor, whose Balaji Telefilms is well regarded for its quality entertainment.

The achievements of none of these, however, come anywhere close to Kiran Mazumdar's. Though her Biocon's pre-liberalization record was by no means unimpressive, the company achieved its full potential only in the post-liberalization period. Well until the beginning of the 1990s, it was still a single product company. With the launching of a number of subsidiaries in 1993 and 1994, Biocon India developed into an integrated business group, producing a variety of biopharmaceutical products. Noted for the excellence of its products, the company was awarded the coveted ISO 9001 certification from RWTUC, Germany, in 1993, much before any other enterprise in the world claimed this recognition. Progress during the 1990s was so fast that by the end of the century Biocon's annual sales touched Rs 100 crore, enabling Mazumdar to buy off her Irish partner. If Mazumdar was simply a successful woman entrepreneur up to the end of the 1980s, she won a place for herself among the nation's corporate leaders by the end of the 1990s, presiding over India's largest biotech company.

Like Mazumdar, the post liberalization resurgence in Indian business has pushed a number of entrepreneurs and family groups, that were still struggling for recognition, into the mainstream of corporate India. According to a recent report in the *Economic Times*, at least eight such groups, all of which trace their origin to the mid-1980s, have registered 100 per cent growth in the last five years to storm into the Rs 1000 crore-plus turnover club. These include the JP group of Jaiprakash Gaur which boasts of a market value of about Rs. 6700 crore—50 per cent higher than the combined market value of Nusli Wadia's Bombay Dyeing and Britannia—and Rajesh Exports of Rajesh Mehta whose revenue is equal to that of the entire Godrej group.

A New Worldview

More important than all that has been said above is the fact that there has been a radical change in the worldview of Indian business since the liberalization process went under way. A basically inward-looking attitude—the result of a long period of colonial subjugation supplemented by severe curbs on the freedom of enterprise continuing for almost forty years after Independence—has yielded place to an outward-looking attitude characterized by confidence and optimism. There is no denying the fact that Aditya Birla and a few other corporate leaders did, in the past, attempt to transcend the physical boundaries of the country while conceiving and implementing their business plans, but an overwhelming majority remained content with exploiting opportunities in the vast domestic market rendered safe by a protective web. As liberalization gradually opened the Indian economy to the world, and the forces of globalization gained momentum, Indian business houses began to look for gainful opportunities in other parts of the world including the developed countries. Interestingly enough Oil and Natural Gas Corporation (ONGC—Oil and Natural Gas Commission until 1996), a public sector company, has become the largest investor abroad. Its wholly owned subsidiary ONGC Videsh Limited (OVL) has operations in Russia, Iran, Iraq, Sudan, Libya, Myanmar, and Vietnam. Indian Oil Corporation operates in Sri Lanka and plans to expand in other Asian countries. Another public-sector giant, Gail (India) Ltd engaged in the exploration, processing, and distribution of natural gas, too has emerged as an important international player in its field of operation in recent years. The liberalized environment, it seems, has generated a competitive worldview among public-sector undertakings as well.

Among private sector firms, Reliance, which claims to be India's first global company, has oil blocks in Yemen and has recently acquired Flag Telecom, an international bandwidth provider, and Treviara, a Hoechst company based in Germany. The Tatas, another private sector giant, have acquired Daewoo's truck operations in Korea, Natsteel in Singapore, and Tyco Global Network with 60,000 kms of undersea cable network in North America, Europe, and Asia. The house has also registered its presence in the United States and a number of countries of Europe and Asia. And the Aditya Birla group, the first to make forays out of India way back in the late 1960s, has expanded its operations in several countries of South East Asia, Egypt, Canada, Australia, and China. Mahindra & Mahindra, Bajaj Auto, and TVS are among other notable Indian groups with global ambitions. While the Mahindras have tractor operations in the United States and China, Bajaj and TVS are planning to set up local operations abroad—the former in Indonesia and the latter in Iran.

It is not only the big houses, but also some of the smaller companies that have been acquiring stakes in businesses abroad. The chemicals major Atul Products Ltd for instance, has wholly owned subsidiaries in the United States, Europe, and China, and Zee TV is planning to launch a global news network. Perhaps the most aggressive about expanding abroad have been the Indian drug manufacturers, who before the liberalization were like second-class citizens in their own country in comparison with the Indian subsidiaries of multinationals. Practically all of them—Dr Reddy's Laboratories, Zydus Cadila (Cadila Laboratories formed in 1951 split in 1992 between the two founders, the name of the other offshoot being Cadila Pharmaceuticals), Nicholas Piramal, and Ranbaxy to name the most important ones—have carved varying degrees of presence for themselves in other countries including the developed West. The most common route to expansion abroad has been the setting up of joint ventures with reputed drug manufacturers to gauge the market at the first stage and then to acquire, after a few years, the foreign partner's holdings in the company. As most of the Indian drug companies have installed manufacturing plants approved by the United States Food and Drug Administration (USFDA) at their home bases—India has the largest number of such plants in the world outside the United States—it is easy for them to penetrate the world market through the production of generic drugs of world standards that their subsidiaries, joint ventures, or strategic partners abroad distribute. Ranbaxy, the most aggressive of them all in this respect, has ground presence in forty-four countries including North American and European countries, and its products are sold in more than a hundred countries. Dr Reddy's Laboratories is not far behind. Significantly, around 50 per cent of the sales of most pharma companies come from their global operations.

Looking at these and other cases of foreign forays by Indian enterprises, it is safe to conclude that having missed out on the chance to partake of global opportunities during the licence-permit raj, the Indian business world is keen to make up for the time lost. The fact that more than twenty-five Indian companies were registered on the British and American stock exchanges by the beginning of the current century as compared to none in 1991 clearly indicates this trend. During the three years since 2001, Indian companies made an investment of about Rs 9000 crore in foreign acquisitions and acquired as many as 120 foreign firms, according to an authoritative estimate. Significantly enough, these acquisitions have been spread over a number of sectors; they have not been restricted to only a few areas, such as information technology, pharmaceuticals, and petroleum industries. And in so doing, at least some Indian companies have emerged as world leaders in their respective fields. Bharat Forge, which became the second largest forging company in the world after acquiring a German forging company in 2004, is a case in point. It has recently acquired another European firm, this time in Sweden. The much younger Infosys has acquired an Australian software company. Foreign acquisition in fact seems to have become a passion with Indian enterprises, both old and new, and hardly a week passes without some report to this effect appearing in the financial newspapers.

The new outward-looking attitude is reflected not only in the Indian companies setting up production facilities abroad but also in modifying their product lines in India with an eye on the world market. Arvind Mills belonging to the Lalbhai group is a case in point. Until almost the mid-1980s this Ahmedabad-based enterprise was still a regional or at best national player, producing cotton goods for the Indian market. Soon after the winds of economic reform began to sweep through India, the company revamped its production strategy to target foreign producers of denim garments. And in the process Arvind emerged as the largest denim manufacturer in the world, supplying the fabric to more than seventy countries. Although the management had to recently shut down the Mauritius subsidiary set up in 1992, this has had no effect on its position as a major textile player in the world. Interestingly, Arvind has carved out a niche for itself in what is usually counted among the so-called sunset industries.

The following statistics, published in a recent issue of the *Economic Times* (21 October 2005) may highlight the impact of liberalization on India's business landscape. The aggregate net sales of the top 100 companies have grown to Rs 976,419 crore in 2004–5 in comparison with Rs 130,448 crore in 1990–1; profits during the same period have leap-frogged to Rs 91,552 crore from a mere Rs 6885 crore; and profit margins have doubled from 5 to 10 per cent—a reflection of the corporate sector's success in cutting costs, streamlining operations, and reducing the cost of capital. The last fifteen years have witnessed the entry of forty-three new companies in the top-hundred list, pushing back many erstwhile illustrious names. The new entrants include firms such as ICICI Bank, Hero Honda, Wipro, Infosys, Jet Airways, Ranbaxy, Satyam Computers, and HDFC Bank, while companies like Escorts, JK Synthetics, Mukund Iron, Premier Auto, Modi Rubber, and BPL have been left behind.

STRATEGIES AND STRUCTURES

In the midst of all these momentous developments, the strategies and structures in the Indian business world have obviously not remained insulated against the forces of change. Although departure from the old ways in these respects is by its very nature slow and not so easily perceptible, one can detect some feeble pointers to the emergence of new trends in the functional areas of management. Perhaps the most visible impact of liberalization is in the realm of marketing. A number of aggressive selling devices, almost absent from the scene or employed sparingly in the age of control, have come into play in recent years in the wake of growing competition. Tempting incentives, blistering publicity through eye-catching hoardings, imaginative advertisements in the print media, a spate of commercials on television channels, hire-purchase facilities, and an unending string of 'sales' offering goods and services at reduced rates—these and many other selling devices so common in the West have now made deep inroads in India. Never before in the business history of India was the Indian consumer an object of such wooing and pampering.

Financial strategies too have undergone some change, though not to the same degree as marketing. As banks, financial institutions, and venture capitalists have developed attractive schemes of business financing; private sources of finance, such as the family, have lost their importance. And a veritable equity cult has gained momentum, as raising capital through stock markets has become much more popular than ever before. This, among other things, is responsible for the increasingly larger number of business splits—there have been about twenty since 1990. Unlike before, when most of the break-ups came after the third generation, splits are now taking place much earlier. The recent spilt in the Reliance group is a most obvious example.

How this would eventually affect the family-centric structure of the Indian business is hard to anticipate but there is no doubt that the value of management professionals even in family-controlled businesses has been going up as the environment has become more competitive. Not only has the demand for the business graduate gone up severalfold and is constantly growing, but also the salary and perks that he expects and is in fact offered have no resemblance with what his pre-liberalization counterpart received. This is because he is considered to be an indispensable resource to maximize the shareholders' wealth. Thus, even though the formal managerial structure has undergone little change since liberalization, a much-needed professionalism is being brought to bear on the operations of the Indian companies. And to make sure that the professionals give their best, many companies have introduced appropriate changes in their personnel policies. A few organizations such as the Murugappa group and Ranbaxy have even experimented with placing professionals at the top. There is no doubt that the professional manager has much greater autonomy today and the working environment in the corporate offices is much more relaxed, much more permissive, and much less authoritarian.

Liberalization has brought about some change in the attitude towards technology development also—an area that remained the weakest link in the Indian business all through the colonial period and to which Independence made little difference. The Tatas' success in producing a passenger car based on indigenously developed technology is the most visible example of change in this sphere. But there are other indicators too. Expenditure on research and development (R&D), a rather dispensable item for most Indian companies until the onset of liberalization, went up to US $ 19 billion, according to

Organization of Economic Cooperation and Development (OECD), placing India among the top ten countries of the world in this respect. Indian companies filed in 2003 as many as 1700 patent applications (up from 1200 in 2002) with the US Patent and Trade Mark Office. The number filed in India that year was 15000. Admittedly, the R& D activity is still too modest for a country of India's size and pool of technical manpower at its disposal. But what is noteworthy is that a beginning has been made in an area that had almost totally been neglected before.

The liberalized India has experienced many other salutary developments in its business climate. Only the most important aspects have been dealt with here. These are sufficient to suggest that even the partial liberalization of the economy has released a massive pent-up urge to perceive and exploit new avenues of gain and offer new products and services. What would have happened if liberalization had come about earlier and with a more comprehensive coverage and less cautious speed can be anybody's guess.

CHAPTER 15

A SUM UP

THE MAIN FOCUS OF THIS VOLUME IS ON THE EVOLUTION OF INDIAN business from trade to industry. We have tried to place our analysis of the transition against the backdrop of the changing social, economic, and political environment from time to time. On the face of it, the strategic-structural dimensions have received somewhat less attention. But given the present underdeveloped state of research in this field, we thought it more appropriate to concentrate on mapping out the entire territory than to delve too deep into specific functional areas. The pace of changes in these respects at any rate has been too slow, and innovations in these areas too infrequent or too inconsequential, to claim a very large space in a work concerned with developments spanning three hundred years.

Even with its limited focus, this account offers much-needed corrections to some misconceptions about Indian business, formulated on the basis of intuitive generalizations instead of hard, durable data. One of these is a suggestion that peddling was the most distinguishing feature of the Indian business on the eve of the European commercial penetration of India. Our account of the activities of the powerful merchants, who operated in almost every part of the country in the eighteenth century and even later, runs counter to this view. The association of merchants representing different trades that existed in many cities would have been wholly unnecessary if the number of participants in these trades was not sufficiently large. Also the hundi network for transferring funds could not have functioned without the presence of a large number of creditworthy merchants and bankers throughout the land.

Even though not much is known about the less powerful actors operating at secondary and tertiary levels, there is no doubt that they existed and flourished. The only peddlers we know of were the banjaras with no sedentary establishments, but their tribe was already diminishing in the eighteenth century.

A preponderant number of these merchants, both big and small, undeniably belonged to the Vaishya stock or were Jains. Business was the prescribed occupation for the former under the Hindu *varnashram* scheme, and Jainism has been traditionally associated with business. Regardless of caste or community origins these merchants, including those who had accumulated enormous capital through trade or moneylending or both, took no step whatsoever to take India to the next stage of capitalist development. It is generally believed that India on the eve of the European penetration was among the most advanced and cost-competitive industrialized countries in Asia, but its merchant class could not sustain the tempo, because of which India continued to lag in the race towards economic progress.

This may give credence to another misconception about Indian business behaviour that holds India's social-cultural values and its social organization primarily responsible for retarding its material progress. On the face of it, the social background of the Indian businessmen at the turn of the eighteenth century and the static character of their operations may appear to support this view. This, however, would be a misreading of the evidence. For, the failure of the merchants to use their commercial gains to move towards industrial capitalism had more to do with the absence of objective preconditions for industrial transition than the religious-cultural orientations of the principal actors. The prevailing state of technology could not have permitted an industrial breakthrough, and given the state and nature of education, no serious quest for new technologies would have been possible. Added to these were the limited size of the markets and various impediments to movement even within the geographical limits of the subcontinent, that would have done little to encourage deviation from the trodden path. Not the lack of material ambition, but the limits that the totality of the material-ideational milieu placed on their plans and exertions was the primary reason for the business behaviour of the mercantile classes undergoing little qualitative change during this period. Otherwise, at least those merchants who were less constrained by Hindu 'otherworldliness', such as the Muslims, would have manifested some tendency towards moving in new directions.

The absence of inducement from the environment also explains why the business profession did not attract new elements to its fold—why new businessmen did not emerge from those groups and sections among the Hindus that, under the time-honoured social division, had been traditionally engaged in other occupations. With the existing opportunities having been already pre-empted by the mercantile classes, for whom business had been a prescribed occupation for generations, others could have thought of transcending their own prescribed occupational boundaries to enter the business profession only if there were a definite expansion of opportunities, generating a sufficiently higher expectancy of reward than what they derived from their existing occupations. This was hardly possible, given the static business situation. The result was a rough equilibrium between the existing business opportunities and social arrangements to exploit them, which the material environment in the eighteenth century was incapable of disturbing.

This equilibrium began to be disturbed by the growing European presence on India's business horizon, coupled with the unchallenged political supremacy that the British established over the entire subcontinent by the first quarter of the nineteenth century. While the Indian operations of the free merchants and the agency houses—their pioneering efforts to open up several new fields that had been left unexplored, the risk-taking propensities and aggressiveness they displayed in their business methods, and the way most of them amassed enviable business power and wealth—opened up new business vistas, the infrastructural developments that the new political masters had to bring about primarily to serve their own selfish ends gradually resulted in a new business climate. The outcome was a great deal of expansion in business opportunities and a consequent breakdown in the equilibrium between the opportunity base and the traditional social arrangements. It is not surprising that the period after 1830, particularly after the collapse of the agency house system, witnessed the entry into business of people traditionally not identified with business castes and occupation.

This trend became increasingly firm as the process of industrialization gained momentum with the access to necessary technology that the imperial connection provided, and the growing size of the market that resulted from the efforts of the new rulers to tie up different parts of the vast land with a view to facilitating efficient governance and colonial exploitation. As the account in these pages bears out, most of the new industries in India were pioneered by the people who should have kept aloof from the business spheres altogether, had they followed the occupational prescriptions in choosing their careers. In fact, it can be safely maintained that at practically every watershed of Indian industrial history the groups and individuals, whom the conventional caste norms should have kept from indulging in business activities, plunged into the modern organized sector more readily than those who were already settled in traditional lines. Neither they themselves nor anybody else ever accused them of compromising their religious-cultural norms and values simply because they chose not to follow the occupations of their forefathers. The emergence of a more conducive business climate also induced large sections of the mercantile community to leave the security of trading and moneylending and enter the more competitive field of industry.

These early founders of modern industries, irrespective of their socio-cultural backgrounds, had one thing in common. This was the exposure to new ideas and values either through education or contact and interaction, direct or indirect, with societies that had a more developed business environment. And many others who followed suit were influenced by the demonstration effect of the pioneers' exploits. Thus, religious-cultural constraints seemed to impede the development of business in India only as long as the objective-material conditions were too weak to generate fresh business opportunities, too stable to cause a disequilibrium between opportunity base and the social arrangement to exploit it, and too static to support a sustained process of change. As the opportunity base expanded, tradition and custom yielded place to a more creative response, leading India into a new age. What happened in the subcontinent was not different from the experiences of other societies that can legitimately boast of much more impressive gains in the realm of business. But the objective-material conditions in India took much longer to take a favourable turn.

The favourable turn in the objective conditions was undoubtedly a consequence of the infrastructural apparatus created to serve the exploitative designs of the colonial regime. But most of the measures to tighten the imperialist noose, or facilitate the exploitation of the vast resources of the subcontinent for the benefit of the metropolitan country, also created in the process, albeit unintendedly, a better climate for enterprise. The British role in India can be likened to that of the pre-Meiji Tokugawa regime in Japan, whose highly regressive policies and programmes aimed at protecting the political-economic interests of the ruling oligarchy also prepared the soil for the Meiji reconstruction to thrive.

The new kinds of businesses that emerged during the colonial era bore a clear imprint of India's interaction with the West in their structures and strategies, although there was no wholesale borrowing of business methods prevailing in Great Britain or practised by the British businessmen in India. The Indian promoters of new businesses in Bengal during the 1830s and 1840s deviated in significant details from the traditional manner of organizing an enterprise. Private proprietorships or partnerships had been the most popular form of business organizations in India until then, and the joint stock principle was hardly known. Departing from the time-honoured pattern, people like Dwarkanath Tagore adopted the company form of organization, making it possible for a number of independent parties to invest in enterprises promoted on their initiative according to joint stock principles, even though there were no legal sanctions for such a structure based on limited liability. While the basic inspiration for this form of ownership came from the West, the managerial system devised for these enterprises was essentially an adaptation of the way Indian proprietary concerns had been managed for generations. Through formal agreements, the partnership firms of the promoters were appointed secretaries and treasurers, which, by virtue of holding controlling interests in the companies entrusted to them, enjoyed an unchallengeable authority over their affairs. Many British agency houses in Bengal used to manage the business affairs and property of absentee owners for a fee, while carrying on their own businesses. The managerial system devised by the Indian promoters of joint stock enterprises seems to have had its origin in this practice of the agency houses.

Whatever the case, the managerial innovation devised by the Indians represented a combination of what must have seemed the virtues of the Western and Indian systems. If that was so, they were not far too wrong. For, from this experiment evolved the managing agency system that stood the test of time and played a critical role in the development of modern industries in India. With the benefit of hindsight, it is now easy to find numerous faults with the managing agency system, but in a country where both capital and managerial ability were in short supply, perhaps no other method for organizing and managing large enterprises would have delivered the goods.

The functional strategies pursued by the organizers of new businesses, including industrial undertakings, also represented a blending of the old and the new. The same age-old sources that supplied finances for mercantile operations in the past also provided industrial finance, although a few business groups promoted their own banking firms at later stages to help them in this regard and made limited use of the stock market. For distributing their goods, most of them continued to depend on commission agents, symbolizing a continuity of the old trading pattern, although some innovations inspired by the practices prevailing in England were attempted. As most promoters of industrial concerns came from trading backgrounds with natural preference for short-term profits rather than long-term goals, they gave greater attention to higher dividends at the cost of depreciation and building reserves, so necessary for periodic upgrading of plant and machinery. A few industrialists introduced some salutary welfare measures on their own, but most of them did so only after they were made obligatory by law. And no Indian firm ever provided in its balance sheets, the principal instruments for educating their shareholders about the state of business, more data and information than the law required. In fact, the early documents looked more like the account books of trading establishments. The annual reports became somewhat more sophisticated as the years passed, but again only to satisfy new statutory requirements.

While the strategies broadly pursued in the functional areas listed above represented a blending of the Indian and British practices, there was no Indian element whatsoever in the production technologies employed in the factories in India. All Indian industrialists depended on the production processes developed in the West. Not only were these processes accepted blindly and uncritically, no attempts were made to modify or adapt them to suit the Indian needs. This was primarily due to the commercial background of a large number of those who founded modern industries in India. Coming as they did from the trading classes, they were primarily concerned with the financial aspects, unlike the founders of industrial firms in Great Britain and other European countries, most of whom had been craftsmen and, thus, possessed keen technological insight.

These structural-strategic stances were common to practically all industrialists during the colonial era, regardless of their socio-cultural backgrounds. There were of course, minor variations in specific cases, but they had nothing to do with the social origins of the promoters of the enterprises concerned. And yet, the development of Indian business is often analysed with reference to the so-called business communities. According to this view, India developed a collection of business communities, unlike other capitalistic societies that developed business classes. The fact of the matter however is, as our account bears out, that the enterprises identified with the so-called different business communities had similar organizational structures, and their managements pursued essentially similar strategies to achieve their goals. The differences pointed out by the proponents of the business communities view pertain to behaviour on the social plane or refer to the pre-colonial age when the Indian markets were much more fragmented. With territiorial consolidation, business elements of various descriptions in India increasingly developed a sense of interdependence, leading eventually to the rise of pressure groups to safeguard their common business interests. An all-India business class thus had already come into being much before India gained independence.

Thus the Indian private sector on the eve of Independence was not as disjointed or fragmented as it was at the beginning of the colonial era. A reasonably strong foundation for its upward progress had already emerged, though without any deliberate support from the state and despite the debilitating effects inevitable in an imperialist set-up. It can be argued that but for the strong foundation, the Indian private sector had already developed it would not have been able to make such good use as it did of the expansion of opportunity base that freedom brought in its wake, coupled with the unprecedented active role of the state to speed up the process of economic transformation. True, the private sector enjoyed much less freedom after Independence, but the luxury of a vast protected market, that the post-colonial dispensation provided, more than compensated for the fetters that came in the form of numerous regulations and controls.

However, with practically no threat of outside competition, there was little pressure to bring about fundamental changes in the realm of structures and strategies. The hold of business families over the private sector remained largely undiluted despite the legal abolition of the managing agency system. According to one estimate, even after fifty years of independence as many as 461 of the 500 most valuable public limited companies were under family management. Although families ceased to be the primary source of industrial finance, and most private sector companies were now dependant on the government-controlled financial institutions for funds, it meant little change in the power of the families, as the institutional representatives on the boards seldom interfered with management. Instances of imaginative marketing strategies to gauge the market and boost sales were few and far between, and in the realm of employees' welfare and public disclosure of business details, statutory requirements rather than voluntary action still played a decisive role. Research and development and technology upgradation, that had remained the weakest link in Indian management throughout the colonial period, still remained the most neglected area. Referring to the situation in this respect, Ashok Ganguly, a past chairman of Hindustan Lever, justifiably lamented in 1990:

We have been lulled by the available access to marginally appropriate or inappropriate technologies from different parts of the world and find ourselves at the mercy of the vendors of technology. Since our information and technology bases are both outdated, we have progressively lost the ability to keep up with the galloping changes that are taking place around the world.

The question of imaginative product development policy could not at all arise under these conditions. Inevitably, most of the products offered by the Indian companies left much to be desired in respect of quality. It is no surprise under these conditions that India, that was far ahead of many Asian countries in terms of business developments at the end of the colonial era, was left far behind by the end of the licence-permit raj. With the benefit of hindsight, the socialist ideology of the government of free India for almost four decades is often considered principally responsible for this state of affairs. If so, the ideological bases of the policies pursued by the post-colonial government of India have not been particularly more helpful for the development of business than the ideological stance of its predecessor. While the colonial administration with its commitment to laissez faire doctrine functioned merely as a night watchman with regard to economic development, inevitably placing limits on business growth, the national government, with its socialist pretensions and concomitant big-brother posture, turned out to be too watchful for the Indian business to realize its full potential. This puts a big question mark against analyses that seek to explain India's business backwardness with reference to colonialism alone.

Momentous changes have been taking place in Indian business since the early 1990s in the wake of the growing liberalization of the economy and the opening of the Indian market to the world. Almost every major department of business bears witness to the nation's free enterprise system responding to the new policy environment most creatively, optimistically, and confidently. Whether this response would have been so vigorous if the post-colonial regime had introduced a less regimented economic order right from the start or freed the economy much earlier will always remain a moot point. For, it can be argued that the Indian business in 1947 was still too weak, both structurally and psychologically, to face unbridled competition from the West in its own homeland, and that it needed a period of protection and care to gain sufficient maturity and self-confidence before exposing itself to the world. According to this perspective the control regime of the earlier years may have been a necessary building block for effective liberalization in the later phase.

The speculations are futile for the course of history cannot be rerun. What, however, cannot be denied is that the Indian private sector has now embarked upon the most progressive, regenerative, and competitive course in its entire history.

APPENDIX

Current Names of Places Mentioned in the Text

Original name used in the text	Current name
Abyssinia	Ethiopia
Baroda	Vadodara
Benares	Varanasi
Bombay	Mumbai
Broach	Bharuch
Burma	Myanmar
Calcutta	Kolkata
Calicut	Kozhikode
Cambay	Khambat
Ceylon	Sri Lanka
Kaira	Kheda
Madras	Chennai
Poona	Pune
Rangoon	Yangon
Tanjore	Thanjavur
Trichinopoly	Tiruchirappalli
United Provinces	Uttar Pradesh
Vizagapattam	Visakhapatanam

Note: This list does not include most other names where only the spellings have been changed to match the correct pronunciations, e.g. Durg (earlier Drug), Jabalpur (earlier Jubbulpore), Kanpur (earlier Cawnpore), etc.

REFERENCES

Andrew Yule & Co., *Andrew Yule and Company, 1863–1963* (Calcutta: Privately printed, 1963).

Amin, B.D., *The Rise and Growth of the Alembic Chemical Works* (Baroda: privately printed, 1939).

Antrobus, H.A., *The Jorehaut Tea Company Ltd* (London: Jorehaut Co., 1949).

——, *A History of the Assam Company* (Edinburgh: Assam Co., 1957).

Arasarathnam, S., *Merchants, Companies and Commerce on the Coromandel Coast, 1650–1750* (Delhi: Oxford University Press, 1986).

Ashton, T.S., *The Industrial Revolution, 1760–1830* (London: Oxford University Press, 1961).

Bagchi, A.K., *Private Investment in India, 1900–1939* (Cambridge: Cambridge University Press, 1972).

Banerjee, Tarashankar, *Internal Markets of India, 1834–1900* (Calcutta: Academic Publishers, 1966).

Basu, Champak, *Challenge and Change: The ITC Story* (Hyderabad: Orient Longman, 1988).

Basu, S.K., *The Managing Agency System* (Calcutta: World Press, 1958).

Bayly, C.A., *Rulers, Townsmen and Bazaars: North Indian Society in the Age of British Expansion, 1770–1870* (Cambridge: Cambridge University Press, 1983).

Bhagawati, J.N., *India: Planning for Industrialization and Trade Policies since 1951* (London: Development Centre of the Organization for Economic Cooperation and Development, 1970).

——, *India in Transition: Freeing the Economy* (New Delhi: Oxford University Press, 1994).

Bhattacharya, Amit, *Swadeshi Enterprise in Bengal, 1900–1920* (Calcutta: Bookland, 1986).

Brown, Hilton, *Parrys of Madras* (Madras: Parry & Co., 1954).

Buchanan, D.H., *Development of Capitalist Enterprise in India* (New York: Macmillan, 1934).

Chandavarkar, Rajnarayan, *The Origins of Industrial Capitalism in India: Business Strategies and the Working Classes in Bombay, 1900–1940* (Cambridge: Cambridge University Press, 1994).

Chaturvedi, Abha and Anil Chaturvedi, *ACC: A Corporate Sage* (Mumbai: Associated Cement Companies, 1977).

Cragg, C., *The New Maharajahs: The Commercial Princes of India, Pakistan and Bangladesh* (London: Century Business, 1996).

Dadabhoy, Bakhtiyar K., *'JEH': A Life of J.R.D. Tata* (New Delhi: Rupa & Co., 2004).

Das, Gurcharan, *India Unbound* (New Delhi: Viking, 2000).

Dasgupta, Ashin, *Indian Merchants and the Decline of Surat, C.1700–1750* (Wiesbaden: Franz Steiner Verlag, 1979).

Desai, A.R., *Social Background of Indian Nationalism* (Bombay: Popular Prakashan, 1966).

Desouza, F., *House of Binny* (Madras: Binny & Co., 1969).

Dobbin, Christine, *Urban Leadership in Western India: Politics and Communities in Bombay City* (London: Oxford University Press, 1972).

Dossal, Mariam, *Imperial Designs and Indian Realities: The Planning of Bombay City, 1845–1875* (Bombay: Oxford University Press, 1991).

Elwin, V., *The Story of Tata Steel* (Bombay: Tata & Sons, 1958).

Erdman, Howard L., *The Swatantra Party and Indian Conservatism* (Cambridge: Cambridge University Press, 1972).

FICCI, *Footprints of Enterprise: Indian Business through the Ages* (New Delhi: Oxford University Press, 1998).

Ghosh, G.C., *Ramdoolal Dey: The Bengalee Millionaire* (Calcutta: K.L. Firma Mukhopadhyaya & Co., 1968).

Ghosh, Suniti Kumar, *The Indian Big Bourgeoisie* (Calcutta: Prachi, 1985).

Gillion, K.L., *Ahmedabad: A Study in Urban History* (Berkeley: University of California Press, 1968).

Gordon, A.D.D., *Businessmen and Politics: Rising Nationalism and a Modernizing Economy in Bombay, 1918–1933* (New Delhi: Manohar, 1978).

Harris, F.R., *Jamsetji Nusserwanji Tata: A Chronicle of His Life* (Bombay: Blackie & Son, 1958).

Harrison, Godfrey, *Bird & Company of Calcutta* (Calcutta: Bird & Co., 1964).

Hazari, R.K., *The Structure of the Corporate Private Sector: A Study of Concentration, Ownership and Control* (London: Asia Publishing House, 1966).

——, *Essays on Industrial Policy* (New Delhi: Concept, 1986).

Hazelhurst, L.W., *Entrepreneurship and Merchant Castes in a Punjab City* (Durham: Duke University Press, 1960).

Heredia, Ruth, *The Amul India Story* (New Delhi: Tata McGraw-Hill, 1997).

Hilding, Per, *Technology in a Controlled Economy: The Match Industry in India* (Stockholm: Nordic Institute of Asian Studies, 1992).

Iyengar, H.V.R., *The Bombay Plan and Other Essays* (Bombay: Forum of Free Enterprise, 1968).

Jackson, Stanley, *The Sassoons* (London: Heinemann, 1968).

Jaju Ram Nivas, *G.D. Birla: A Biography* (New Delhi: Vikas, 1985).

James Finlay & Co., *James Finlay and Company Limited* (Glasgow: Jackson & Co., 1951).

Jones, Stephanie, *Merchants of the Raj* (London: Macmillan, 1992).

Joshi, Arun, *Lala Shri Ram: A Study in Entrepreneurship and Industrial Management* (New Delhi: Orient Longman, 1975).

Karaka, D.F., *The History of the Parsees* (London: Macmillan, 1884).

Karanjia, B.K., *Godrej: A Hundred Years, 1897–1997* (New Delhi: Viking, 1997).

Karkaria, Bachi J., *Dare to Dream: The Life of Rai Bahadur Mohan Singh Oberoi* (New Delhi: Viking, 1992).

Khanolkar, G.D., *Walchand Hirachand: Man, His Times and Achievements* (Bombay: Walchand & Co., 1969).

Khera, S.K., *Government in Business* (New Delhi: National Publishing House, 1977).

——, *The Establishment of Heavy Electrical Plant at Bhopal* (New Delhi: Indian Institute of Public Administration, 1953).

Kirloskar, S.V., *Yantrikanchi Yatra* in Marathi (Kirloskarwadi: Kirloskar Brothers, 1958).

Kling, Blair B., *Partner in Empire: Dwarkanath Tagore and the Age of Enterprise in Eastern Indian* (Berkeley: University of California Press, 1976).

Kochanek, Stanley, *Business and Politics in India* (Berkeley: University of California Press, 1974).

Kudaisya, Medha M., *The Life and Times of G.D. Birla* (New Delhi: Oxford University Press, 2003).

Kulke, Eckehard, *The Parsees in India: A Minority as Agent of Social Change* (New Delhi: Vikas-Bell Books, 1978).

Kumar, Dharma (ed.), *Cambridge Economic History of India: Vol. II* (Cambridge: Cambridge University Press, 1982).

Lala, R.M., *The Creation of Wealth: A Tata Story* (Bombay: IBH Publishing Co., 1981).

Little, J.H., *The House of Jagat Seth* (Calcutta: Calcutta Historical Society, 1967).

Lokanathan, P.S., *Industrial Organization in India* (London: Macmillan, 1935).

Mahindra, K.C., *Sir Rajendra Nath Mookerjee* (Calcutta: R.K. Ghoshal, 1962).

Markovits, Claude, *Indian Business and Nationalist Politics, 1931–1939: The Indigenous Capitalist Class and the Rise of the Congress Party* (Cambridge: Cambridge University Press, 1985).

——, *The Global World of Indian Merchants, 1756–1947. Traders of Sind from Bukhara to Panama* (Cambridge: Cambridge University Press, 2000).

Mehta, S.D., *Cotton Mills of India, 1854–1954* (Bombay: Textile Association, 1954).

Merchant, Minhas, *Aditya Vikram Birla: A Biography* (New Delhi: Viking, 1997).

Misra, Anna Maria, *Business, Race and Politics in British India 1860–1960* (Oxford: Clarendon Press, 1998).

Misra, S.C., *Muslim Communities in Gujarat* (Bombay: Asia, 1964).

Mody, J.R.P., *Jamsetji Jejeebhoy: The First Parsee Baronet* (Bombay: The Author, 1959).

Mohnot, S.R., *Reliance: An Industrial Legend* (New Delhi: Centre for Industrial and Economic Research, 1987).

Moraes, Frank, *Sir Purshotamdas Thakurdas* (Bombay: Asia, 1957).

Moreland, W.H., *From Akbar to Aurangzeb* (New Delhi: Oriental Books Reprint Corporation, 1972).

____, *India at the Death of Akbar* (Delhi: Reprints and Trans Publications, 1974).

Muthiah, S., *Getting India on the Move: The 150 Year Saga of Simpsons of Madras* (Madras: Higginbothoms, 1990).

Nanda, H.P., *The Days of My Years* (New Delhi: Viking, 1992).

Narola, Gurmeet, *Entrepreneurial Connection* (New Delhi: Tata McGraw-Hill, 2001).

Pandit, Srinivas, *Thought Leaders: The Source Code of Exceptional Managers and Entrepreneurs* (New Delhi: Tata McGraw-Hill, 2001).

Patel, Sujata, *The Making of Industrial Relations: The Ahmedabad Textile Industry, 1918–1934* (New Delhi: Oxford University Press, 1987).

Patwardhan, V.S., *The House of Garwares* (Bombay: Popular Prakashan, 1990).

Pavlov, V.I., *The Indian Capitalist Class* (New Delhi: Peoples' Publishing House, 1964).

Pearson, M.N., *Merchants and Rulers in Gujarat* (Berkeley: University of California Press, 1976).

Piramal, Gita, *Business Legends* (New Delhi: Viking, 1998).

____, *Business Maharajas* (New Delhi: Penguin, 1996).

Piramal, Gita and M. Herdeck, *India's Industrialists* (Bombay: India Book Distributors, 1986).

Ray, Prafulla Chandra, *Autobiography of a Bengali Chemist* (Calcutta: Orient Books, 1958).

Rao, P. Chentsal, *Lakshmipat Singhania: His Concepts and Creations* (New Delhi: Vikas, 1986).

Ray, Aniruddha, *Merchants and the State: The French In India, 1666–1739* (New Delhi: Munshiram Manoharlal, 2004) 2 vols.

Ray, R.K., *Industrialization in India: Growth and Conflict in the Private Corporate Sector, 1914–1947* (New Delhi: Oxford University Press, 1979).

Raychauduri, T. and Irfan Habib (eds), *Cambridge Economic History of India, Vol. I* (Cambridge: Cambridge University Press, 1982).

Rudner, D.W., *Caste and Capitalism in Colonial India: The Nattukottai Chettiers* (Berkeley: University of California Press, 1995).

Rungta, R.S., *Rise of Business Corporations in India, 1850–1900* (Cambridge: Cambridge University Press, 1970).

Sarkar, Sumit, *The Swadeshi Movement in Bengal, 1903–1908* (New Delhi: Peoples' Publishing House, 1977).

Sen, S.K., *The House of Tatas, 1839–1939* (Calcutta: Progressive Publishers, 1975).

Seshadri, R.K., *A Swadeshi Bank from South India: History of the Indian Bank* (Madras: Swadeshi Bank, 1983).

Singer, Milton (ed.), *Entrepreneurship and Modernization of Occupational Culture in South Asia* (Durham: Duke University Press, 1973).

Singh, S.B., *European Agency Houses in Bengal* (Calcutta: Firma Mukhopadhyaya & Co., 1966).

Subramanyam, Sanjay (ed.), *Merchants, Markets and State in Early Modern India* (New Delhi: Oxford University Press, 1990).

Taknet, D.K., *Marwari Samaj* in Hindi (Jaipur: Kumar Prakashan, 1989).

Tandon, Prakash, *Banking Century: A Short History of Banking in India and the Pioneer, Punjab National Bank* (New Delhi: Penguin, 1989).

Timberg, T.A., *The Marwaris: From Traders to Industrialists* (New Delhi: Vikas, 1978).

Tirumalai, R., *TTK: The Dynamic Innovator* (Madras: T.T. Maps, 1988).

Tripathi, A., *Trade and Finance in Bengal Presidency* (Bombay: Orient Longman, 1956).

Tripathi, Dwijendra, *The Oxford History of Indian Business* (New Delhi: Oxford University Press, 2004).

———, *Dynamics of a Tradition: Kasturbhai Lalbhai and His Entrepreneurship* (New Delhi: Manohar, 1981).

———, *Historical Roots of Industrial Entrepreneurship in India and Japan: A Comparative Interpretation* (New Delhi: Manohar, 1997).

——— (ed.), *Business Communities of India: A Historical Perspective* (New Delhi: Manohar, 1984).

———, *State and Business in India: A Historical Perspective* (New Delhi: Manohar, 1987).

———, *Business and Politics in India: A Historical Perspective* (New Delhi: Manohar, 1991).

Tripathi, Dwijendra and M. Mehta, *Business Houses in Western India, 1850–1956* (New Delhi: Manohar, 1990).

Tripathi, Dwijendra and Priti Misra, *Towards a New Frontier: History of the Bank of Baroda* (New Delhi: Manohar, 1985).

Vedavalli, R., *Private Foreign Investment and Economic Development* (Cambridge: Cambridge University Press, 1976).

Venkataramani, Raja, *Japan Enters Indian Industry: The Maruti Suzuki Joint Venture* (New Delhi: Radiant Publishers, 1990).

Venkatasubbiah, H., *Enterprise and Economic Change: 50 Years of FICCI* (New Delhi: Vikas, 1977).

INDEX